# LIBERTY'S
# FIRST CRISIS

Also by Charles Slack

*Hetty: The Genius and Madness of America's First Female Tycoon*

*Noble Obsession: Charles Goodyear, Thomas Hancock, and the Race to Unlock the Greatest Industrial Secret of the Nineteenth Century*

*Blue Fairways: Three Months, Sixty Courses, No Mulligans*

# LIBERTY'S
# FIRST CRISIS

ADAMS, JEFFERSON,
AND THE
MISFITS WHO SAVED
FREE SPEECH

## CHARLES SLACK

Atlantic Monthly Press
*New York*

*Published simultaneously in Canada*
*Printed in the United States of America*

FIRST EDITION

ISBN 978-0-8021-2342-8
eISBN 978-0-8021-9168-7

Atlantic Monthly Press
an imprint of Grove/Atlantic, Inc.
154 West 14th Street
New York, NY 10011

Distributed by Publishers Group West

www.groveatlantic.com

15 16 17 18   10 9 8 7 6 5 4 3 2 1

*For My Father, Dr. Warner Slack*
*Whose Words and Actions*
*Have Taught Me the Beauty of Freedom*

*Who would have believed it, had it been foretold, that the People of America, after having fought seven long years to obtain their Independence, would, at this early day, have been seized and dragged into confinement by their own government?*

—*The Aurora*, Philadelphia, Nov. 22, 1798

*Congress shall make no law respecting an establishment of religion, or prohibiting the free exercise thereof; or abridging the freedom of speech, or of the press; or the right of the people peaceably to assemble, and to petition the Government for a redress of grievances.*

—*The First Amendment to The Constitution of the United States*

**Se·di·tion** (sǐ-dǐsh-ən). n. **1.** Conduct or language inciting rebellion against the authority of a state.

—*The American Heritage Dictionary of the English Language*

# CONTENTS

# Author's Note

To avoid a needless distraction for contemporary readers, I have removed the eighteenth-century convention of using "f" for "s" when quoting from period publications. Otherwise, I have preserved the authors' spelling, capitalization, and punctuation. Italics, unless otherwise noted, are in the original.

# PART I

# THE ROAD TO SEDITION

# CHAPTER ONE

The greatest enemy of liberty is fear. When people feel comfortable and well protected, they are naturally expansive and tolerant of one another's opinions and rights. When they feel threatened, their tolerance shrinks. By 1798, the euphoria surrounding the American Revolution, the sense of a common purpose and a common enemy, was gone. Everyone agreed that the new nation founded amid high hopes and noble ideas was in danger of collapse. The one thing they could not agree on was who to blame.

The Federalists, who dominated most of New England as well as both houses of Congress, the John Adams presidency, and the Supreme Court, viewed themselves as the protectors of family, faith, education, and country. Though the term "federalism" refers only to the system of shared powers between individual states and a centralized government forged by the Constitution, under the leadership of men such as Alexander Hamilton, principal author of the Federalist Papers, it had come to imply a decisive tipping of the scales in the direction of centralized power. Hamilton and other Federalists believed in a strong national military to protect the fledgling country from foreign invaders, a centralized bank to stabilize and grow the economy, and a government with the muscle to tax and to direct the destiny of the nation. They had little faith in the intelligence or morals of average men. As such, they believed in liberty, yes, but liberty as informed and guided by a natural aristocracy consisting of themselves.

Yet everywhere they turned, they saw their orderly utopia of English-descended freemen under siege, rapidly devolving into something more volatile and chaotic. For this, Federalists blamed an unofficial, disparate but growing collection of citizens referring to themselves as Republicans, or Democrats, or Democratic-Republicans, or Jeffersonian Democrats. In the interest of simplicity, they'll be referred to henceforth as Republicans, but with no inference of a connection or lineage to the modern party of the same name. Indeed, the word "party," now so firmly rooted in our political language that one might assume party structure was written into the Constitution, was an epithet in 1798. Men in power used "party" interchangeably with "faction" and "interest" to designate outliers, troublemakers, and enemies of good government.

In their innocence, the founding generation assumed that a government chosen by the people would represent *all* the people. Federalists, who had controlled most of the national government from its inception, never considered themselves to be a political party; to oppose the Federalists was to oppose the very idea of America. In his farewell address at the end of his second term in 1796, President George Washington, the great unifier, had warned against "the baneful effects of the Spirit of Party," and "the alternate domination of one faction over another, sharpened by the spirit of revenge natural to party dissention."[1]

Yet to those calling themselves Republicans, Federalist efforts to unify the country were beginning to look a lot like what they had just fought a war to overturn. Everything from Washington's fancy carriage to John Adams's thin-skinned reaction to criticism to Alexander Hamilton's emerging master plan for a muscular national bureaucracy had the whiff of privilege and elitism, if not incipient monarchism. Federalists, to Republican minds, were "aristocrats" and "royalists" bent on consolidating power and replicating English class divisions on American soil. Like the Federalists, Republicans believed their American utopia to be under siege, but their greatest fears surrounded the very measures that Federalists saw as the country's salvation. The idea of a powerful national military (a "standing army" in the parlance of the day) raised the fresh specter of British troops forcibly quartered in the homes of colonists. A federal government capable of taxing at will elicited memories of usurious taxes imposed by a distant monarch.

Against this background of internal divisions, Americans were panicked over a possible imminent invasion by a great European power. The trouble was they could not agree on which European power, England or France, would do the invading. Fueled by hatred for the English monarchy, Republicans felt a spiritual connection with the French, who had not only aided the American Revolution but also launched a revolution of their own.

Federalists, for their part, had watched in growing horror as the French Revolution degenerated into a procession of rolling heads and bloodlust. They saw in that revolution a chilling forecast of what the United States could expect from its own population without strong, principled leadership from the elite. Indeed, they saw themselves as the last barrier against Republican-driven chaos. Radicals, revolutionaries, and malcontents from around Europe were streaming onto American soil and stirring things up.

Federalists mistrusted foreigners in general and immigrants in particular, especially of the poor and non-English variety. Alarmed by the numbers of Germans, French, and Irish pouring each year into their cities and towns, Federalist politicians had proposed a ban on anyone born outside the United States holding government office, along with a twenty-dollar naturalization fee for immigrants—no small amount at a time when an American farmhand might get by on six to twelve dollars a month.[2] In July 1797, Congressman Harrison Gray Otis of Massachusetts sounded the alarm on immigration in what became known as the "Wild Irish" speech, warning that while he had nothing against "honest and industrious" immigrants, the country could not afford to "invite hordes of wild Irishmen": "The mass of vicious and disorganizing characters who could not live peaceably at home, and who, after unfurling the standard of rebellion in their own countries, might come hither to revolutionize ours."[3] Everything that Otis and his fellow Federalists feared, hated, and scorned could be summed up in three words: Congressman Matthew Lyon.

A native of Ireland, Lyon had schemed and brawled his way from indentured servitude to the upper layers of business and politics in his adopted country. Everything about his life was outsized: his ambition, his intelligence, his enemies, and his flaws. He never let an insult pass without returning it twofold. Put simply, Matthew Lyon couldn't keep his mouth shut. It was this quality above all others that resulted in his greatest, albeit unintentional, contribution to the American experiment. His belligerence in the face of Federalist power would help push the United States into a constitutional crisis, forcing a generation that had soured from idealism to bitterness to confront a few epic questions. Would they live up to the words they themselves had forged, upholding freedom of expression as the highest form of liberty? Did they truly mean what they had said, that Congress shall make no law abridging free speech, or freedom of the press?

Records of his early life in Ireland are murky, so it's impossible to say for sure what prompted Lyon to leave his native country at age fifteen, alone and indentured. His descendants in America claimed that Lyon fled after English authorities hanged his father for agitating for the rights of farmers. If true, that experience would help explain Lyon's hatred for England, as well as his visceral contempt for anyone in his adopted country whom he believed to be putting on aristocratic airs.[4]

Lyon landed in Connecticut in 1764. His indenture seems to have changed hands several times. He ultimately arrived in Litchfield County, in northwestern Connecticut, where a farmer purchased him for a pair of bulls. While such transactions were fairly common in colonial times, the particulars of this trade would serve as a source of pride and pain for the rest of Lyon's life. He often boasted of "the Bulls that redeemed me" as evidence of just how far he had risen.[5] Yet he was quick to attack anyone who used the tale to mock him, whether Litchfield County boys when he was still in his teens, or, much later, his Federalist enemies who claimed he was untamed, uncouth, and unfit for office; indeed, that this "wild Lyon," having once been traded for livestock, was more animal than human.

For a young man of sharp ambitions and no social standing, Connecticut in the early 1770s already felt too confining. So in 1774, the twenty-five-year-old Lyon, freed from his indenture and with a young wife and a little savings to his name, headed north to a territory bounded by New Hampshire on the east and Lake Champlain on the west.[6] If visitors today think of Vermont as a land of soft green fields and gently eccentric politics, the pre-statehood territory more closely resembled a Wild West frontier. The colonial governments of New Hampshire and New York simultaneously laid claim to the territory. They sold grants to prospective settlers, often to the same or overlapping properties—with predictable results. Settlers having staked their life savings to a plot of land would travel for weeks or months over crude or nonexistent roads, prepared to carve a new life out of the forest, only to find someone bearing a title from a different colonial authority already building a homestead. With little recourse to law enforcement or courts, the settlers relied on frontier justice to settle such disputes. Ethan Allen and Seth Warner today are best remembered as heroes of the Revolutionary War. But the Green Mountain Boys they commanded fought their first bloody battles not against the English but against bands of "Yorkers."[7]

Geography added its own imperative in the form of the Green Mountains, which cleaved the Vermont territory into two starkly different worlds. To the east, residents were more like their cousins from Massachusetts or Connecticut: staid, conservative, with a steadfast belief in law and order as exemplified by English common law. West of the mountains, closer to the New York boundary, were a more varied lot of individualists. The west was an amalgam of immigrants from other colonies and from overseas, more likely to judge a man by his skill with a plow and a musket than by his family name or church affiliation.[8] Settlers living under the daily threat of skirmishes with Yorkers regarded the Green Mountain Boys as heroes and protectors. Over to the east, residents took a dimmer view of such men; removed by a mountainous barrier from the turmoil, they saw the Green Mountain Boys as lawless, uncivilized thugs.[9]

The western side of the mountains practically called out Lyon's name. He paid the New Hampshire colonial government twenty pounds for ninety acres near the hamlet of Wallingford, just a few miles from the New York line.[10] There, he fell in with the Green Mountain Boys. Within a few years the militia's mission shifted to the more momentous fight for independence from England. Rising in the ranks during the Revolutionary War, Lyon led a company of the Green Mountain Boys in battle against the British at Fort Ticonderoga and Crown Point.[11]

Lyon's Revolutionary War service was marred by an incident in 1776, when men under the command of Lyon and other officers, hearing reports of an imminent attack by hundreds of Indians on their position near Lake Champlain, mutinied and fled. Lyon was among several officers arrested, tried, and cashiered for cowardice. Lyon vigorously fought the charges, insisting he had done everything in his power to stop the revolt. Though the incident would come back to haunt his political career years later, Lyon was reinstated within a matter of months and served out the remainder of the war.[12] In 1777, he took part in the Continental Army's decisive Battles of Saratoga, resulting in the surrender of British general John Burgoyne and more than five thousand British troops and a huge cache of arms and equipment—a major turning point in the war. Lyon took special joy in being one of those responsible for relieving the surrendered British troops of their weapons.[13]

As the long war wound to a close and other veterans dreamed of returning to the peaceful rhythms of life on their farms, Lyon was already plotting to grab a share of the victors' spoils. He parlayed his military prominence into a position as clerk for the Court of Confiscation, part of the provisional Vermont government (formal statehood would not come until 1791). As the draconian name implies, the Court of Confiscation's task was to seize and sell property held by loyalist landowners. An order signed by Thomas Chittenden as president and Matthew Lyon as clerk shows the court seizing estates from fifteen Tories on a single day in April 1778.[14] Lyon and other court administrators were not shy about purchasing Tory property that they had taken part in confiscating.[15]

As evidence of Lyon's growing influence in the area, in 1782 the Vermont General Assembly named him one of seventy-six founding proprietors of a new town, Fair Haven, to be forged out of the wilderness along the New York border at the extreme southern tip of Lake Champlain. With a personal share totaling more than four hundred acres, Lyon built a homestead on the north bank of the Poultney River, sold off small portions of his land to newcomers, and then set his attentions on manufacturing goods to sell to the swelling population.[16]

He built a dam and an ironworks and forge, where he produced axes, hoes, and other tools. He also built a slitting mill capable of turning slender rods of iron into finished nails—a rare commodity that traditionally had to be imported from England. To shore up his competitive position, Lyon petitioned the Vermont Assembly to impose a duty of two pence per pound on imported nails (the petition was denied). Lyon added a sawmill and a tavern, as well as a paper mill, helping to pioneer the use of wood pulp instead of linen or rags to make paper. Taken together, his budding empire came to be known as "Lyon's Works."[17]

In the mid-1780s, following the death of his first wife, Mary, Lyon married Chittenden's daughter, Beulah. By this time Thomas Chittenden was the first governor of pre-statehood Vermont. Chittenden, like Lyon, was a man of low birth and little formal schooling. He had left Connecticut as a young man and made his fortune through land speculation in western Vermont.[18] Under Chittenden's tutelage, Lyon paired financial successes with growing political ambitions. He served as head of the Fair Haven board of selectmen, as an assistant county judge, and as a representative in the Vermont legislature.[19]

Lyon's ambitious, competitive nature meant that he always made enemies as well as friends. For years, he feuded with a Fair Haven Federalist named Joel Hamilton, who accused Lyon of fixing local elections by importing instant "residents" from just over the state line in New York to vote for him. Through protracted lawsuits Lyon charged Hamilton with damaging his reputation, while Hamilton charged Lyon's supporters with stealing into his orchard and damaging his fruit trees.[20] In addition to these local spats, Lyon was making enemies among powerful Federalist Vermonters who viewed the likes of Thomas Chittenden and Matthew Lyon as bumptious peasants who had gotten above their place.

Lyon's greatest enemy was Nathaniel Chipman. Like Lyon, Chipman had arrived in the Vermont territory from Connecticut as a young man full of ambition. The similarities ended there. Unlike the self-taught Lyon, Chipman arrived in the wilderness armed with a degree from Yale and a tacit belief not just in the opportunities his education represented, but in the noblesse oblige it implied. Whereas Lyon had come to western Vermont to escape conservative Connecticut and the limitations of his humble background, Chipman had come to make it more like home, to convert a rugged backwater into the next bastion of New England morals and virtue. As he wrote to a friend, "think what a figure I shall make, when I become the oracle of law to the state of Vermont."[21]

Given their ambition and conflicting goals, Lyon and Chipman were destined to clash. In 1780, just a year after arriving in the territory, a twenty-eight-year-old Chipman issued a report to the provisional Vermont legislature favoring a return of confiscated land to its loyalist owners without consideration to the settlers who in many cases had been working the land for years. From the Federalist perspective, these settlers were little more than trespassers.[22] Encountering Chipman in a law office in Westminster, Lyon announced that "no man who had a spark of honesty" could have presented such a report. Chipman responded that he had no intention of listening to the complaints of "an ignorant Irish puppy." Lyon leaped from his chair and grabbed Chipman's hair, snapping the comb holding it in place. Chipman, who had been mending a pen with a whittling knife, waved the knife at Lyon. Stephen Bradley, the owner of the law office, grabbed Lyon and pulled him away. With Bradley holding his shoulders, Lyon kicked at Chipman, who grabbed his legs. Together, Chipman and Bradley dumped Lyon in a corner.[23]

The fight ended without serious injuries. Vermont passed a Redemption Act in 1780, restoring some confiscated land to loyalists. After five more years of haggling, a Betterment Act provided limited compensation for the improvements settlers had made while on the land. But for Lyon and Chipman, the episode marked the beginning of a political and personal feud that would lead from rural Vermont to the nation's capital and back again over the next two decades.[24]

To Chipman and many Federalists, the rise of men such as Matthew Lyon in business and, particularly, in politics represented a direct assault upon the natural order of the world. True, the late war had secured independence from England and the most burdensome aspects of royalty. But did not an orderly society still depend upon the leadership of its best class of citizens, its most well-bred, wise, and learned members? During the framing of the Constitution, New Englanders had unsuccessfully opposed a provision in Article VI prohibiting religious tests for anyone serving in the federal government. Without the ability to restrict non-Christians, they warned, the government might soon be teeming with "Jews Turks & infidels."[25]

Now, they were forced to confront an equally unsettling reality. Men whose immigrant status or lack of formal education suited them to productive lives as itinerant laborers, servants, or farmhands seemed incognizant of their moral duty to be ruled by their betters. This astonishing loss of "consciousness of humility" was, as historian Gordon Wood has noted, perhaps the most radical product of the American Revolution.[26] It stripped away hierarchies that had structured nations throughout history and left in their place a few noble words about liberty and unalienable rights—along with vast uncertainties about whether this new system would survive or explode. Lyon wasn't waiting to find out. He may have been a lowly indentured servant, a son of Ireland traded for a pair of bulls, but some deep well of pride, stubbornness, and gall told him those words applied to him. He held this truth to be self-evident: Matthew Lyon was created equal.

However laudable this quality was, it made Lyon thin-skinned and caustic to a fault on the subject of social distinction. Anyone with family money or even a college degree was an "aristocrat." His least favorite aristocrats were "law characters" such as Chipman, whose slick tongues and legal chicanery, he believed, enabled them to cheat settlers out of land that honest toil had made productive. Lyon's assumptions about class were, in their own way, as ignorant and foolish as his enemies' assumptions about him. Chipman, the son of a blacksmith and farmer who had scraped to send him to Yale, was hardly the aristocrat that Lyon branded him. To be sure, Chipman was as content to play the gentry as Lyon was in his role as renegade outsider. Yet the chasm between them wasn't as wide or deep as either imagined. In addition to everything else, this first generation in the American experiment would set in motion that marvelously porous "class system" whereby one generation's despised immigrant upstart is the next's country squire.[27]

With the arrival of statehood in 1791, Lyon was determined to represent Vermont in the first Congress. He marshaled his supporters from around the western part of the state, promising to represent the interests of average citizens against the moneyed lawyer class. But his influence was insufficient against Chipman who, true to his own prediction, had risen meteorically and amassed powerful friends. By 1791, Chipman had already served in the Vermont House of Representatives, and been elected a judge in the state supreme court and appointed its chief justice. In 1791 he was named judge of the U.S. District Court. Chipman threw his weight behind another candidate, Israel Smith, who won the congressional seat Lyon was after.

Lyon ran again in 1793 and 1795, failing both times. For the 1797 campaign he tried a new tactic. For years, he had been making paper; now, he decided to start one, founding a Fair Haven newspaper, *Farmer's Library*. The paper served as a rare Anti-Federalist sheet in Vermont and also unabashedly promoted the political ambitions of its founder. It gave Lyon precisely the megaphone he needed. At last, in 1797, Lyon won his coveted seat in Congress—as the lone Republican representative from all of New England.

Republicans arose not so much as a formal organization but a loose affiliation of individuals chafing under the consolidated power of Federalists. Often this made for strange alliances. If aristocrat-hating Matthew Lyon was a Republican, so, too, were Virginia plantation owners and Founding Fathers Thomas Jefferson and James Madison, men whose claim on "aristocracy" was far greater than that of John Adams or Nathaniel Chipman. Jefferson and Madison feared the Federalists not for their elitism but for what they perceived as their disdain for the rights of individuals and states.

In any case, Republicans were sorely outnumbered in Philadelphia when Lyon set off for the capital city in 1797. Federalist editors, primed in advance by Lyon's enemies from Vermont, gave him a taste right away of the sort of reception he could expect. William Cobbett, the most vituperative of the Federalist editors, warned readers the day before Lyon took his seat:

> To-morrow morning at eleven o'clock will be exposed to view the Lyon of Vermont. This singular animal is said to have been caught in the bog of Hibernia, and when a whelp, transported to America; curiosity induced a New Yorker to buy him, and moving into the country, afterwards exchanged him for a yoke of young bulls with a Vermontese. He was petted in the neighbourhood of Governor Chittenden, and soon became so domesticated, that a daughter of his excellency would stroke and play with him as a monkey. He differs considerably from the African lion, is more clamorous, and less magnanimous. His pelt resembles more the wolf or the tiger, and his gestures bear a remarkable affinity to the bear; this, however, may be ascribed to his having been in the habit of associating with that species of wild beast on the mountains: he is carnivorous, but not very ferocious—has never been detected in having attacked a *man*, but report says he will *beat women*.[28]

Matthew Lyon was undaunted and ready for the national stage. At age forty-eight, he was wealthy, seasoned, battle hardened, yet still youthful enough to have lost none of his anger or ambition. Rather than being cowed by being surrounded by so many potential enemies, Lyon, characteristically, picked his first political fight on the national stage with the most powerful Federalist of all.

# Chapter Two

With about forty thousand residents, the Philadelphia in which Matthew Lyon landed in early 1797 was the nation's second-largest city (after New York), its capital, and a seat of culture and education. And it was deeply divided politically and seething with hostilities. As the nation's political center, Philadelphia contained in concentrated form all the anxiety and fear of a nation at once immense and weak, conflicted and uncertain over the meaning of the word "united" and whipsawed between two perpetually warring powers, England and France.

Given the tangled, overlapping involvement of both countries in America's founding, it was inevitable that the United States would find itself drawn, politically and economically, if not militarily, into any major conflict between the two countries. But for Americans in the 1790s, supporting France or England became much more than a matter of picking sides. The countries seemed to present vivid, stark symbols of two opposite destinies for the American republic. From the earliest constitutional debates, Americans had disagreed furiously over whether the greatest threat to liberty lay in a powerful central government or in the chaos of the mob. Now, virtually every American felt compelled to have a strong opinion on England and France. To declare oneself for one and against another was to stake a claim in the future of one's own country.

During the early parts of the 1790s, public sentiment favored France. Most Americans, regardless of political stripe, greeted the

French Revolution in 1789 with approval and even jubilation. The storming of the Bastille, the Oath of the Tennis Court, the Declaration of the Rights of Man, and other early developments of the revolution struck Americans as evidence of the inevitable advance of individual liberty across nations, as if carried on a benevolent wind.

American newspapers printed the French constitution, and Americans from Boston to Charleston held parades, drank toasts, and greeted French citizens visiting or living in the United States as fellow travelers on the road to freedom. Fashionable Philadelphians addressed one another as "Citizen" or "Citess" and sported the French cockade, a rosette of tricolor satin ribbons that became the symbol of the revolution after the storming of the Bastille.[1] Americans were, at least at first, predisposed to approve of whatever methods the revolutionaries chose to cast off generations of royal oppression. Toy guillotines sold briskly in Philadelphia shops.[2]

Philadelphia was also home to a large and growing French-speaking population, many of them colonists who had fled Saint-Domingue (now Haiti) in the French West Indies, following uprisings in 1791. Home to some three thousand French immigrants by 1794,[3] the city had French schools, restaurants, and booksellers, and during the early 1790s supported no fewer than eight French-language or bilingual newspapers, many of them overtly political and supporting French interests.[4] Those sentiments carried over into the pages of sympathetic English-language Philadelphia newspapers such as the *Aurora* and the *National Gazette*, which beat a relentless drum for closer U.S. ties with France and greater distance from England.

Rising pro-French sentiments in the early 1790s alarmed and provoked the British and made life exceedingly difficult for President Washington, who was trying to maintain a delicate neutrality. Considering the relish with which England threw its weight around, one might have been hard-pressed to know who had won and who had lost the Revolutionary War. British tariffs prevented imports of American goods to England, or made them unduly expensive, even as English goods captured a large share of the American market. As England restricted American trade with the British West Indies, high-profile British trade reports, endorsing and promoting such policies, made their way across the Atlantic and inflamed American indignation. Meanwhile, on the high seas, British vessels used war with France as an excuse to press U.S. sailors into service for the Crown and to seize U.S. military supplies from ships.[5] England declared the authority to detain grain-bearing ships bound for French ports—a policy that left the door wide open for British harassment of American merchant vessels.[6] By early 1794, when Great Britain raised the ante by threatening to blockade all American ships bound for the French West Indies, the United States and Great Britain were in serious danger of going to war.[7]

President Washington, hoping to protect American shipping and avoid a costly war, dispatched Supreme Court chief justice John Jay to England to negotiate a treaty. The agreement Jay reached with his British counterparts in the fall of 1794 ignited a passionate American debate extending over the next two years, from the floors of Congress to newspapers to street corners and taverns.

The treaty did nothing materially to address the matter of British seizures of American personnel and equipment and, if anything, created an even greater imbalance in trading rights. One of the few concessions Jay managed from the British was an agreement to abandon several forts in northern territories—something they had already promised but failed to do eleven years earlier in the Treaty of Paris.[8] Even the Jay Treaty's singular accomplishment for the American side, avoiding war, was, initially at least, a tough sell to a public with still-fresh memories of the successful revolution.

To many, the treaty made the country look weak, fearful, and too eager to give up without a fight. Jay was burned in effigy across the country and had stones thrown his way when he appeared in public. And Washington, who had emerged from the Revolutionary War as a demigod, suffered his first taste of unrestrained hostility from the press. The *Aurora*, Philadelphia's most stridently anti-British, pro-French newspaper, took Washington's support for the treaty as clear evidence that the president, despite his service in the war, was a closet royalist looking to establish his own English-style aristocracy on this side of the Atlantic. The *Aurora* claimed that Washington's expensive tastes, right down to his "cream coloured coach, drawn by six bay horses" and his "servants in livery" showed that the president was no man of the people.[9]

The Jay Treaty had equally passionate defenders who believed the measure was the only way to ensure peace and strong ties with the country that was not just America's most vital trading partner but remained the cultural, linguistic, and spiritual wellspring of the American nation. The final showdown occurred in 1796, when Madison and other Republicans appeared ready to deal Washington a devastating setback. Although the Constitution gives the House no formal role in the treaty process and the Senate had already consented to it, the Jay Treaty required the House to approve the funding to implement it. James Madison, now serving in Congress as a representative from Virginia, argued vehemently against the treaty.

It was Fisher Ames, a congressman from Dedham, Massachusetts, who saved the day for Washington in dramatic fashion. Beset with a chronic illness that would soon force his premature retirement, Ames rose from his sickbed on April 28, 1796, and slowly made his way to Congress Hall. "I entertain the hope, perhaps a rash one, that my strength will hold me out to speak a few minutes," he told the assembly.[10] Gathering strength as he spoke, Ames delivered his speech in an emotional crescendo that touched on everything from the nature of human frailty to the rights of nations. He blasted the "strange sort of independence" advocated by Republicans who feared that the treaty would anger France.[11] Rejecting the treaty, he warned, would expose the United States to such dangers that "it is forbidden to human foresight to count their number, or measure their extent."[12]

When Ames finished to thundering applause, Supreme Court justice James Iredell turned to Vice President John Adams and gushed, "Bless my stars, I never heard any thing so great since I was born!"

"It is divine," Adams replied.[13]

Two days later the House approved funding for the Jay Treaty, 51–48.[14]

This endorsement was more than just a signature victory for Washington and the Federalists; it marked a turning point in American popular sentiment.[15] Public fury against England was subsiding as Americans became increasingly disenchanted with France. France's revolution had descended into a savage, arbitrary, and incoherent bloodbath known as the Reign of Terror.[16] Along with an endless procession of beheadings by guillotine came a wave of quasi-official mob violence, tacitly sanctioned by various competing factions and often aimed at victims who bore little or no responsibility for the oppressions that had sparked the revolution.

In September 1792, French mobs armed with pickaxes, clubs, knives, and swords slaughtered some twelve hundred inmates at several prisons. The "traitors" who met their deaths included low-level clergy, former servants to royal families, and justices of the peace, along with petty criminals, including adolescents being held for routine transgressions such as prostitution and begging.[17]

During the American Revolution John Adams had written to a friend in France about "the horrible Perfidy and Cruelty of the English," and the "natural Friend" that France was to the United States.[18] For Adams and others, the affinity with France had been much more than political or practical. Beyond France's aid in winning the revolution, there was the sense of kinship. When the French cast off the burdens of royalist government in their own revolution, Americans could claim at least partial responsibility for the reinvention of one of the world's great powers. Far from being a shaky, unsteady flicker that might blink out at any moment, the United States was looking like a strong flame of liberty to light the world.

By 1792, Vice President Adams was changing his mind on France. One precipitating event was the death of the Duc de La Rochefoucauld, an old friend from his Parisian days, who had traveled widely in the United States, supported the revolution, and translated the Declaration of Independence into French. Now his countrymen saw him as just another royalist oppressor. A French mob stoned him to death in the street.[19] The Marquis de Lafayette, beloved by Americans for his military role in the Revolutionary War, was forced to flee France as an enemy of the state and spent several years languishing in an Austrian jail.[20]

To Adams and other Federalists, spiritual kinship between the United States and France was looking more like chains than bright destiny. If democratic ideals could so quickly collapse into chaos and bloodshed, what was to stop their own fragile republic from going the same way? It was no great leap for a successful Philadelphia shipowner, New York merchant, or Boston clergyman to imagine himself being similarly hunted down. Adams's growing cynicism was captured in an observation following the execution of Louis XVI in 1793: "Mankind will in time discover that unbridled majorities are as tyrannical and cruel as unlimited despots."[21]

As American enthusiasm for the French wavered, the French themselves at times seemed determined to push the relationship off a cliff. In 1793, thirty-year-old Edmond-Charles Genêt landed in South Carolina as the French minister to the United States. Though American crowds at first welcomed Genêt, his overweening arrogance quickly wore out his welcome. He recruited American ships to serve as privateers against British ships, and organized U.S. citizens to participate in invasions against British-held territories in the Deep South and in Canada.[22] When Genêt arrived in Philadelphia, he drove President Washington to distraction by disrupting the president's careful efforts to remain neutral.[23] Thomas Jefferson, an admirer of the French, saw the damage that Genêt was causing to relations between the countries and tried to rein the Frenchman in—only to be rebuffed. Genêt was ultimately silenced not through American protests or warnings but when he himself fell victim to the French Revolution's latest arbitrary witch hunt. Ordered home by the revolutionary government to answer for some transgression allegedly committed before he left home, Genêt ignored the summons and settled in New York, married an American woman, and lived quietly for the remainder of his life.[24] But the damage to France's image, in the eyes of many Americans, had already been done.

By now, an American sporting a French cockade on the streets of Philadelphia might find himself called, with disgust, not just a Francophile but a "Jacobin" or "Sans Culottes" after two of the more strident and brutal French factions competing for power in postrevolutionary France.[25] The implication was inescapable: the man wearing a French cockade today might be driving a guillotine wagon along Chestnut Street tomorrow.

These tensions deepened and intensified through every layer of society, through to the highest reaches of the U.S. government. What Washington had envisioned as leadership devoid of party and faction, unified around the idea of public service, was becoming a government of competing interests and divided loyalties. The fractures were deepest in his own cabinet, among men in whom he placed the highest trust. Thomas Jefferson, Washington's secretary of state, had spent four years as minister to France leading up to the French Revolution. He viewed the revolution as the antidote to European aristocracy and as the next logical step in the march toward "The liberty of the whole earth." In his zeal, he discounted reports of French atrocities, even when a former protégé reported that "the streets literally are red with blood."[26] Jefferson discreetly financed Philadelphia newspapers such as Philip Freneau's *National Gazette*, which lambasted Washington for his supposed British sympathies. When Washington questioned Jefferson over rumors of his involvement with Freneau, Jefferson denied any role.[27] For all his brilliance as a writer and thinker, Jefferson was also a politician, a survivor who avoided direct confrontation. When things got nasty, he managed to stay above the fray as surrogates did his dirty work (and suffered the consequences).

Jefferson's principal enemy in the Washington administration was Treasury Secretary Alexander Hamilton, in some ways the greatest visionary of all the Founders. It was Hamilton who most clearly predicted the country's destiny as a mighty power. His plans to establish a national bank, to have the new government assume the Revolutionary War debts of individual states, and to repay at face value all holders of war bonds were among the most important early steps in solidifying the financial future of the federal government and the nation.

To Jefferson and, increasingly, to James Madison, Hamilton's plans seemed to trample liberty in the interest of creating a federal goliath on the model of the British government. Madison had been Hamilton's essential partner in creating the Federalist Papers, but Madison now watched Hamilton's energetic efforts on behalf of national power with a growing alarm. Hamilton's federal whiskey tax led in the early 1790s to violent confrontations in western Pennsylvania between federal tax collectors and enraged farmers. Only the arrival of massed U.S. troops, led by George Washington himself, with Hamilton at his side, had prevented large-scale bloodshed.

If Jefferson saw in Hamilton's plans incipient tyranny, Hamilton viewed Jefferson's vision of an agrarian nation of gentlemen farmers and decentralized government as a guileless, Francophile fantasy. In the end, both were right. Though they viewed their battle as a fight for the soul and survival of America, either approach, taken to extremes, might have spelled disaster for the young country. If Hamilton's big government machinations implied tyranny of one sort, the dangers inherent in Jefferson's overabundant faith in states' rights had already been made clear by the Articles of Confederation and the First and Second Continental Congresses, whose weakness and impotence called into question the very meaning of "united" in United States. As it was, these competing ideologies kept each other appropriately in check. Trembling beneath the surface was a question just as vital as the proper role of government: Could free people accommodate such radically opposing views without yielding to the temptation to forcefully silence each other?

When Washington left office in 1797, these fractures were destined only to grow under the incoming president, John Adams. Adams was nothing like the unifying figure that Washington had represented. Adams's election over Thomas Jefferson was by a slim margin of 71 to 68 electoral votes.[28] Because national politics had yet to recognize parties, presidential candidates did not campaign with vice presidential running mates; rather, the second-place finisher became vice president. As party differences emerged and hardened, this arrangement meant that Adams had as his vice president a man who had come to fundamentally disagree with him on what Adams saw as his most immediate challenge: containing the threat from France.

# CHAPTER THREE

Philadelphia's Congress Hall, home of the U.S. House of Representatives and Senate from 1790 until 1800, was a rectangular building and quite small considering the outsized historical events that took place there. The House of Representatives occupied the first floor, where members sat at long rows of shared desks facing the raised dais of the Speaker of the House. The Senate gathered in more elegant and refined quarters up a long double set of wooden stairs. Though it had less than one-third the members (32 versus 106 in 1798), the Senate commanded equal square footage with the House, offering expansive room in the chambers, along with capacious offices and committee rooms. The House, with just a door and a small alcove separating members from the public on the street outside, felt comparatively crowded and cramped—especially when the Senate was called down for a joint gathering.

On May 16, 1797, a little after noon, Speaker Jonathan Dayton sent word to members of the Senate upstairs to join them in the House chamber. Soon thereafter, the senators entered and took their assigned seats. The room was packed. The new president, John Adams, strode in and took Dayton's seat at the dais. Neither Federalists nor Republicans knew quite what to expect. Few men in the history of politics ever had a tougher act to follow. George Washington, the first and to this day only U.S. president to be elected unanimously (twice) to office had left a void in the public spirit that no man could be expected to fill.

Adams had called this special meeting of Congress to address the subject on everyone's mind. Tensions with France had intensified in recent months with the capture of hundreds of American merchant vessels by French privateers in the West Indies. Though not officially part of the French navy, the privateers operated with tacit approval from the government. The West Indies represented vital trade for American ships, who supplied the islands with timber, fish, grain, and other commodities, and returned home with holds groaning with sugar.

France, for its part, considered itself to be the aggrieved party in the deteriorating relations. Having helped secure American independence, France had been stung by Washington's signing of the Jay Treaty with England in 1794. It mattered little that Washington had done so as an act of self-preservation; the French saw it as taking sides with a sworn enemy. As one French journalist noted of the United States, "In vain have we hoped for some time that gratitude, or at least self-interest, would make of that federal republic a loyal ally of France."[1]

Still, the situation was quickly becoming untenable for American commerce. The cost of insuring a voyage jumped from 6 percent of the combined value of the ship and cargo in 1796 to as high as 25 percent in 1797.[2] Not only did the United States lack the naval power to protect its ships, but efforts at diplomacy were being rebuffed in humiliating fashion. Most recently, news had returned to Philadelphia that the French had refused to accept Charles Cotesworth Pinckney, appointed by Washington in one of his final acts as president, to serve as U.S. minister to France. Instead of treating Pinckney as a duly appointed representative of a foreign power when he arrived in Paris, French officials dismissed him as a pariah and ordered him out of town.[3]

Now, all eyes turned to John Adams. Would he stand up to the French, or cave in? Adams sat for a moment, as if to collect his thoughts, and then rose to deliver the first major speech of his presidency. He started on a note of optimism, sounding like a president assuming the reins of a happy and peaceful land. Adams thanked

> the Supreme Dispenser of national blessings, for general health and promising seasons; for domestic and social happiness; for the rapid progress and ample acquisitions of industry, through extensive territories; for civil, political, and religious liberties. While other States are desolated with foreign war, or convulsed with intestine divisions, the United States present the pleasing prospect of a nation governed by mild and equal laws, generally satisfied with the possession of their rights.[4]

Moments later, his tone darkened and rolled like thunderheads over the placid scene he had just painted. "It is with extreme regret that I shall be obliged to turn your thoughts to other circumstances, which admonish us that some of these felicities may not be lasting," he warned. The French government had refused to recognize an American minister sent in good faith to settle growing differences between the two countries. Such a move "is to treat us neither as allies, nor as friends, nor as a sovereign State." Americans owed it to themselves to show the French, and the world, "that we are not a degraded people, humiliated under a colonial spirit of fear and sense of inferiority, fitted to be the miserable instruments of foreign influence."[5]

The only way to ensure national security was through a navy, Adams said. While pledging to continue peace efforts with France, Adams raised the prospect of war by calling on Congress to appropriate funds for a strong navy capable of patrolling nearly two thousand miles of coast, to stem the rise of French privateering attacks on U.S. vessels. "A Naval power, next to the Militia, is the natural defence of the United States."[6]

By the time Adams concluded, hardline Federalists who had doubted whether he had the backbone to stand up to France were overjoyed. The House quickly proposed a response praising the words of "the Supreme Executive," and warning the French that "No attempts to wound our rights as a sovereign State will escape the notice of our constituents."[7]

Republicans hoping that Adams's position on France would soften the harder edges of Federalist belligerence were just as deeply disappointed. They saw in the president's words a direct slap at an ally whose support had helped secure American independence. Just as troubling was Adams's call for a strong navy, which played directly into Republican fears of a standing army and its potential for abuse in the hands of an overpowerful federal government. Republicans wanted no part of the Federalists' fawning endorsement of the president's speech. For the next two weeks, both sides furiously debated the official House response to Adams's words. One might have expected a freshman congressman thrust from the backwoods of Vermont into the national legislature in America's most sophisticated and cultured city to be a bit cowed, or, at least, to hang back for a while and get his bearings. Not Matthew Lyon. He waded eagerly into the debate, and every petulant, Gaelic-tinted syllable that left his lips struck Federalist ears as a gross indecency.

At one point, Lyon and fellow Republican Albert Gallatin, a native of Switzerland, simultaneously objected to the wording of a specific clause in the Federalist draft. In his personal background and bearing, Gallatin was urbane, elegant, and gentlemanly. He had studied at some of the finest institutions in Europe and taught at Harvard. Though still in his midthirties, Gallatin displayed the poise and deliberative nature of a much older and more seasoned politician. He had learned to choose his battles carefully and to overlook passing slights and setbacks in favor of long-term victories.

Just four years earlier, in 1793, Gallatin had been elected to the U.S. Senate from his adopted home in western Pennsylvania, only to be evicted three months into his first term by Federalists claiming he had not lived in the country for the requisite nine years. The party-line vote was a sham; Gallatin had come to the United States in 1780, a full thirteen years before running for the Senate. Without apparent rancor, Gallatin regrouped. He bided his time and returned as a member of the House, as polite and deferential as ever.[8]

To a native-born Connecticut Yankee such as John Allen, though, Abraham Alfonse Albert Gallatin and his suspiciously French accent had no more business than Matthew Lyon trespassing on this sacred floor of American statesmanship. Allen rose to his feet and assured his fellow congressmen that, regardless of Lyon's and Gallatin's objections, there was "American blood enough in the House to approve of this clause, and American accent enough to pronounce it."[9]

On June 2, the House adopted a strong endorsement of Adams's speech, accusing the French of endangering the peace and tranquillity of the United States and pledging to Adams their "zealous cooperation in those measures which may appear necessary for our security or peace."[10] Many Republicans, reluctant to openly rebuke the new president, joined the Federalists in approving the statement by a vote of 62–36.[11] Among these was Gallatin. Overlooking Allen's personal insult from the previous day, Gallatin made a prudent, reasonable decision to preserve his political capital for another fight.

The House and the Senate requested a formal audience with the president in order to present their responses to his address. Adams agreed to greet the lawmakers that day at noon. Members of both bodies would gather outside Congress Hall on Walnut Street, form a processional, and march one long block north to the president's home on Market Street to deliver their words. To ensure a respectable showing, a House rule dictated that no member, unless excused for illness or leave of absence, could skip the ceremony. Modeled on traditional homage paid by British Parliament to the king, the parade had been incorporated into American practice during the Washington administration. Adams, a man of plain dress and habits, had taken pains to present himself as a man of the people. He had dispensed with Washington's fancy carriage and six white horses, and with most of the quasi-regal trappings that always seemed to surround the revered general. But the processional struck Lyon as royalist pomp.

Lyon, one of the thirty-six members who voted against the endorsement, rose before the House to announce that, rule or no rule, he had no intention of marching with the group. He wondered drily whether he would be arrested for breaking the House dictum, and chided "our magnanimous President," who, having "spent a great part of his life amongst a people whose love of a plainness of manners forbids all pageantry," would surely "despise such a boyish piece of business." As for himself, Lyon said he could not participate even if he wanted to, since all eighty thousand plain-speaking, equality-loving Vermonters in his district would condemn him.[12]

Such flagrant disrespect caught Federalists and moderate Republicans alike off guard. One can imagine Gallatin sinking in his seat, glancing furtively from one stony Federalist face to the next, calculating the damage he would have to undo for being associated by party and by foreign birth with Matthew Lyon. But Lyon wasn't finished.

Invoking John Allen's insult, he said, "The gentleman from Connecticut yesterday hoped there would be American blood enough to carry the question." If members of Congress insisted on bragging about something as ridiculous as the quality of their blood, Lyon continued, he should point out that he had as good blood as any of them, having been "born of a fine, hale, healthy woman." As for their English lineage, Lyon was just as glad to say that he was *not* "descended from the bastards of Oliver Cromwell, or his courtiers, or from the Puritans, who punished their horses for breaking the Sabbath, or from those who persecuted the Quakers or hanged the witches." But nobody could tell him he was not an American. Lyon proclaimed "this was his country, because he had no other; and he owned a share of it, which he had bought by means of honest industry; he had fought for his country."[13]

Beyond having their ancestry boiled down to an assortment of Cromwellian bastards and horse-abusing Puritan witch-hangers, what surely galled Federalists even more was this lowbred servant boy's claim to full and equal ownership of *their* country. Nonplussed, Connecticut's Samuel W. Dana responded that "the House would not wish to do violence to the gentleman's feelings" by forcing him to attend. As if opening a window to let out a bad smell, exasperated members quickly and unanimously approved Lyon's motion to be excused from the ceremony.[14]

His public slap at the president and Federalist Congress made Matthew Lyon, overnight, the most controversial Republican politician in the United States. Nathaniel Chipman, newly elected senator from Vermont, wrote to Cephas Smith Jr., a prosperous attorney back in Rutland, of Lyon's behavior in the capitol: "You can not with all your knowledge of the man easily conceive how ridiculous a figure he makes." But Chipman spotted a silver lining. "I think however he will be of use, as by aspiring to take the lead among the jacobins he will make many more decent men of that party ashamed of their association."[15]

Over the next several months Lyon's notoriety only grew. He took every opportunity to highlight what he viewed as Federalist pretensions and hypocrisy—the more sensitive the issue, the more boldly he spoke. And if the flap over the Adams ceremony amounted to so much pomp, when the issue carried greater moral weight Lyon proved capable of defending principled positions with eloquence and grace.

That July, the House debated the twenty-dollar naturalization fee for new immigrants to stem what Federalists saw as an alarming tide of newcomers. Since the proposal was tucked in as an amendment to a revenue-raising stamp tax bill, Republicans accused Federalists of trying to reshape America's immigration policies on the sly. The arguments might have been ripped from a twenty-first-century debate on the same subject. John Swanwick, a Pennsylvania Republican and poet, argued that the tax unfairly targeted the poor, who were entitled to at least as much consideration as the "rich moneyed corporations" upon whom the Federalists always seemed willing to bestow favors.[16]

Massachusetts Federalist Samuel Sewall shot back that no foreigner deserved to become a citizen who "did not think the privilege worth twenty dollars." David Brooks of New York assured Republicans that he had nothing against foreigners in general, but wanted only to keep "fugitives from justice" and other undesirables out. And Robert Goodloe Harper of South Carolina questioned the wisdom of "inviting immigrations from all parts of the world." The time for liberal immigration policies had come and gone, Harper said. "There was a moment of enthusiasm in this country, when this was thought to be right," but that moment had clearly passed. "An experience of ten or fifteen years . . . convinced us we were wrong." Harper proposed that foreigners be allowed in, but that "no man should become a citizen of this country but by birth."[17]

But it was Matthew Lyon who rhetorically carried the day, calling the proposed fee "injurious, cruel, and impolitic." The fee was, he said, "injurious, because we had dealt out a different kind of language heretofore; we had told the world, that there was in this country a good spring of liberty, and invited all to come and drink of it. We had told them that the country was rich and fertile, and invited them to come and taste of our fruits." How could such a nation "turn round to them and say, you shall not be admitted as citizens unless you pay twenty dollars"?[18] At length, the Federalists tired of the debate. They lowered the proposal from twenty dollars to five dollars, but the House adjourned before taking a final vote on the stamp bill, and the proposal died.[19]

As Lyon grew more strident, Federalist newspaper editors ramped up their attacks. Fed by Chipman and other Vermont Federalists, William Cobbett, editor of *Porcupine's Gazette*, dredged up the

Revolutionary War episode in which Lyon's troops had deserted and Lyon been charged with cowardice. Cobbett included in his article the colorful but apocryphal tale that Lyon, as a symbol of cowardice, had been forced to wear a wooden sword.[20]

Rising tensions between Lyon and the Federalists finally erupted spectacularly on January 30, 1798. The House had spent much of the day debating impeachment proceedings against Tennessean William Blount, a former delegate to the Constitutional Convention who had been ejected from his Senate seat for his part in a tangled conspiracy to help the British to seize Spanish territories in Louisiana and Florida. During a break in the debate, Lyon leaned against the House bar in conversation with Speaker Jonathan Dayton. In a voice "loud enough to be heard by all those who were near him, as if he intended to be heard by them," Lyon held forth on the poor quality of representatives from his original home state of Connecticut. He accused them of acting against the interests and beliefs of their constituents and of seeking personal gain from public office. What Connecticut lacked, Lyon continued, were good, strong opposition newspapers to give the people the truth.[21]

Sitting within earshot throughout Lyon's monologue was thirty-six-year-old Congressman Roger Griswold of Connecticut. Born and raised in Lyme, educated at Yale, and a Connecticut representative since 1795, Griswold had heard enough.

"If you go into Connecticut," he called, "you had better wear your wooden sword."

When Lyon either ignored or did not hear the slight, Griswold rose from his seat and walked over to Lyon and Dayton. Still addressing the Speaker, Lyon noted that he had lived among Connecticut people for much of his life, and fought with them, and always managed to convince them that he was right.

Griswold asked, "Do you fight them with your wooden sword?"

This charge of cowardice could not be ignored. A gentleman would have demanded satisfaction with dueling pistols at daybreak.

That custom, dragged across the Atlantic from Europe, was still in vogue for Americans with aristocratic pretensions. Six more years were still to pass before Aaron Burr leveled a dueling pistol at Alexander Hamilton and fired, thus giving America its signature duel and ending the life and career of the most brilliant Federalist of them all.

But Matthew Lyon was no gentleman, and his anger could not wait for sunrise. What Lyon did next was ungentlemanly in the extreme, but for a man who had been street fighting his entire life it seemed like the only thing to do: he turned and spit in Roger Griswold's face.

# Chapter Four

For a few moments, Griswold and the rest of the House stood in stunned silence. Then the members snapped into action, clearing the public gallery of spectators while debating a proper response to what Samuel Sewall called "a violent attack and gross indecency."[1] After briefly considering whether to continue discussing the matter in secrecy, the House voted unanimously to refill the galleries. With the public reseated, Sewall read a hastily prepared resolution demanding that Lyon be expelled from Congress. Some demanded that he be arrested on the spot and held by the sergeant at arms until further notice. But cooler heads prevailed, and the motion garnered only 29 votes, with 62 against.

For once, even Lyon seemed humbled by his own actions. Two days later he submitted an archly formal apology to Speaker Dayton. He feigned surprise that spitting in another member's face on the House floor might be viewed as a breach of conduct, since it did not directly pertain to matters of state. The apology had no effect whatever on the Federalist majority in Congress, which finally saw an opportunity to rid itself of this interloper.

Despite the looming crisis with France, revenue and taxation matters, immigration bills, and the need to address any number of other issues before them, House members spent the next two weeks transfixed by Lyon's airborne gob of saliva. Nathaniel Chipman, only too pleased to watch his old enemy twist, came down from the Senate to testify that Lyon was a notorious hothead. Chipman recalled a conversation back in Vermont, in which Lyon, preparing for his new role in Congress, had supposedly vowed revenge on anyone in Philadelphia who dared to mention wooden swords.[2]

Lewis R. Morris, Vermont's other congressman, represented the Federalist eastern side of the mountains. Amid the conflict, he wrote home to a friend, bemoaning "the disgrace Vermont & the United States have suffered by the conduct of my colleague."[3] Republicans, too, were dismayed by Lyon's behavior. No doubt more than a few wished he had never emerged from the Green Mountains. Albert Gallatin observed that Lyon's action "shows a want of manners—a want of good breeding." But he argued that although some members may choose not to fraternize with Lyon, "we do not come here to associate as individuals, but to deliberate upon legislative subjects in our representative capacity."[4]

Robert Goodloe Harper, the South Carolina Federalist, responded that a mere insult was not the same thing as an assault. "The distinction between words and a personal [physical] attack, is a distinction well understood." Those words would come to drip with irony.[5]

Harrison Gray Otis took the prize for bombastic silliness by suggesting that Lyon's spittle had shaken the foundations of the republic. Permitting Lyon to remain in office, Otis proclaimed, would be tantamount to "sealing the infamy of the National Legislature." Lyon was guilty of "conduct which could not be suffered in a brothel or in a den of robbers!"[6]

As the attacks on his character and questions about his fitness to serve mounted, Lyon recovered from his brief bout of humility. He requested time to bring forth witnesses from Vermont who would testify as to his strong character. When this approach got him nowhere, he barked, "I did not come here to have my [arse] kicked by every body."[7]

After two weeks of debate, Federalists mustered 52 votes for eviction against 44 nays. It was enough to demonstrate that a clear majority of Lyon's House colleagues wanted him gone, but eight votes short of the two-thirds required for expulsion. Matthew Lyon survived.[8]

Griswold had remained largely silent throughout the hearings. But when the House failed to provide satisfaction, his personal honor demanded action. On a Thursday morning, shortly before the House was called to order, Griswold entered the chamber carrying a hefty wooden cane.[9] Lyon, writing at his desk, looked up just in time to see Griswold striding toward him. Before he could react, Griswold swung and landed several blows. Bleeding from a gash on his head, Lyon fought his way to the fireplace behind the Speaker's desk and grabbed a pair of metal tongs. For the second time in as many weeks, the House of Representatives stood in awestruck silence. The tongs came crashing toward Griswold's head. Griswold diverted the blow and grabbed the tongs. Pulled off balance, the pair tumbled to the floor, with Griswold on top, as House members at last intervened. Two members, each holding one of Griswold's legs, managed to pull the Federalist off the Republican and bustled them both from the chamber. As Speaker Dayton ordered members to take their seats, Lyon and Griswold again flew at each other in the outer room, only to be separated by the assistant doorkeeper and some onlookers.[10]

The next day, Thomas Terry Davis, a Kentucky Republican, moved to have both Griswold and Lyon ejected from the House for conduct "so grossly violent, and so notorious to most of the members of the House, that there need be no hesitation in deciding upon it."[11] But now that one of their own had made the leap from words to physical assault, Federalists lost their appetite for expulsion. As a compromise, Lyon and Griswold, bloodied but otherwise not seriously injured, swore not to fight anymore under threat of arrest from the sergeant at arms. The motion to expel the pair garnered just twenty-one votes.[12] Hardliners had to settle for an official reprimand of the two, for "riotous and disorderly behavior."[13]

If these extraordinary events mortified members of Congress, they came as a great gift to Philadelphia's newspapermen, who recorded every spit-streaked, bloodstained moment, as well as every syllable of pompous speechifying that followed. Congressmen claimed the journalists were deliberately trying to make them look like fools. Journalists countered that members of Congress had only themselves to blame.

In one form or another, that same debate had been going on since Congress first opened its doors in 1789. Unlike the Senate, which for the first several years conducted its business sealed off from the press and the public, the People's House had always invited onlookers. Rank-and-file visitors packed a public gallery. Reporters sat in chairs on the floor itself or lounged next to the windows. The relationship was based on mutual need. Journalists, often doubling as their own printers, needed copy to fill their pages. House members separated from their constituents by hundreds of miles of bad roads and treacherous river crossings needed to stay current in the minds of folks back home. Reports from Philadelphia newspapers found their way into local newspapers in towns around the country.

Yet the relationship was never easy. Journalists scribbled furiously to capture long-winded speeches, motions, and votes. They complained that House members mumbled, spoke too fast, turned away from them when speaking, and generally made their task impossible. Congressmen charged that reporters misquoted them through incompetence or malice, twisted and distorted their speeches, omitted key facts and invented others out of thin air. On September 26, 1789, members debated a resolution introduced by Aedanus Burke of South Carolina, charging journalists with having "misrepresented these debates in the most glaring deviations from truth," and with "throwing over the whole proceedings a thick veil of misrepresentation and error."[14]

The timing was ironic, to say the least. Two days earlier, on September 24, the House approved the final wording of what would become the First Amendment to the Bill of Rights, guaranteeing freedom of the press.[15] Another irony is that our detailed knowledge of the debate comes courtesy of the very reporters who so angered Congress. The Annals of Congress, the single best resource on the workings of the early House, was compiled entirely from old newspaper accounts. The Constitution issues only a vague mandate that each house of Congress keep and publish a journal of its proceedings "from time to time," while allowing exceptions for "such Parts as may in their Judgment require Secrecy," and with the yeas and nays of each member recorded only "at the Desire of one fifth of those present."

Thus there was no official stenographer recording the most revealing and dramatic elements, the debates. When House members suggested hiring one, James Madison, serving as a representative from Virginia, pointed out that such a move would saddle members with the colossal homework assignment of correcting and amending each day's proceedings before the record could become official.[16] Other arguments against a full-time stenographer included the expense, along with fears that whoever was in power at the moment would in essence have the power to write history.[17] So the job of recording the history of Congress was left to reporters.

And now, as the Lyon-Griswold feud unfolded, Congress was again stewing over a licentious, seemingly out-of-control press. The Federalists did most of the complaining, even though much of the reporting was favorable to their side. For all the caterwauling, between 1797 and 1801 (the years of John Adams's presidency) Federalists enjoyed an outsized advantage in the press. Of 318 newspapers published during those years in the United States, 171 leaned or were strongly Federalist, compared with 89 that leaned or were strongly Republican, with the rest either professing neutrality or devoting little or no attention to politics. In some states, the Federalist advantage was overwhelming. Of 23 Connecticut newspapers, 11 were strongly Federalist, compared with just 1, the weekly *New London Bee*, which leaned strongly Republican.[18]

Pennsylvania, with its large numbers of Irish and German immigrants, presented a more balanced mix, with 16 solidly Federalist versus 14 solidly Republican papers.[19] But there was no shortage of strident journalists lambasting the Republican bête noir, Matthew Lyon, whom Federalists had taken to calling "the spitting Lyon." A Boston editor wrote that all true patriots should "feel grieved that the saliva of an Irishman should be left upon the face of an American & He, a New England-man."[20] The *Connecticut Gazette* published an elaborate parody in biblical prose, detailing the adventures of a member of "the Tribe of Irishites" who carried a sword "made of costly Wood, even of the Pine of the Green Mountains," and who, faced with battle, "ran mightily."[21]

Still, Federalists were infuriated by one of the few stalwart Republican newspapers that came to Lyon's defense. For the past several years, the *Aurora* had been the most consistent thorn in the side of those in power. Its publisher, Benjamin Franklin Bache, was absolutely fearless. Attacks only strengthened his resolve to fight. Staunchly Republican, the *Aurora* was one of the most popular and, without question, the most controversial newspaper in America. If Matthew Lyon had competition at the head of the list of men the Federalists most wished to silence, it was Benjamin Bache.

Bache's advocacy for Lyon amounted to an eloquent defense of the American immigrant experience. On February 5, the Federalist *Gazette of the United States* had published a letter signed only by "An admirer of the true American character." The letter derided Lyon as "not a native American, but an imported patriot" whose election was a "disgrace" to his adopted land. Bache reprinted the letter in the *Aurora*, and asked, in response: "In reason and in fact, what is the distinction between the foreign-born and the native citizen? Truly it is in favor of

the former; he is the United States from *choice* the latter from *chance*."
Bache continued: "It surely is to the honor of Mr. Lyon, that from a
low beginning he has raised himself to competency by industry and
acquired such a standing among those he lives with . . . None but a
proud, prejudiced and selfish being, an aristocrat in grain, will quar-
rel with a man because he did not draw his first breath on the same
spot with himself, or will reproach him because the consequence he
has acquired in wealth and station, was not bequeathed to him by
his ancestors, but by his own industry and merits."[22]

Bache delighted in recording and printing every word of the
daily congressional debate. A few days after the spitting incident,
Speaker Dayton, weary of the close coverage, proposed that journalists be required to submit their notes to members of Congress before
writing their stories. Dayton insisted that he had no desire to censor
the press, and was merely demanding "the opportunity of correcting" notes, in advance, in order to ensure accuracy of statements that
would be presented to the American public as fact. In one instance,
Dayton said, his own words had been reduced to "utter nonsense."
David Brooks, a New York Federalist, declared, "a regulation of this
kind would be extremely proper."[23]

The complaints only incited Bache, who counted proudly
among his enemies George Washington, John Adams, Alexander
Hamilton, and Secretary of State Timothy Pickering—strong men
with powerful friends and long memories. He was hardly going to be
intimidated by Jonathan Dayton and Samuel Dana. When Dayton
ordered Bache from the House floor, the editor happily relocated
from the floor to the gallery, where he whipped out his pen, craned
his neck to hear, and took more notes.

# CHAPTER FIVE

Considering his deeply ingrained need to criticize those in power, and his sympathy with the plight of poor immigrants, Benjamin Franklin Bache might be assumed, like Matthew Lyon, to be a born outsider salving childhood wounds of poverty and low birth. On the contrary, as his first and middle names attested, Bache was the second grandson of perhaps the most celebrated Founding Father. Bache's mother, Sarah (called "Sally"), was Benjamin Franklin's beloved only daughter. His father, Richard Bache, was a mild-mannered, unsuccessful merchant of whom Franklin initially disapproved but later came to accept.[1]

Though Ben Franklin, the son of a poor soap maker, had started out as an apprentice printer, by the time his grandson Benjamin Bache was born in 1769, Franklin's celebrity was so firmly entrenched, his years of comparative poverty so far in the past, that even the old man himself might have been loath to say where actual life experience left off and Poor Richard's aphorisms began. The Franklin that his grandson knew was a portly, wealthy man of the world, whom one historian would call "America's first international celebrity."[2] He was enjoying his golden age; a lover of bonbons and fine wines, he was as comfortable in a European salon filled with perfumed wigs as in a Yankee town hall meeting.

In the epochal year 1776 the seventy-year-old Franklin sailed for France on a nine-year diplomatic mission to shore up French support for the American cause. He decided to take Bache ("Benny," Franklin affectionately called him) and Bache's older cousin, William Temple Franklin, along for company. Bache was the perfect companion for a grandfather whom he would come to worship. His mother wrote of the boy, "I look upon Ben to be of a temper that will be easy to govern. He will do a great deal out of affection."[3] Not long after his seventh birthday, Bache kissed his parents good-bye and sailed off on a journey that would largely define his life, bestowing on him an abiding fondness for France and the French, and a deep, idealistic commitment to liberty as filtered through the fertile mind of his grandfather.

The journey started inauspiciously, to say the least. So as to avoid raising British suspicions, Franklin, Bache, and William traveled by night carriage out of Philadelphia, without fanfare. South of the city they boarded the warship *Reprisal*.[4] For the next thirty days, packed into tight, inelegant quarters, Franklin and his grandsons gnawed salt beef and fought illness as the ship endured storm after storm on the rough winter seas of the North Atlantic. Already racked by ailments owing to his age and the age in which he lived, Franklin suffered a flare-up of boils covering much of his body. When at last the ship came in sight of French land, unfavorable winds kept them from approaching their chosen destination. After four days of waiting Franklin paid a local fisherman to row the three ashore and deposit them, unceremoniously, near the small village of Auray on December 3.[5]

For security purposes, the trip had never been announced.[6] But as soon as the French became aware of the man in their midst, everything changed. From the dark purgatory of eighteenth-century ocean transportation, Franklin and his grandsons were delivered into the dazzling light of French culture and sophistication. By the time the trio had passed through Nantes and Versailles, word had spread to the point that Parisians turned out on the streets to see the carriage as it arrived in the capital on December 21.[7]

If Franklin was famous in the United States as a practical phi-losopher, printer, and political figure, in France he was on the order of a demigod, equally revered for his scientific breakthroughs and plainspoken truths. He was known as the man who tamed lightning itself. No less a figure than Voltaire had proclaimed him a genius.[8] Franklin's Poor Richard book, *The Way to Wealth*, recast with the mellifluous title *La science du Bonhomme Richard*, ran through multiple printings.[9]

Franklin made elegant camp in the Paris suburb of Passy, on the estate of Jacques-Donatien Leray de Chaumont, a wealthy trader, hater of the English, and sympathizer with the American cause. Chau-mont took special interest in seven-year-old Bache, helping to enroll him in Le Coeur's *pension*, a small, highly regarded boarding school nearby. The lessons were taught in French, and with his scholastic immersion Bache quickly became as comfortable in his adopted lan-guage as in English.

If the positive French reception was gratifying to Franklin, France seemed, in the eyes of a seven-year-old who had crossed the dark seas, a veritable wonderland. A quiet, serious, studious child, Bache visited Franklin in Passy on weekends, where he saw his grand-father being doted on by French dignitaries, and was introduced to frequent American visitors, including Thomas Jefferson and John Adams. Adams's son, future president John Quincy Adams, was enrolled at the same school, two years ahead of Bache.[10]

Distracted and consumed with the cult of his own celebrity, Franklin seems to have had little real time for the boy, despite his genuine affection for him.[11] If he was (and is) sometimes portrayed by detractors as a bit of a fop and a dilettante, particularly during his Paris days, Franklin in fact faced an extraordinarily difficult task in helping to win the French over to the American side in the war during the late 1770s. Despite the long-standing antipathy of the French and English for each other, the two countries were maintain-ing a precarious truce. There were clear advantages to the French in providing military support to the colonies, should they emerge victorious. But reports of American defeats, such as British general William Howe's capture of Philadelphia in 1777, intensified the difficulties of Franklin's mission. Should the French commit themselves to a losing cause, they might hinder their own international diplomacy at a highly delicate time.[12]

When Bache was nine years old, Franklin shipped him off to a boarding school in Geneva.[13] During Bache's first lonely year there, letters from his beloved grandfather came like gifts. "I am very glad that you write to me very often," he wrote. "I pray you to continue it."[14]

The longer he stayed in Europe, the more Bache identified with European customs and the French language. "I try as much as I can to regain my English in writing to you," he informed his mother in a letter home.[15] Three years later he blamed a sloppily written note on his bad pen and on having become "a Franco Anglois/Anglois Franco" to the extent that "you can not expect good English."[16] The claim of losing his English was overstated, a youthful attempt to emphasize his Continental sophistication or excuse lazy letter writing, but his affiliation with Europe and, in particular, the French would remain for the rest of his life.

If young Bache was missing extraordinary events of the Revolutionary War back home, it was nevertheless an exciting time for an alert, observant adolescent to find himself in Geneva, then an independent republic in the throes of its own revolutionary turmoil. In the spring of 1782, when Genevans revolted against an authoritarian local government, alarmed monarchs in France, Switzerland, and Sardinia sent some twelve thousand troops to restore order.[17]

Bache's diary from these years intermixes boyhood high jinks with a growing awareness of politics and the violence of his age. Some entries find him enraptured with ice-skating, bored with enforced attendance at balls, and pondering revenge on a neighborhood cat that had run off with one of his pet guinea pigs. Elsewhere, he chronicles a darker side of life in Geneva. With a natural reporter's eye for detail, Bache, still just thirteen years old, roamed the city, detailing descriptions of drunken brawls and duels among the Swiss, French, and "Piedmontese" (Sardinian) troops occupying the city. In September he attended the public execution of a Sardinian soldier convicted of stealing some copper coins. "This was the mode of procedure," Bache reported. "The regiment surrounded the criminal who marched accompanied by a priest. Arrived at the place of execution, he was seated on a bank of turf and was tied to a picket. The priest continues to speak as he retires, the officer gives the sign, the soldiers fire, the regiment marches around the dead body and they carry it away."[18] Though he related that episode with clinical detachment, he could also show, for a boy his age, a rare sensitivity to others' emotions. Moved no doubt by his own homesickness for his grandfather in Passy and his parents in Philadelphia, Bache noted one day: "The Swiss are changing their soldiers who were in Geneva. I went to see those arriving, they looked very sad because they had just left their families; on the contrary those who quitted Geneva were very joyous."[19]

At the end of his term in 1783, a teenage Bache returned to Franklin's home in Passy. He swam in the Seine and flew kites with his grandfather.[20] Fascinated by an emerging French passion, Bache attended balloon launchings whenever he could. And he luxuriated in his grandfather's world of concerts, scientific lectures, and celebrated guests.[21]

As Franklin began to consider a profession for his grandson, he naturally steered Bache toward the vocation that had consumed so much of his own life: printing. Despite all of his other pressures and involvements, Franklin had set up a printing house in Paris, producing bank orders, passports, and other documents. Franklin's French print master, Maurice Meyer, took Bache under his wing, showing him the intricacies of setting type and printing. Franklin, now in his late seventies and with the weight of endless diplomacy beginning to wear on him, took refuge from his cares in the reassuring smell of ink and the sound of the press. His relationship with his grandson matured into a more adult friendship. As Bache's skills developed, he recounted proudly in April 1785, "My grandfather has induced Mr. Didot, the best printer of this century, or that has ever been seen, to take me into his house for a time to teach me his art. I take my meals at his house, and lodge at Mr. Le Roy's, a friend of my grandfather's."[22]

Later that year Franklin's diplomatic mission ended, and with it the happiest, most enchanting period of Bache's life. On the journey home, in August 1785, the ship encountered a fierce storm. When a gale tore free the bowsprit sail, "We remained without a single sail, driven at the mercy of the wind which happily was not unfavorable. The sea was in a frightful state of agitation. The waves rose to such a height that the mainmast plunged three times into the water, and the water was so blown about by the wind that we could not see 50 feet ahead of us," Bache wrote, "and the sailors and Captain acknowledged, they had never seen anything to equal it." The next day, thankfully calm and sunny, Bache was still animated by the experience, full of youthful enthusiasm and courage. "I was quite satisfied to have enjoyed such a beautiful scene, and to have escaped from such peril. I believe that all my life I shall keep in remembrance that moment, rendered so interesting by its danger."[23]

Though Bache reunited joyfully with his parents upon returning to Philadelphia, he and Franklin had grown close enough that the two were never far apart. Franklin saw to it that Bache capped his European education by enrolling at the University of Pennsylvania, where he studied Euclidean geometry and moral philosophy. But there was never much question about what profession he would ultimately enter. After finishing his studies in 1787, the nineteen-year-old Bache took a direct role in building a printing business, financed by Franklin, in a series of buildings on Market Street.[24]

As Franklin's health by now was failing, Bache served as aide as well as companion and private secretary. Through his grandfather's eyes, he witnessed the birth of the Constitution in Philadelphia during the convention of May 1787. Though Franklin's practical participation in formulating the document was limited due to age, he, like George Washington, provided enormous symbolic power to the proceedings. His closing speech, described by biographer Walter Isaacson as "the most eloquent words Franklin ever wrote," expressed his own reservations about certain parts of the document, as a means to encourage dissenters to overcome theirs. His words, added Isaacson, were "perhaps the best ever written by anyone about the magic of the American system and the spirit of compromise that created it."[25]

A fall down his garden steps in 1788 left the eighty-two-year-old Franklin in constant pain. That combined with gout and kidney stones left him unable to write. Bache patiently transcribed his grandfather's correspondence through the final months of his life. In April 1790, as Franklin lay dying, it was Bache who took down his final letter, an affectionate response to a letter from Thomas Jefferson. "Tho' it was with great difficulty that he could breathe, yet he dictated a letter of a folio page and an half, upon business that required every exertion of his memory & judgment, without once requiring me to read back what I had written, or obliging me to correct more than one small error," Bache wrote to his future wife, Margaret Markoe, two weeks after Franklin's death. "The letter was as good a one as he ever wrote, notwithstanding the several difficulties he labored under at the time." Over the next several days, as Franklin slipped into semiconsciousness, Bache was a constant presence, quietly holding Franklin's hand to comfort him.

When his grandfather died, Bache told Margaret, "He has left us, I hope, to live in a happier country." As for the twenty-year-old Bache, he declared the pain of his loss to be "irreparable."[26]

Franklin bequeathed to Bache his personal library and all of his printing equipment.[27] By pedigree, education, and early life experience, Bache might have led a long, pleasant life of privilege. Having inherited his grandfather's wide range of intellectual interests, he could have been a gentleman property owner, spending his days dabbling in the arts and sciences. That he lived instead a short, tempestuous life, sometimes violent and always passionate, is one of the great ironies of the Sedition Act drama. Armed with these implements provided by Franklin, he was to become one of the most controversial and contrarian figures of his time, stirring up no end of trouble for the government. And that was nothing compared with the trouble he created for himself.[28]

# CHAPTER SIX

In October 1790, within six months of his grandfather's death, Bache launched the *General Advertiser, and Political, Commercial, Agricultural and Literary Journal.*[1] The newspaper proclaimed in its first issue: "The Freedom of the Press is the Bulwark of Liberty."[2]

The editorial office was on the first floor of 322 Market Street, a three-story brick house built in 1787, part of the small complex of buildings Franklin had erected along the most prestigious and busiest thoroughfare in Philadelphia. The building, which had originally housed rent-paying tenants, featured the sort of architectural innovations, such as advanced fireproofing techniques, that one might have expected from Franklin. The framing was designed so that no woodwork from one room would touch the woodwork from another. The brick outer walls separating Franklin's property from its neighbors extended above the roof line, making it that much more difficult for flames to leap from one house to the next. Beyond making the house more secure, these features lowered the insurance bill for the famously thrifty Franklin.[3]

The actual printing of the paper took place in the print shop out back that Franklin had built, and behind that stood the mansion where Franklin had lived and died. For a time after starting his newspaper, Bache lived in the Franklin house with his parents, Sarah and Richard. In 1791, Bache, age twenty-two, married twenty-one-year-old Margaret Markoe, the same woman to whom he had written the heartrending letter about his grandfather's death.

Margaret and Bache had met in the summer of 1788, when he was eighteen and she seventeen. Born on Saint Croix (the same island where Alexander Hamilton had been raised), Margaret, the daughter of a sugar planter, had moved to Philadelphia as a girl following the death of her father. The Markoes were a family of faded gentry—Margaret's cousin had squandered the family's sugar fortune.[4] Margaret's widowed mother married Dr. Adam Kuhn, a prominent but quiet and reserved Philadelphia physician. Though Bache must have represented to her and to her family the opportunity to gain connection through marriage to one of America's most illustrious founding families, he was at first perhaps too ardent a suitor. In 1789 Margaret returned with her mother to Saint Croix. Distance cooled the relationship for a time, but when Margaret returned to the United States in 1791, Bache succeeded in breaking through her reservations.[5]

In 1792, the young couple moved out of the Franklin homestead and into rooms above the printing office.[6] Bache worked slavishly at his presses, writing to a friend in 1792 about the pressures of running a daily newspaper: "Do you know how I am situated? Publisher of a large, large (I speak only of mathematical dimensions) newspaper— every day—even Sundays, never a day at home."[7] Margaret cared for a growing brood of sons—Franklin Bache, born in 1792; Richard Bache III, in 1794; and Benjamin Bache in 1796.[8]

The *General Advertiser* started off as a wide-ranging publication devoted to the sciences, agriculture, literature, and politics. It might have stayed that way but for the fates of timing and geography, specifically, the fact that the newspaper launch coincided with the move of the national government in 1790 from New York to Philadelphia. For the next decade, among the most contentious years in the history of the federal government, Philadelphia would be the seat not just of culture and wealth, but also of politics, influence, and intrigue.

Pitched brawls, figurative and literal, would play out on the streets, in the taverns, and, in the case of Lyon and Griswold, on the floor of the House. The government's move to Philadelphia put the *Aurora* and its publisher at the nexus of these events. The office was two blocks east of the house that George Washington and then John Adams would occupy, and two blocks northeast from Congress Hall. Over the next several years amid the politically charged atmosphere, the newspaper's name changed to the *Aurora and General Advertiser* and, eventually, the *Aurora*. The focus, likewise, narrowed. It became more political and partisan.

Even back in school in Switzerland, Bache had been known among his schoolmates as a young man with a sense of justice that was unyielding to the point of brittleness.[9] These qualities only intensified during his newspaper days. Bache's greatest weapon, and, ultimately, his undoing, was his unbending idealism. Having formed a purist's conception of liberty and democracy at the knee of one of the greatest thinkers of the revolutionary era, Bache would spend most of the 1790s in a state of perpetual indignation at the messy compromises, backroom deals, and accommodations of an emerging American political class. Death spared Benjamin Franklin the hazard of testing his ideals against the contentious realities of running a government. Other Founders could not escape that fate. One after another, great men of the revolution took office, failed to live up to Bache's lofty expectations, and suffered the indignities of his poison-tipped pen.

Critics found in Bache's anger evidence of a man haunted by the desire to live up to his impossibly accomplished grandfather. He was, in the estimation of Federalist William Vans Murray, "obliged to act a part for which he had not talents."[10] Still, Bache had talent, conviction, and courage enough to vex the mighty.

As George Washington made his way from Mount Vernon to New York for his first term as president, adoring crowds along the way only filled him with foreboding. "I greatly apprehend that my countrymen will expect too much of me," he wrote to a friend.[11]

At first, Bache was inclined to trust Washington's leadership. His grandfather and Washington had not known each other well personally, but they shared a deep mutual respect. When Washington arrived in Philadelphia in May 1787 for the Constitutional Convention, his first act, before even unpacking his bags, had been to visit Franklin's home to pay his respects.[12] During the early years of Washington's presidency, a twenty-one-year-old Bache wrote optimistically if not fawningly that Washington "presides over us with as much dignity & wisdom as man is capable of exerting."[13]

Five years later, Washington was, in Bache's eyes, a weakling, a phony, and a cad. Washington's great failings were his declaration of neutrality in the war between England and France in 1793 and, later, his signing of the Jay Treaty. Bache even assailed the unassailable: Washington's record in the Revolutionary War. He suggested that Washington's tactical victories had been small and overblown, that his timidity as a military leader had cost precious time and lives, and that the French had saved his bacon.[14] Absurdly, he challenged Washington to name a single instance in which he had been a friend to American independence.[15]

Though he nurtured a reputation for stoic indifference to critics, Washington was acutely aware of such attacks and resented them, calling criticism by Bache and other Republican editors "outrages on common decency."[16] Washington charged that Bache's "Calumnies are to be exceeded only by his Impudence." Consternation over Bache's criticisms was said to play a role in Washington's decision not to run for a third term in 1796.[17]

If anything, Bache's invectives against Washington's successor were even more intense. After a brief honeymoon during which he praised President Adams as a man of "incorruptible integrity" and a welcome antidote to Washington's "ostentations," Bache soured when the new chief executive actually began to govern.[18] In no time, Adams was an English toady, guilty of nepotism, gross vanity, and seeking war with France. In his most colorful attack, Bache referred to the president as "old, querilous, Bald, blind, cripled, Toothless Adams."[19]

Much as these attacks irked Adams, they positively infuriated his most loyal advocate and confidante. First Lady Abigail Adams called Bache a "wretch." Most ominously, considering the dark days ahead for Bache and the country, she predicted in a private letter written in the spring of 1798 that Bache would soon get his comeuppance, when "the wrath of an insulted people will by & by break upon him."[20] Cobbett's *Porcupine's Gazette* claimed Bache "has outraged every principle of decency, of morality, of religion and of nature." John Fenno's the *Gazette of the United States* called the *Aurora* "that detestable sink of pollution."[21]

The French, meanwhile, weren't making things easy for Bache and other Republicans intent on defending the importance of Franco-American friendship. Their dismissive treatment of U.S. diplomats, starting with Charles Pinckney, took an ominous turn for the worse with a diplomatic scandal that came to be known, infamously, as the XYZ Affair. In 1797, as one of his first acts as president, Adams had appointed John Marshall and Elbridge Gerry to travel to France and, together with Pinckney, make another effort at a peaceful end to French harassment of U.S. shipping. The French had upped the ante by assuming the right to search American ships and seize English goods found on board, to claim as a prize any ship unable to hand over formal documentation of passengers and crew in the French *rôle d'équipage* format, and to consider any American found serving on an English ship a pirate.[22] This final point presented American sailors with the prospect of being kidnapped and pressed into hard labor on an English ship, only to be captured by the French and hanged for the offense of serving in the British navy.

Instead of greeting the American delegates as serious diplomats when they arrived in the fall of 1797, the ruling French Directory let Pinckney, Marshall, and Gerry wait incommunicado for several days before granting them a dismissive, fifteen-minute meeting with

Charles-Maurice de Talleyrand-Périgord, French foreign minister and leader of the Directory. In the days and weeks that followed, three French agents delivered a series of progressively more humiliating demands as a pretext to further negotiations: the Americans would have to formally apologize for and disavow President Adams's stern speech to Congress the previous May, provide France with a sizable loan for pursuing its own wars, and even offer Talleyrand a $250,000 personal bribe.[23]

The Americans balked at the demands. In dispatches, the three French agents who had presented them were described only as X, Y, and Z. As details made their way through Philadelphia and around the states in the spring of 1798, the episode—soon dubbed the XYZ Affair—stirred new and ever more intense waves of anti-French feeling among the population. The American envoys were greeted as heroes upon returning to the United States. Congressional Federalists hosted a dinner for Marshall. Among a series of toasts, one— "Millions for defense, but not one cent for tribute"—became a potent rallying cry for Federalists around the country.[24]

For Republicans the XYZ Affair was a disaster. Not only did it damage their already weakening case for a U.S. alliance with France against Great Britain, it exposed them personally more than ever to charges of disloyalty to their country. In May, Bache published a conciliatory letter to President Adams from Talleyrand, the French minister of foreign affairs. If Bache's goal was to show that the French had no desire for war, his plan backfired. Secretary of State Timothy Pickering was at a loss to explain how readers of the *Aurora* had access to a letter that had yet to be delivered to the president himself, and Federalists promptly labeled Bache a traitor.[25]

Republican newspapers came to the editor's defense, answering in particular the charge that Bache had committed treason by publishing the French minister's letter. In New York, the Republican *Time-Piece* asked how a man could commit treason by simply showing "industry, and interest enough, to procure an important State Paper"

before the Federalists. But such voices were no match for those insisting that Bache was trying to destroy the country. On the floor of
Congress, Harrison Gray Otis warned that Bache's poisonous words
were spreading like a disease around the country, infecting innocent
and susceptible citizens with seditious thoughts and "disturbing the
silence of the woods and tranquillity of the cottage."[26]

Bache's explanation that the document had been leaked to him
by an unnamed American politician hardly mollified his critics. On
June 18, when President Adams delivered to the Senate and House the
official copy of Talleyrand's letter, Massachusetts Federalist George
Thatcher, on the floor of the House of Representatives, complained
that the letter had already been printed in the "French paper" (i.e.,
the *Aurora*) and accused its printer not just of being sympathetic to
the French but an agent of the French "Executive Directory"—an
accusation tantamount to treason. When Republican Thomas Claiborne demanded proof, Thatcher responded that he "hoped soon to lay
before the House satisfactory evidence of the fact." Federalist Robert
Goodloe Harper called Bache one of the "secret agents in this country"
trying to "excite resistance to the measures of our Government."[27]

Bache answered the charges with a twelve-page, two-cent pamphlet with the long-winded title: *Truth Will Out! The Foul Charges of
the Tories Against the Editor of the* Aurora, *Repelled by Positive Proof and
Plain Truth, and His Base Calumniators Put to Shame.*[28]

The pamphlet leveled some of the harshest words Bache had
ever directed toward a politician. Thatcher was a man "devoid of *honor*
and *spirit* . . . whose *cowardice* stood upon record." As for Thatcher's
promise to produce evidence of Bache's treachery, Bache wrote: "We
*dare* him to the scrutiny, even before the tribunal he has chosen, and
shall not cease to call on him for the evidence which he pretends to
be in possession of."[29] Bache published a sworn affidavit signed by
Hilary Baker, the mayor of Philadelphia, stating that the Talleyrand
letter had been delivered to Bache not by French officials but by "a
gentleman of this city."

Whether these represented journalistic coups or acts of treason was a debate as controversial in the eighteenth century as the
Pentagon Papers were in the twentieth, or WikiLeaks and Edward
Snowden's NSA revelations in the twenty-first. But there is no question that Federalists had come to see Bache as a man intent on
destroying the country. Worse still, every new and damaging article
printed in the *Aurora* went viral, eighteenth-century style, making
its way into Republican newspapers from Georgia to Kentucky to
Vermont—where the Federalist *Rutland Herald* accused Bache of
being "paid out of the French treasury, for abusing the government
of the United States, deceiving the public with artful lies."[30]

One day that May, some twelve hundred young loyalists of John
Adams appeared outside of the president's home in a show of support. Adams received them wearing a military uniform and sword.[31]
That evening, a smaller, mischievous remnant of that crowd, fueled
by alcohol, arrived at Bache's home. "My doors and windows were
battered, and the women and children in the house (I happened to
be from home) somewhat terrified," Bache reported. Intervention
by neighbors and passersby prevented the mob from doing further
damage. Without naming Adams specifically, Bache blamed the incident on older Federalists for egging such mobs on and encouraging
"young men, not of age, to meddle in politics." Once bloodlust is
unleashed, "who will say where it would stop." At the same time,
Bache vowed not to yield to threats, and to remain true to "the voice
of my conscience; which tells me it is my duty to remain firm at my
post when the liberties of my country are endangered."[32]

# CHAPTER SEVEN

Bache may have been the most controversial journalist in America but he was not the most despised. That distinction belonged to James Thomson Callender, a native Scotsman who spent his career taking revenge with his pen for every indignity that life sent his way. His legion of enemies called him a "nasty beast,"[1] "that wretch Callender,"[2] and "a dirty little toper."[3] Abigail Adams, incensed by Callender's attacks on her husband, wrote that "When such vipers are let loose upon society, all distinction between virtue and vice are leveled, all respect for character is lost."[4]

Given the fierce animosities between Republicans and Federalists, Callender's greatest mistake was to attack both sides at one time or another with equal fervor. A craftier, more ambitious journalist would have attached himself to one party or Founder and basked in the reflected prosperity of the great man's political successes. But Callender was the opposite of a climber. He was a political faller. He recoiled from authority and was incensed by the very idea of political power. Though he harbored a special distaste for Federalists, his enthusiasm even for his fellow Republicans inevitably waned as their fortunes rose. In a reflective moment in the Richmond jail after one of his many scrapes with the law, Callender explained, "It is a part of my constitution, it is interwoven with my intellectual existence, that the greater opposition is, I become the more perfectly determined to Strike it in the face . . ."[5] Whatever troubles this trait caused for his illustrious victims, invariably it redounded most severely on Callender himself, in the form of misery, poverty, and abiding loneliness.

What is truly remarkable about Callender, though, is the extent to which modern historians and latter-day guardians of this or that Founder's reputation have carried a visceral contempt for him into our own time, assailing the journalist as if he were still actively besmirching their hero's reputation from the grave. They've called him "notorious,"[6] "the most abusive and the most irresponsible of the Republican journalists,"[7] a "scandalmonger," and "an ugly, misshapen little man who made a career of spewing venom."[8] One scholar wrote, "Few more unsavory and generally obnoxious figures than James Thomson Callender ever set foot on American soil . . ."[9] Another declared, "Of all the foreigners who were connected with journalism in the United States at the beginning of the [eighteenth] century, James Thomson Callender was easily first in the worst qualities of mind and character."[10] Even the rare nods to Callender's journalistic skills have come wrapped in layers of invective, as when twentieth-century editor and scholar Virginius Dabney labeled Callender "a drunken, vicious and depraved, albeit talented, Scotsman."[11]

A man who excites such passions centuries after his death is worth knowing more about in any case, but it so happens that Callender was also an astute, fearless journalist whose writing placed him at the center of the most important political events of his time. He was in his own tortured way a man of principle. According to biographer Michael Durey, author of the most complete and balanced portrait of the man, "Callender was fueled by an inner rage which impelled him to risk all in vain attempts to cleanse society of what he perceived to be blatant wrongs."[12]

There is no question that Callender was a highly objectionable man in many ways. He was brittle, superior, defensive, and paranoid—qualities that were intensified by his heavy drinking. He turned on people with only the slightest provocation, and used journalism as a way of settling personal scores. Yet for all that, Callender understood essential elements of freedom that his adopted country, despite its Bill of Rights, had yet to fully ascertain; namely, that free speech belongs to each individual wrestling with his own conscience, and is meaningless unless the people one most hates can have their say without fear of official reprisal.

William Cobbett, editor of the Federalist *Porcupine's Gazette*, berated Callender mercilessly, calling him "a little mangy Scotsman" and speculating that Callender's nervous tic of jerking his shoulders was evidence of fleas and lice.[13] Cobbett even published a mock will in which he bequeathed to Callender "twenty feet of pine plank, which I request my executors to see made into a pillory, to be kept for his particular use, till a gibbet can be prepared."[14] Yet when Cobbett found himself in legal jeopardy for articles angering the powerful Republican chief justice of the Pennsylvania Supreme Court, Callender, instead of gloating, leaped to Cobbett's defense and publicly criticized the judge for misusing his powers to take revenge. "If a man is attacked from the press, let him reply through the same channel," Callender wrote.[15] Later, when Callender attacked the opinions of another Federalist editor, he was careful to note the editor's right to publish his foolish opinions: "It is the happy privilege of an American, that he may prattle and print, in what way he pleases, and *without any one to make him afraid*."[16] In a sense, he had been preparing his whole life to help America learn those lessons.

Born in Scotland in 1758, Callender spent the first eight years of his career as a sub clerk in an Edinburgh municipal office. While other sub clerks grumbled quietly about corruption and dishonesty, Callender openly accused his politically appointed boss of misusing public money. The boss threatened to kill Callender but fired him instead.[17] As an aspiring writer in an age when fawning patronage shaped careers, Callender declared war on one of the most revered authors of the eighteenth century. In a sixty-three-page pamphlet entitled *Deformities of Dr. Samuel Johnson*, Callender, at age twenty-four, showed no deference whatsoever to the seventy-three-year-old Johnson, whose dismissive comments and writings about Scotland had infuriated him. Callender combed through Johnson's famed *A Dictionary of the English Language*, exposing errors and contradictions.[18]

By the early 1790s Callender graduated from literary figures and provincial bureaucrats to a more dangerous foe, the British Crown. In 1792 he published *The Political Progress of Great Britain*, a compendium of British misdeeds, intended to make the case for Scottish independence. The pamphlet tabulated the cost of England's foreign wars in lives and in treasure drawn from Scottish industries to pay for them. Beyond its copious facts and figures, the book showed Callender already honing his keen eye for melodramatic detail. He wrote of a young wife whose husband had been pressed into military service, and who, reduced to begging to support her infant children, was sentenced to hang for stealing a piece of linen from a shop. "*The hangman dragged her sucking infant from her breast, when he straitened the cord about her neck . . . ,*" Callender wrote. "Such were the fruits of what Englishmen call *their inestimable privilege of a trial by jury.*"[19]

When the government responded with a warrant for his arrest, Callender fled first to Ireland, then to the United States, landing in Philadelphia in May 1793, when he was thirty-five years old. Having supported the American Revolution and admired the United States from afar, he settled in Philadelphia with his wife and children, about whom little is known. He quickly found a position as an assistant on a Philadelphia newspaper, the *American Daily Advertiser*, where he became an outspoken commentator on American policy and interests. "In an infant government like ours, to hazard a foreign war, unless from the very last necessity, would be the height of madness," he wrote.[20] Within a few months, Callender moved from the *American Daily Advertiser* to the *Philadelphia Gazette*, where he was assigned to report on the doings of the House of Representatives.

Over the next several years, Callender wrote for several prominent Republican newspapers. While working for the *Gazette*, he moonlighted for Bache's *Aurora*, cranking out political pamphlets attacking powerful figures he viewed as too eager to instill British-style systems of class and political power in the United States. In 1797, he picked his first high-profile fight with Alexander Hamilton, the "aristocrat" that every Republican loved to hate.

In terms of pedigree, Hamilton was, ironically, the least aristocratic of the leading Founders. Born to an unwed mother in the West Indies, with little social standing and fewer economic prospects, the precociously brilliant Hamilton attracted the notice of patrons who helped him immigrate to New York and gain admission to King's College (now Columbia University). Later, Hamilton distinguished himself as one of George Washington's most trusted officers in the Revolutionary War. By dint of his brilliance, courage, and deep ambition, he had reached the top levels of American power and society. His marriage to Eliza Schuyler, daughter of a leading New York family, brought him a level of happiness, stability, and social respectability that he had never known.

Perhaps because of the things he had seen growing up poor in the West Indies, Hamilton harbored few romantic notions about the nobility or innate wisdom of everyday folks. "His faith in Americans," notes biographer Ron Chernow, "never quite matched his faith in America itself."[21] Given a choice between the messiness of democracy and an orderly system with clear divisions between the rulers and the ruled and a clear path to the prosperity he saw as America's destiny, Hamilton would have chosen the latter without hesitation. As lead author of the Federalist Papers and architect of the U.S. Treasury, Hamilton was a brilliant, indispensable advocate for a strong federal government. Yet his enthusiasm for class structures alarmed critics such as Callender who viewed Hamilton as trying to re-create England on the American continent. In particular, Callender viewed Hamilton's plan for a Bank of the United States, modeled on England's central bank, as a dangerous step toward institutionalized aristocracy and centralized control of wealth.

Callender shared with Hamilton a deep pessimism about the intelligence and morals of average men. "In this country, the stile of writing is commonly so gross, that I do not think the majority of such a public worth addressing," he wrote.[22] Yet where Hamilton found solace in the idea of a powerful central government run by a wise elite, Callender thought even less of the elite than he did of the rabble. By the tender age of twenty-four he had already seen enough puffery, stupidity, and despotism emanating from the upper classes in his native Scotland to write: "The laurels which human praise confers are withered and blasted by the unworthiness of those who wear them."[23] That sense of doom, pessimism, and indignation would only grow in his later years.

In a pattern that would mark Callender's most explosive journalism, he chose to attack Hamilton's personal behavior as a way of pointing out what he saw as the man's dangerous public flaws. He focused his attention on a long-rumored but never publicly exposed extramarital affair with a mysterious dark-haired beauty named Maria Reynolds. The affair had begun around 1791 when Reynolds knocked on Hamilton's door (his wife and children were away) asking for financial help. For the normally careful and fastidious Hamilton, the Reynolds affair, which continued throughout 1791 and into 1792, represented astonishing misjudgment. And his choice of paramours could not have been more reckless. Her husband, James Reynolds, was a con man who, upon learning of Hamilton's affair with his wife, started blackmailing him.[24] If these surreptitious payoffs weren't dangerous enough for a man in Hamilton's public position, the plot thickened when Reynolds and a business partner were arrested on charges of defrauding the U.S. government of $400. While the fraud case was unrelated to the affair and blackmail, the charges were levied by the Department of the Treasury, which Hamilton, as secretary, oversaw. In his delicate role as the first secretary of the Treasury, crafting fiscal policy for a new nation, Hamilton had scrupulously avoided even the appearance of personal gain or conflict of interest. From jail, Reynolds renewed his threats to expose the affair.

As gossip swirled through the capital, in 1792 Hamilton gathered a small group of political leaders, including James Monroe, and admitted the affair and blackmail payments to Reynolds—while forcefully denying any political component to the scandal. The leaders were satisfied, and the whole affair seemed to blow over when Maria and James left Philadelphia following his release from prison.

Then, in 1797, Callender brought the scandal roaring back to life with a 312-page tome entitled *The History of the United States for 1796.* The first two hundred pages offered a tedious recounting of government doings for the year, drawing heavily on his notes as a congressional reporter. Then came the bombshell, starting on page 204: a methodical, piece-by-piece description of Alexander Hamilton's affair with Maria Reynolds.[25] This was no secondhand rumor but a painfully documented exposé, including verbatim correspondence among Hamilton, Reynolds, and the three politicians who had met with Hamilton to resolve the matter five years earlier. Callender didn't stop at detailing what was easily the most embarrassing and humiliating chapter in Hamilton's career. The author suggested that Hamilton's infidelities were a mere smoke screen hiding more serious crimes of bribery and financial misdealing involving James Reynolds—exactly the sort of innuendos Hamilton had hoped to avoid. To Callender, the volume of paperwork that Hamilton and others generated over the affair indicated something other than the purely carnal. "So much correspondence," he noted, "could not refer exclusively to wenching."[26]

Callender never revealed his sources. But the minute details and verbatim documents implied a source with direct access to sensitive information. Hamilton had no doubt about the culprit: Thomas Jefferson, his philosophical opposite and his chief rival for influence in the Washington administration. James Monroe, one of the three

politicians to whom Hamilton had quietly confessed in 1792, was
a fellow Virginian and close friend of Jefferson's. Not long before
Callender's book appeared, Hamilton had publicly supported Monroe's recall as minister to France. Now Hamilton was convinced that
Monroe had paid him back by giving Jefferson the documents related
to the Reynolds affair.

Considering the conclusive detail in Callender's reporting, there
was no point in Hamilton's denying the affair with Maria Reynolds.
Instead, he issued a lengthy rebuttal, which came to be known as
simply as the Reynolds Pamphlet.[27] As he had in private, Hamilton
conceded the affair but flatly denied any financial improprieties. The
payments he made to James Reynolds, he insisted, were purely in the
interest of keeping his sexual affair a secret. It was a painful admission
both publicly and personally, especially since Hamilton was otherwise, by all appearances, happily married, and his wife, Elizabeth,
the same year gave birth to the couple's sixth child. Although Hamilton was never charged with any financial wrongdoing, and would
continue to be a major voice in shaping policy from the wings, his
hopes of returning to politics in a high elective office were essentially
dashed, thanks to Callender.

For a short time, Callender basked in his journalistic triumph
against one of the most combative, powerful, and well-connected
figures in the United States. He took special pleasure in having forced
Hamilton to write his confessional pamphlet. "If you have not seen
it, no anticipation can equal the infamy of this piece," he gloated
in a letter to Jefferson. "It is worth all that fifty of the best pens in
America could have said against him."[28]

Callender's reporting intensified the Federalist voices calling
for formal restrictions on the wayward press. Clearly, something
had to be done to silence Matthew Lyon, Bache, Callender, and
others. Vice President Jefferson sensed the coming storm, noting in
a letter to James Madison that President Adams "May look to the
Sedition bill which has been spoken of, and which may be meant

to put the Printing presses under the Imprimatur of the executive. Bache is thought to be a main object of it."[29] On June 13, Bache's *Aurora* issued what amounted to a fervent plea for himself and for the country: "We ring the alarm. Papers of freedom, you that have not sold yourselves, you that forget not your revolution and the constitution . . . —take up the sound before it dies, and let the peal rouse the spirit and reflection of the land . . ."[30]

As Jefferson predicted, Federalists were indeed planning such a bill, but they decided that getting Bache simply couldn't wait. On June 26, federal district judge Richard Peters issued a warrant for his arrest, charging him with libeling the president and the government "in a manner tending to excite sedition." Bache immediately posted bail set at $4,000 and vowed to continue publishing the *Aurora* as he awaited trial set for the fall.[31]

Because there was as yet no federal bill covering criminal libel, the charges were issued under the common law, the ancient legal system handed down from England to the colonies and inherited by the young republic. Common-law offenses were determined not by specific statutes passed by legislatures, but by long-standing tradition and the accrued weight of judicial precedents. In the early days of the United States, common law guided much criminal as well as civil law. Today, as local, state, and federal legislatures have enacted innumerable criminal (as well as certain civil) statutes, the common-law system remains in place largely for civil cases.

A common-law libel case, even against so controversial a figure as Bache, presented some challenges for prosecutors. For one thing, the piecemeal history of libel cases in the seven-year-old country offered few obvious indications as to whether Bache had actually committed a crime. Moreover, there was some question as to whether this new entity known as the U.S. government possessed the authority to pursue common-law cases at all against individual Americans. Still, Federalists believed that with the proper judge and jury, they had a good chance of putting Bache away and disrupting the *Aurora*.

Had they pursued a similar strategy to silence the rest of their critics, Federalists might have intimidated their enemies and corroded press and speech freedoms almost on the sly. A series of unrelated libel cases might never have forced the country into a reckoning over the meaning of the First Amendment. But the Federalists decided to shoot much higher. Emboldened by their strong majorities, inflamed by the looming possibility of a war with France, and egged on by multitudes of sympathizers around the country, they saw their opportunity for a decisive show of power. They would make clear that American leadership was unified, strong, and determined enough to vanquish those who would threaten the survival of the United States, whether those threats emanated from overseas or from traitorous forces within the country.

First, they cracked down on undesirable foreigners, with a series of laws that came to be known as the Alien Acts. The first, implemented on June 18, 1798, increased from five to fourteen years the amount of time that a foreign-born resident needed to be in the United States in order to become naturalized. The act applied not just to newcomers, but also to those already in the country. All were required to register as aliens. The second act gave the president power to deport any alien, without trial, even if the alien was from a country the United States was at peace with. If the president chose not to deport, he was free to intern them, also without trial. The third act essentially continued the second, specifically authorizing the president to deport any aliens during a time of war, or even threat of war.[32]

Next, the Federalists turned the gaze inward, to America's own wayward citizens. They would make clear that the government would not tolerate those who would verbally assault their leaders and undermine the leaders' ability to govern. By taking this fight to the next level, Federalists ensured a momentous showdown between themselves and Republicans and over the very nature of liberty.

# CHAPTER EIGHT

The Senate struck first.

On June 26, 1798, the same day that Bache was arrested, Federalist James Lloyd of Maryland, a Revolutionary War veteran, asked for and received permission from his fellow senators to introduce a "bill to determine more particularly the crime of treason, and to define and punish the crime of sedition."[1]

Cast in elliptical, run-on legalese, the Senate version of what would become known as the Sedition Act makes for painful reading. Yet it's worth wading into because beneath the arch language, the "manner aforesaids," "thereofs," and "induces," lay a piece of legislation breathtaking in its capacity for tyranny and mischief.

The heart of the bill stated:

> That if any person shall, by any libellous or scandalous writing, printing, publishing, or speaking, traduce or defame the legislature of the United States, by seditious or inflammatory declarations, or expressions, with intent to create a belief in the citizens thereof, that the said legislature, in enacting any law, was induced thereto by motives hostile to the constitution, or liberties and happiness of the people thereof; or shall in a manner aforesaid, traduce or defame the President of the United States, or any court or judge thereof, by declarations tending to criminate their motives in any official transaction;

the person so offending, and thereof convicted, before any
court of the United States having jurisdiction thereof, shall
be punished by a fine, not exceeding two thousand dollars,
and by imprisonment, not exceeding two years.[2]

Defining libel in the context of criticizing public officials is hard
enough. But how does one adequately define "scandalous" writings,
or "inflammatory declarations," or speech that might "criminate
the motives" of those in power? The scope would seem to include
virtually any speech or writing that a government official felt made
him look bad.

The wording of the proposed law would make it a crime even
to ask whether a politician had the highest motives in mind when
introducing a bill. Indeed, by declaring it off-limits to suggest that
a lawmaker had "motives hostile to the constitution," the law as
written would seem to forbid even asking whether the law itself
was constitutional.

After a second reading the next day the Senate appointed members to review the bill in committee. Among these was Vermont's
Nathaniel Chipman, for whom the Sedition Act and the chance to
destroy his enemy Matthew Lyon could not come fast enough. After
what was by all indications a perfunctory and favorable review, the
committee referred the bill to the whole Senate. The Senate read
the bill for a third time on Tuesday, July 3.[3] All that remained for
the next day, July 4, was a final vote.

All of this had taken place with slippery speed. It's hard to imagine that the Senate's outnumbered Republicans didn't voice objections, but the Senate Journal offers no details on the discussions. Nor
were any nosy reporters hanging around. If the House was steerage
on the ship of state, everything about the Senate spoke of first class.
The senators sat in leather-bound chairs and each enjoyed a private
desk, as compared with the long, benchlike desks shared by members
of the House of Representatives. In contrast to the raucous scene

that often transpired downstairs, the Senate's operations were calm, orderly, and secretive. And this was entirely by design.

The Senate in the early days of the republic was the product of an uneasy compromise between those who feared an incipient monarchy and those who feared the ignorance of the people. During the constitutional debates of 1787, Alexander Hamilton had famously argued for the president and senators to be appointed by electors rather than popular vote, and to serve for life, on good behavior. In England, Hamilton explained, the king's wealth and hereditary position kept his personal interests in line with those of the nation. The hereditary House of Lords was "a most noble institution," he felt, one worthy as a model for the U.S. Senate. Such leaders would be essential to counterbalance the "men of little character" who would inevitably covet power through popular elections to the House of Representatives.[4]

Hamilton didn't get those lifetime appointments. Presidents would serve four-year terms, senators six. But in other respects, the early U.S. Senate manifested the remoteness and elitism he and others envisioned. Voters wouldn't get to popularly elect their senators until the passage of the Seventeenth Amendment in 1913. More remarkable still, for the first five years the Senate barred reporters and spectators, conducting all of its business away from leering galleries and the taint of popular opinion. Senators would be wise men, answerable only to their knowledge and conscience, and rich men, above the lure of corruption—"a body of carefully selected men who represented the country's wisdom and good judgment and who would deliberate confidentially without regard for special interests."[5]

From the start, being governed by a band of would-be philosopher kings struck some Americans as downright undemocratic. Some newspaper editors smelled aristocratic pretensions, with one accusing senators of adopting "the secret privileges of the House of Lords" and another blasting "This *Patrician* stile, this concealment, this affection of preeminence."[6] Republican editor Philip Freneau of the *National Gazette* urged his readers to demand public access, challenging them, "Are you freemen who ought to know the individual conduct of your legislators, or are you an inferior order of beings incapable of comprehending the sublimity of Senatorial functions, and unworthy to be entrusted with their opinions?"[7]

After defeating several internal resolutions over the years to open its doors, the Senate in early 1794 bowed to pressure—and then dragged its feet for nearly two years over construction of a modest public gallery. When the doors finally opened in December 1795 for some Senate functions (debates on treaties and nominations would remain secret until the twentieth century), journalists soon found that listening in wasn't worth the trouble. Journalists weren't permitted to lounge on the floor as in the House, and catching details from the gallery was difficult at best. And anyway, the senators seemed to have made all of their important decisions behind closed doors in committee. So journalists continued to focus their limited manpower on the House of Representatives.[8]

What remains as a record of proceedings is the Senate Journal—crisp, businesslike, and dull. As rendered in the Journal, the Senate's deliberations carry all the drama of a private men's club deciding where to locate the new billiards room. This, too, was by design: men removed from the storm and stress of public debate, protected from prying eyes, would be all the better equipped to make the wisest decisions on behalf of the people.

And on July 4, 1798, twenty-four senators mounted the long wooden steps to their chambers on the second floor of Congress Hall. Eight members were absent. The first item on the Senate's agenda for the day was a proposal to establish an office of purveyor of public supplies for the War Department. After passing the proposal on for a second reading, the senators took up their second item of the day, final consideration of its sedition bill.[9]

That this final vote would take place on Independence Day may have been by coincidence or design. Nothing in the Senate Journal indicates that senators viewed this particular Wednesday as anything besides another day at the office (federal recognition of the Fourth of July as a holiday wouldn't come until 1870). Even so, the Senate's decision to decimate the Bill of Rights on the twenty-second anniversary of the signing of the Declaration of Independence invites consideration of what other Americans were up to on that day. How did those average Americans who were not to be fully trusted with freedom, the ones in need of appointed rulers, spend their Fourth of July?

If the residents of Mendham, New Jersey, are any indication, they approached Independence Day with respect bordering on reverence. The celebration began in late morning, when nearly five hundred residents gathered outside the home of a local dignitary. At noon, the celebrants marched to the town meetinghouse. After an opening prayer by the Reverend Amzi Armstrong, John M. Carter read aloud the Declaration of Independence. Later, Dr. William Leddel read the U.S. Constitution, as well as the New Jersey law ratifying the Constitution and the Bill of Rights.[10]

Other residents offered prayers and poems. When the readings ended, the local militia fired artillery in salute. The crowd reassembled around a recently erected flagstaff bearing the American flag. After three cheers, the large crowd dispersed. Town leaders then sat down to an outdoor dinner under the shade of a bower. The feast was punctuated by more artillery salutes, and one after another, men rose to toast: "The 4th of July, '76—May the spirit of that day be the enduring characteristic of the patriots of '98"; "Our sovereign, the *People*—May their voice and their will be one, in defense of their Liberties"; "The memory of the heroes who fought without *shoes*, and bled without *medicine*—the martyrs of British tyranny."

Elsewhere on the Fourth, speakers at Federalist gatherings struck a more ominous tone. In Boston, Josiah Quincy, twenty-six years old and newly appointed as town orator, rose to address residents at Faneuil Hall. Built in 1742, Faneuil Hall had been the scene of seminal speeches and gatherings during revolutionary days. Now, Quincy warned that the country had lost its way. "The principle of our revolution was simple; a passion for Independence; a high sense of the eternal right of a great people to govern themselves after their own choice and manner," he told the gathering.[11] But Americans had gotten lazy. They lacked the toughness and resolve of previous generations. Their forefathers had secured liberty, he said, but as yet the current generation had proven itself incapable of protecting it.[12]

Though he never mentioned Republicans by name, Quincy compared opponents of federalism with Tory traitors of the revolutionary period. "[G]ive them new weapons and new cloaks, and the tories and royalists of Seventy Five are the Jacobins . . . of Ninety Eight," he said.[13]

A few miles south of Boston, in Dedham, Massachusetts, about sixty residents gathered for a dinner with speeches and patriotic songs.[14] The organizer of the event was Fisher Ames, the leading Federalist in a sharply divided town. Until his premature retirement because of a chronic illness (probably tuberculosis) a year earlier, Ames had been one of the most powerful members in the U.S. Congress. It was Ames whose soaring oratory on the House floor had helped rescue the Jay Treaty for George Washington, whom Ames revered. Since returning to Dedham to rest and practice law, Ames had been alarmed by rising Republican sentiments in town.

As part of the July 4 festivities, the revelers signed a letter to President Adams, declaring their support should the United States enter war against France. France "will learn that we bear no foreign yoke—we will pay no tribute."[15] Heartened by the turnout, Ames wrote confidently to Secretary of State Timothy Pickering that "the progress of right opinions" in his divided town was winning against "perhaps the most malevolent spirit that exists"—the Republican influence.[16]

Intensifying Ames's passions was the fact that the most prominent Republican in Dedham was his own brother and next-door neighbor, Nathaniel Ames. The town physician, Nathaniel was as reserved as Fisher was outgoing. Nathaniel hated anything suggesting pomposity, phoniness, or putting on airs. He disliked and mistrusted politicians and politics and never coveted public office. When Dedham residents drafted him as a representative to the general court in 1790, he refused to serve. A year later he acquiesced, under the condition that he not have to attend any sessions. Some in Dedham called him "Grumbleton." He hated Federalists as deeply as his brother hated Republicans. On this Independence Day, Nathaniel scratched into his diary that Fisher had corralled "a few deluded people" into signing the Adams letter by "squeezing teazing greazing" them with food and drink. Despite his brother's claim of victory in the fight for the town's hearts and minds, Nathaniel insisted that in Dedham, "the Great Mass of People said, 'Alliance with France and defiance to Britain.'"[17]

Thus spun the carousel of freedom on Independence Day 1798. Americans celebrated after their own fashion, intensely aware of the preciousness of their liberties but disagreeing, then as now, as to who were the champions and who represented the threats. The debate unfolded in public spaces and in the privacy of homes and diaries. It was angry and reasoned, raucous and reverent. The debate marched on, not among a nation of ignorant sheep in need of rulers, but of free people working things out, turning ideas over in their minds and having their say, state to state, town to town, brother to brother.

Back in Mendham, New Jersey, the celebration wound down with a few final toasts acknowledging the growing hostilities in the capital, and the rising possibility that lawmakers might try to silence dissent: "The next Congress—May the liberality and the goodness of their laws, supercede the necessity of *Sedition* bills," and "May it never be *Sedition to toast honest men*."[18]

And then the residents raised their glasses, unaware that even as they drank, senators in Philadelphia were confirming their deepest fears. With little apparent conflict or controversy, twenty-four senators, appointed rather than elected, approved their law by a decisive margin of 18–6. The vote was almost exclusively by party line. Of the eighteen yeas, all were Federalists except for Alexander Martin, a North Carolinian who counted himself as Anti-Administration. Among the nays, five were listed as Democratic-Republican, Republican, or Anti-Administration. Just one Federalist, John Eager Howard of Maryland, broke ranks and voted against the Sedition Act.[19]

Given the rancor of the moment and the number of Federalists clamoring for Republicans' heads, it would be wrong to suggest that those eighteen senators sank lower than the basest passions of their times. But certainly they rose no higher, these men who were to have been so wise. In the end, what separated them from the great swath of humanity was not a superior endowment of vision or wisdom, but the fact that they were enabled to do their work in the dark. Now the bill would move on to the House of Representatives, where at least it would get a full public hearing. Journalists would make certain of that, recording every moment of the debate ahead, revealing in full the raw, unedited, conflicted state of the American mind.

# CHAPTER NINE

The legislative fireworks started on July 5, when the Senate bill made its way downstairs to the House. Edward Livingston, a prominent Republican from New York, moved to reject it out of hand. John Allen, the Federalist who a year earlier had taunted Matthew Lyon and Albert Gallatin about American blood and American accents, rose in defense of the proposed law. "If ever there was a nation which required a law of this kind, it is this," Allen told his colleagues. Something had to be done to stop the "unwarrantable and dangerous combination" of Republican newspaper editors and members of Congress.

Allen, a thirty-five-year-old lawyer from Connecticut, cited a recent article in Bache's *Aurora* accusing President Adams of seeking war with France for political purposes. Since pursuing a war for such reasons would amount to treason, Allen observed, the president should be hanged (if the charges were true) or Bache should be forcibly silenced (if they were false).[1] For what kind of country, he wondered, allowed its citizens to destroy one another with vicious lies and call it freedom? Allen also discounted the argument by Bache and others that citizens should resist a sedition act, if passed, as unconstitutional. Americans could not just pick and choose which laws to follow and which to ignore, based on their own homegrown philosophies of constitutionality, he said. Rather, responsible citizens should be more concerned about stopping "this infamous printer"

from spreading his "tocsin of insurrection." Bache's brand of liberty
"is calculated to destroy all confidence between man and man."[2]

Having spent himself in a flurry of adjectives and rising indignation, Allen yielded the floor to Republican William Claiborne of
Tennessee, who noted drily that Allen was a paid subscriber to the
*Aurora*, thus voluntarily exposing himself to Bache's deadly "tocsins"
on a daily basis. Yet somehow, the Connecticut representative's own
ligaments to family, neighbor, society, and government remained
remarkably intact. Might not other Americans have the fortitude
to read or ignore the *Aurora* at will, recognize it as an opinionated
publication, and make their own decisions without succumbing?
How was it that John Allen alone possessed such rare strength? Allen
responded indignantly: "I take [the *Aurora*] for the purpose of seeing
what abominable things can issue from a genuine Jacobinic press."[3]

In hindsight, it's easy to dismiss Allen as an alarmist and a blow-
hard—in part because the issues that so inflamed the times (fear of
France!) are so removed from our own experience. Still, his concerns
were valid, his fears genuine. President Adams, his cabinet, and the
Federalist Congress were dealing with enormous challenges: France,
a global power, was disrupting U.S. commerce by seizing American
ships; America *was* on the verge of being drawn into a terrifying conflict with France; and the Republicans who opposed the Federalists
were indeed creating no end of trouble and consternation for men
who, with their backs against the wall, were trying to do the right
thing as they saw it.

Robert Goodloe Harper, the moderate thirty-three-year-old
Federalist from Maryland, professed himself to be less concerned
with the wayward newspapers than with his fellow members of Congress who were egging them on, promoting "insurrection" from the
floor of the House. This was a not-so-subtle swipe at Matthew Lyon,
who remained curiously subdued throughout the debate, though still
at the top of the Federalist enemy list. While carefully insisting that
he would not support a bill to forcibly silence opposition members

of Congress, Harper said muzzling newspapers was the only practical way of preventing dangerous thoughts uttered by those members from reaching a wider audience.[4]

Harper was correct in noting the close connection between Republican leaders and newspaper editors who reliably parroted their causes and published their anonymous political writings—usually in exchange for financial support. James Madison and Thomas Jefferson supported the founding of the first Republican political paper, the *National Gazette*. Editor Philip Freneau, an old friend of Madison's from the College of New Jersey (now Princeton University), was often sharply critical of Federalists. Bache counted Jefferson among his wealthy and powerful patrons.[5] Of all the politicians of the era, it was Jefferson who mastered the sly art of quietly supporting writers and editors to promote his views and discredit his enemies and their policies. In personal encounters Jefferson remained polite and carefully nonconfrontational. He left the distasteful and nasty side of his dealings to paid mouthpieces whose writings actively subverted policies and people Jefferson disagreed with, including President Washington at a time when Jefferson was serving in Washington's administration. This habit served Jefferson well, as he rode to higher offices with clean coattails. His opponents, and the editors in his quiet pay, rarely fared so well.

Still, the suggestion that such arrangements amounted to "treasonable combinations," as Allen put it, was hypocritical considering the close ties between Federalist leaders and their own like-minded editors. Alexander Hamilton privately backed John Fenno's *Gazette of the United States*, which matched the *Aurora* insult for insult and reliably supported each and every Federalist cause.

Often, the relationships went beyond private patronage. Federalist politicians rewarded favored printers with lucrative government printing contracts that today would be recognized as gross conflicts of interest, while politically appointed postal officials gave special breaks on mailing to Federalist newspapers. To promote the free flow of information around the country, an act passed in 1792 allowed newspaper editors to send one copy of every issue to as many other newspapers as they wanted, postage free. Beyond that, mailing rates for newspapers were 1 cent for distances up to a hundred miles and 1.5 cents for anything beyond.[6] Deputy postmasters frequently invoked their franking privileges to waive mailing costs for Federalist papers, while charging Republican papers full fare or even delaying or disrupting mailings.[7]

Edward Livingston, who had put forth the motion to reject the Sedition Act, warned his colleagues that Americans would simply refuse to follow any law so blatantly unconstitutional, adding ominously that he would "with pride" support any citizen so inclined.

If citizens could decide for themselves which laws were constitutional and which were not, "who were to be the judges?" asked Harrison Gray Otis, a prominent Federalist from Massachusetts.

Livingston snapped back: "The people of the United States . . . We are their servants, when we exceed our powers, we become their *tyrants!*"[8]

Nathaniel Macon, a forty-year-old North Carolinian and veteran of the Revolutionary War, joined Livingston in condemning a bill he termed clearly unconstitutional. Pass this law, he said, and Congress might as well establish a state religion, or prohibit citizens from worshipping freely, since both prohibitions are contained in the same First Amendment. If Congress could not see the fundamental contradiction contained in the Sedition Act, it might as well abandon the idea of adhering to the Constitution altogether.[9]

At the same time, Macon warned that passing the law would infuriate an American public that was deeply aware of its rights, even if Congress was not. While Europeans were accustomed to bowing to powerful rulers, Americans, "almost to a man, understand the nature both of the State and Federal Governments," he said. They will therefore "much sooner discern and repel any encroachments upon their liberty, of which they, as freemen, ought to be extremely jealous."[10]

Other representatives defended the journalism of Benjamin Franklin Bache. Joseph McDowell, another North Carolinian, called Bache "a citizen of respectable character and connexions." He then pointed to an unnamed Federalist printer (obviously William Cobbett of the *Porcupine's Gazette*) who "boasts of being a subject of King George, and who is generally supposed to be in the pay of the British Minister." Cobbett's paper, McDowell insisted, contained "more libels and lies than any other in the United States."[11] Cobbett was at least as objectionable to Republicans as Bache was to Federalists. Clearly both, in the eyes of many people, were viciously, arrogantly wrong. So, who was the outlaw? Did that depend only on who held the reins of power?

The most eloquent defender of free speech and critic of the proposed act on that day was surely Albert Gallatin. The man who chose his battles carefully knew that this was a time to be heard. Gallatin attacked John Allen for implying that criticism of government debt amounted to sedition. Can it be a crime to suggest that wars drive up debt and taxes, or that politicians often seek to expand their own power, or presidents the power of the presidency?[12]

Gallatin understood American freedom at a level that many of his native-born compatriots did not. Although a Republican, he freely admitted the flaws in his side's arguments. In particular, he referred to the *Time-Piece* article Allen had cited, which had been so contemptuous and personally insulting toward President Adams. The article was bad, Gallatin readily acknowledged, but Allen's solution was infinitely worse: "What was the remedy proposed by the gentleman from Connecticut, in order to rectify and correct error? Coercion: a law inflicting fine and imprisonment for the publication of erroneous opinions." Could the Federalists be so powerless as to lack the means of fighting erroneous opinions with the truth?[13]

Echoing Macon's warnings that Americans would openly rebel against abridgments of their rights, Gallatin said, "God forbid that we should ever see that day!" He added, "But it is above all in the power

of Government to avert such an evil by refraining from unconstitutional and arbitrary laws."[14]

Not every member of Congress shared Gallatin and Macon's
concern over constitutional rights. Connecticut Federalist Samuel W.
Dana chided Gallatin for fixating on what was, after all, only "one of
the articles adopted as amendments to the Constitution." He wondered, "Why is the gentleman from Pennsylvania so very anxious on
the subject?"[15] Dana posed another question: What does free speech
mean? "Can it be anything more than the right of uttering and doing
what is not injurious to others? . . . Indeed, can it, in the nature of
things, be one of the rights of freemen to do injury?"[16] Federalist
George Thatcher of Massachusetts concurred, adding that if free
speech was truly an absolute right, any criminal defendant wanting
to have his way in court would be within his rights to threaten the
life of his judge.

Republican Thomas Claiborne of Virginia countered by drawing a crucial distinction between speech that directly endangers life
and limb versus speech that is merely insulting. To wit: you can't use
your own rights to destroy someone else's. Such is the requirement
of living as a free person in an orderly society. The law already rec-
ognizes this reality, Claiborne said. Threatening the life of a judge
is already a crime, he noted, and no sedition act would make it more
so.[17]

Harper, who had introduced the House version of the bill, was
apparently swayed by the passion of the Republicans' concern over
damage to the Constitution. He offered an amendment: "Provided,
that nothing in this law shall be construed to extend to abridge the
freedom of speech and of the press, as secured by the Constitution
of the United States."[18] But, given the aims of the bill, the amendment seemed so absurd that few men of either party supported it,
and Harper withdrew his motion.

When the House resoundingly overruled Livingston's motion
to reject the bill, Republicans shifted to damage control, seeking to

minimize its scope. Claiborne moved to include language explicitly permitting juries sitting on sedition cases to consider whether the law was just. Federalist Harper responded that such an amendment would be unnecessary, since juries always judged the law when making a decision. Delaware Federalist James Bayard believed that juries should only find in matters of fact and that judges, educated in the law, were the only ones capable of determining matters having to do with the law itself.[19]

Claiborne argued that consistent application of the law would be impossible, since the entire area of libel law in the United States was vague. The crucial matter of whether the truth of the writing under consideration implied a defense had yet to be fully established. Although today factual accuracy provides the ultimate wall of defense in libel cases (particularly when the writings concern public figures such as politicians), a significant body of the English common law from which U.S. laws derived actually argued that truth of a libel only intensified the guilt.

Claiborne managed to persuade a number of Federalists, along with the solid bloc of Republicans, and his amendment passed, 67–15.[20] This was a significant softening of the Senate's stance against questioning the constitutional motives of leaders. In reality, though, this would amount to a hollow victory when the Sedition Act came into effect.

# CHAPTER TEN

As the debate continued and passage seemed more and more certain, Secretary of State Timothy Pickering began laying the groundwork for prosecutions. Since Bache was already facing trial in September under common-law charges, Pickering focused on other Republican editors. He organized a network of friends and informers to keep him abreast of offensive materials published around the country. When the incoming mail delivered a likely target from one of his sources, Pickering would write to the U.S. attorney in that state, suggesting that he investigate and prosecute. Like most suggestions issued from powerful men to underlings, these were treated as direct orders.

The son of a pious, unpopular farmer and church deacon in Salem, Massachusetts, Timothy Pickering graduated from Harvard at age eighteen and made his way through life with a sense of moral superiority unmitigated by wit, irony, or the slightest awareness of his personal shortcomings. He was vain, suspicious, and thin-skinned, and when he suspected someone was against him (as often he did), he used every power at his command to destroy that person. Even the twentieth-century biographer who set out to rescue Pickering from his legacy as "one of the principal villains of early American history" realized partway into his research that the reputation was, alas, richly deserved.[1]

Among the most remarkable things about Pickering was his endurance, his ability to craft a long government career in spite of his many enemies. An officer in the Revolutionary War, Pickering had been chosen by President Washington as secretary of war and then as acting secretary of state following the resignation of Edmund Randolph. But his volatility and self-righteousness rubbed everyone the wrong way.[2]

Wherever he went, Pickering carried the whiff of paranoia and self-righteous double-dealing. Randolph's resignation enabling Pickering's ascension had come about in part through Pickering's own machinations. During the long deliberation on the Jay Treaty, Pickering provided Washington with captured French documents suggesting that Randolph sympathized with the French and might accept bribes in order to help advance French interests with the president. Pickering was not Washington's first (or even fourth) choice to fill the vacant post. At least five qualified candidates turned Washington down first. In the early days of the republic, cabinet posts were not always sought-after assignments. Many viewed them as thankless roles involving low pay and arduous travel. And, in the wake of Randolph's embarrassing resignation, such positions seemed personally risky and fraught with danger. Candidate Rufus King turned down Washington's offer to avoid being subjected to "foul and venomous shafts of calumny" from potential critics.[3] At last, a desperate president offered Pickering the full-time position. Pickering repaid Washington by lamenting (behind his back) that the president was a weak administrator, an overrated general, and a man of only middling intelligence. Upon his election in 1797, John Adams kept Pickering on as his own secretary of state, a decision he came to regret.[4]

Like many Federalists, Pickering believed himself and a few other leaders to be all that stood between the new republic and complete ruin. He hated and mistrusted the French, and believed that equipping an army to stave off a French invasion was the highest priority of government. The second-highest priority was weeding out the seditious elements within the United States who might support an invasion.

Among Pickering's earliest actions was a letter to Richard Harison, the U.S. attorney for New York, alerting him to an offending item from June 19, 1798, in the *Mount Pleasant Register* in Westchester County. The *Register* was no hotbed of Republican unrest but an obscure weekly printed by a man named William Durrell. The offending matter amounted to a single paragraph not even original to the *Register* but reprinted from another paper, the *New-Windsor Gazette* of New York. Pickering enclosed the copy of the *Register* and instructed Harison, "if in your opinion it contains libelous matter, to enter a prosecution against the Printer of that paper."[5]

Within three weeks, Pickering's request had made its way through Harison to New York District Court judge John Sloss Hobart, who ordered Durrell's arrest.[6] No surviving copy of the *Register* or *Gazette* from the day in question is known to exist.[7] But according to the indictment, the offending paragraph compared John Adams to the traitor Benedict Arnold, suggesting that both men wanted the United States to revert to its former position as "an appendage of the British Monarchy."[8] Nor is much known about William Durrell. A former printer and bookseller in New York City, he had recently moved to Mount Pleasant, a quiet hamlet north of the city, married a woman named Sarah Street, and begun publishing the *Register*.[9] For Durrell, Pickering's terse, one-page note was the start of a nearly two-year ordeal that would end with the loss of his newspaper and financial straits for his growing family.[10] But Pickering's attention was already drifting to bigger targets—namely John Daly Burk, editor of the *New York Time-Piece*. After the *Aurora*, the *Time-Piece* was the most outspoken Republican newspaper in the United States.

Burk had been a leader of the anti-British group the United Irishmen, founded in 1791 when Burk was a student at Dublin's Trinity College. Its message of home rule had struck a chord with thousands of his countrymen. Burk formed secret societies to promote deism and revolution against Great Britain, and wrote articles for a variety of papers on the virtues of democracy. When several members of Burk's secret societies were arrested, tried, and hanged, Burk hid for a time in a bookseller's shop in Dublin. Disguised as a woman, he boarded a ship bound for Boston. He arrived in the New World in 1796 with a new middle name ("Daly," in honor of the woman who had given him her clothes for his escape) and a self-styled mission to protect democracy in a country that he had admired from afar.[11]

The influx of United Irishmen into the United States was particularly vexing for Federalists because of the group's close philosophical connection with the aims of the French Revolution. They feared the Irish would foment revolution in the United States. But they misread the motives of Burk and others like him. Whereas the struggles in Europe had been about casting off oppressive governments, the United Irishmen saw the United States as a land where people were free to live according to their ideals. The American Society of United Irishmen, formed by immigrants, saw themselves as trying to preserve the American government, not overthrow it.[12]

Not long after arriving, Burk migrated to New York and took the helm at the *Time-Piece*, where he immediately began criticizing Federalist policies. Even had the Federalists understood the motivations of Burk and others like him, this understanding would only have made them angrier. Burk's editorial voice was strong and, at its best, forcefully elegant; but he could also be self-righteous and pedantic. Federalists considering passage of the Sedition Act were "coward traitors" to the American ideal.[13] One need not be a reactionary to understand the Federalists' chagrin at being lectured on their betrayal of American principles by men so freshly off the boat.

Burk's invectives against the Adams administration as editor of the *Time-Piece* had been harsh and unrelenting, but the issue of Monday, July 2, particularly caught Pickering's attention. One article concerned a letter written by Elbridge Gerry, a U.S. envoy to France, about rising tensions between the two countries. Burk insinuated that Adams, before forwarding the letter to Congress, had altered certain passages to make them more inflammatory, to stir up passions in Congress for "a war of aggression, a war produced by the basest arts, wicked in its purposes."

There was plenty more to choose from. Virtually every item with the exception of advertisements contained some form of attack or ridicule against Federalists, often in militant terms. "Perish the traitors that would surrender the Independence of America to foreign enemies! Perish the traitors that would surrender the independence of America to Domestic traitors!" said one piece, notable mainly because it closely mirrored what Federalists were saying about Republicans. A short poem accused Federalists of trying to hold the common people down by preventing them from reading; another item labeled Federalists "ignorant defenders of aristocracy." Still another appealed to "friends of Liberty" to contribute toward a defense fund for Benjamin Franklin Bache.

One item struck directly at Pickering: "We have strong reason to believe that T. Pickering and William Cobbett, have been closetted together for the purpose of organizing a system of *Espionage*. Citizens beware of Spies and Informers."[14] What sounds like paranoid hyperbole from an impassioned editor was in fact—and this, surely, galled Pickering most—completely accurate. Earlier in the year the Federalist publisher of *Porcupine's Gazette* had sent some papers to Pickering through a mutual acquaintance about the doings of the American Society of United Irishmen. Pickering responded quickly. Promising "perfect confidence," he instructed Cobbett to communicate directly through Pickering's personal assistant any further information that might "support a prosecution."[15]

Pickering on July 7 wrote again to Harison, asking him to investigate and prosecute Burk for his "most false & inflamatory" article about Adams, and other pieces "of a similar seditious tendency." He alerted Harison to a Federalist newspaper, the *New York Commercial Advertiser*, which had recently published an article claiming that Burk had given "a treasonable speech" overheard by one of its writers. Pickering assured Harison that the writer "has left his name with the printer of the *Commercial Advertiser*" and would be glad to provide further details.

Not content just to suggest prosecution, Pickering mused over the best methods: "If Burke [*sic*] be an Alien, no man is a fitter object for the operation of the Alien Act," he wrote. "If on the other hand he be a citizen, & you should be of opinion, that the speech attributed to him is proved, & constitutes an offense against the laws, you will institute a prosecution against him." Then, in a postscript, Pickering added that even if Burk turned out to be an alien, simple deportation might rob the government of a chance to make a proper example of him. Perhaps, he suggested, the government should "punish him for his libels, before he is sent away."[16]

On July 6, Harison formally charged Burk with seditious libel, similar to the charges leveled against Benjamin Franklin Bache. As editor of the *Time-Piece*, Burk had made some influential friends among New York Republicans, including Aaron Burr, the future vice president and Alexander Hamilton duelist. Burr helped arrange a deal with Pickering under which Burk, rather than facing criminal charges, would leave the country. Instead, Burk slipped quietly down to Republican-friendly Virginia, where he changed his name and rode out the next several years teaching.[17]

On Tuesday, July 10, the final day of House debate, Virginia Republican John Nicholas made a final plea against the Sedition Act. Nicholas had, he said, combed through every word of the Constitution looking in vain among the enumerated powers for some authority that would enable Congress to pass this law. Instead, he found only "an express prohibition against passing it." Nicholas scoffed at the Federalists' claim that they could distinguish liberty of the press from licentiousness, and spare the one while punishing the other. All such regulations start with the same ostensibly harmless motives, he argued, while ultimately destroying "the only means by which the people can examine and become acquainted with the conduct of persons employed in their government."[18]

But it was too late. The two sides had hardened and were no longer listening to each other. In the end it was not the zealots on the Federalist side who tipped Congress into this violation of free speech. It was the silent go-alongs such as John Wilkes Kittera, a Federalist from Pennsylvania. Representing a politically divided state, Kittera said, "On one side it is said, this bill is a violation of the Constitution; on the other, it is said to be founded on common law principles. If the latter is true, it may be wise and proper to pass this bill."[19] At the end of the day, Kittera joined other Federalists in approving by a vote of 44 to 41 the law that would become known as the Sedition Act.[20]

The House bill toned down some key aspects of the Senate version. Gone was the stipulation against questioning the constitutional motivations of officials. And the hurdle defining guilt was made slightly higher and more focused. The stricture against "inflammatory" writings was gone, along with prohibition of "criminating motives." To blunt criticism, the House bill also included a section specifically stating that a defendant charged under the act could "give in evidence in his defence, the truth of the matter contained in the publication charged as libel."[21] Federalists would point to this provision as an example of the liberality of their law. The bill also specifically gave juries the power to determine the justness of the law itself when deciding the guilt or innocence of a defendant.

Despite these modifications, the final wording left Federalists plenty of room to ensnare their opponents almost at will. The heart of the act read as follows:

> *And be it further enacted*, That if any person shall write, print, utter or publish, or shall cause or procure to be written, printed, uttered or published, or shall knowingly and willingly assist or aid in writing, printing, uttering or publishing any false, scandalous and malicious writing or writings against

the government of the United States, or either house of the Congress of the United States, or the President of the United States, with intent to defame the said government, or either house of the said Congress, or the said President, or to bring them, or either of them, into contempt or disrepute; or to excite against them, or either or any of them, the hatred of the good people of the United States, or to stir up sedition within the United States, or to excite any unlawful combinations therein, for opposing or resisting any law of the United States, or any act of the President of the United States, done in pursuance of any such law, or of the powers in him vested by the constitution of the United States, or to resist, oppose, or defeat any such law or act, or to aid, encourage or abet any hostile designs of any foreign nation against the United States, their people or government, then such person, being thereof convicted before any court of the United States having jurisdiction thereof, shall be punished by a fine not exceeding two thousand dollars, and by imprisonment not exceeding two years.[22]

The naked politics behind the law can be seen in the fact that it was illegal to speak against both houses of Congress and the president, offices then held by Federalists, but, notably, not the vice president, Thomas Jefferson, a Republican. A final section accentuated this point by giving the Sedition Act an expiration date of March 3, 1801, which just happened to coincide with the inauguration of the next president and the next House and Senate. In case they should lose, the Federalists did not want to fall victim to their own law.

The Federalist press lauded the new bill. The *Albany Centinel* assured its readers that the law would provide an effective check against the "mad licentiousness" of Republican editors.[23] The *New Hampshire Gazette* trumpeted the bill's passage as "a GAG for JACOBINISM!"[24]

All that remained was the signature of the president of the United States.

# CHAPTER ELEVEN

Though he insisted until the end of his life that the Sedition Act and the Alien Acts were necessary "wartime measures," Adams blamed others for their execution and portrayed himself as a reluctant bystander. In 1809, eight years removed from office, a seventy-four-year-old Adams claimed that Alexander Hamilton came up with the idea in an unsolicited letter instructing the incoming president on how to conduct his affairs. The letter, which "had no influence with me," was so presumptuous that Adams believed Hamilton must have been "in a delirium" when he wrote it.[1] "Nor did I adopt his idea . . . ," Adams continued. "I recommended no such thing in my speech. Congress, however, adopted both these measures. I knew there was need enough of both, and therefore I consented to them."[2]

Adams chroniclers have reinforced this image of the president as a reluctant bystander. Adams's grandson, who edited a ten-volume collection of Adams's papers in 1854, wrote that Hamilton and other "ultra members of the federal party" had deemed Adams to be "lukewarm, if not unfriendly" to the laws. "Yet the entire responsibility for the measures has been made to fall on him!" Charles Francis Adams lamented.[3]

In the ages since, sympathetic biographers, while acknowledging Adams's signing of the laws as a terrible decision, have downplayed his active involvement—and quickly moved on.[4] The website for the

Adams National Historic Park in Quincy, Massachusetts, succinctly captures what has become the standard defense: "Adams played no part in the formation of these acts nor did he take steps to enforce them, but he was held responsible for these unpopular measures in the public mind."[5]

Yet the events of 1798 suggest that if John Adams suffered any angst or self-torment over whether to support the laws, he quickly recovered. On July 14, Adams signed the Sedition Act into law. His behavior in the ensuing years of his presidency, far from describing reluctant or conflicted "consent" to the law, reveals a politically embattled leader who eagerly embraced the Sedition Act to silence his critics. True, Adams did not personally issue any arrest warrants, but his secretary of state, Timothy Pickering, would prove to be one of the most zealous enforcers.

Over the next two years Adams would enthusiastically support and conspire in at least one of the prosecutions, and refuse in another case to pardon a defenseless loner convicted in the worst sort of kangaroo court in Boston. In yet another case, he would attempt to reward with high federal office a New Jersey prosecutor who showed particular zeal in pursuing a private citizen for the crime of making a derogatory offhand remark about Adams on a public street. The list goes on. Even without these gestures, it has to be said: John Adams left his fingerprints all over the Sedition Act by letting it happen. Most of those convicted of sedition would be prosecuted for criticizing Adams. If the chief law enforcement officer of the land, a man sworn to uphold the Constitution, knowingly allows officials to throw people in jail for criticizing him, does it even matter whether he took an "active role" in the prosecutions?

For another politician, signing the Sedition Act might have amounted to a political mistake. Adams's signature on this legislation rises to the level of tragedy because it represents a stark, personal betrayal of his deepest held beliefs, one of those moments when a great man under pressure contradicts his conscience.

Few if any of the Founders had been as consistently forceful as Adams on the subject of freedom and on the corrosive potential of concentrated power to destroy rights. Few understood as viscerally that the essence of liberty lay in protecting the rights of besieged individuals against groups, whether an overpowerful government body or a vengeful mob. In 1770, he risked his career and his reputation by defending eight British soldiers charged in the deaths of five citizens in the Boston Massacre. The public was in a hanging mood, and no other lawyer wanted the case. But Adams told the jury, "Facts are stubborn things, and whatever may be our wishes, our inclination, or the dictums of our passions, they cannot alter the state of facts and evidence."[6] Six of the eight defendants were acquitted.

In 1765, a thirty-year-old Adams published articles in the *Boston Gazette* extolling the "indisputable, inalienable, indefeasible divine right" of individuals to criticize their leaders.[7] The series, compiled as *A Dissertation on the Canon and the Feudal Law*, contains some of the founding generation's most cogent, reasoned, and courageous arguments for freedom of the press—courageous because he tossed these words into the teeth of Boston's controlling British authorities. "None of the means of information are more sacred, or have been cherished with more tenderness and care by the settlers of America, than the Press," he wrote. Far from discouraging a free press, the government should encourage the free and unrestrained sharing of ideas. He added, "It should be easy and cheap and safe for any person to communicate his thoughts to the public."

Adams's praise for journalists eerily forecast the central conflicts of 1798. One passage, addressed to printers, reads like a fervent warning from a young, idealistic Adams reaching through time to his future self:

> The stale, impudent insinuations of slander and sedition, with which the gormandizers of power have endeavored to discredit your paper, are so much the more to your honor; for

the jaws of power are always opened to devour, and her arm is always stretched out, if possible, to destroy the freedom of thinking, speaking, and writing.[8]

In his private journals, a thirty-six-year-old Adams made clear that the greatest threat to free speech and other liberties came not from those who would abuse their freedoms, but from those in government who might attempt to curtail them. "Ambition is one of the more ungovernable passions of the human heart. The love of power is insatiable and uncontrollable," he wrote. He went on to say, "The only maxim of a free government ought to be to trust no man living with power to endanger the public liberty."[9]

How, then, does one reconcile the firebrand in his thirties with the crabbed, dyspeptic sixty-three-year-old president who now believed that it was not the people who needed protection from abuses by the government, but the other way around? Certainly, Adams had good reason for feeling besieged on all sides. He was caught in a pincer between hawkish Federalists such as Hamilton, Pickering, and Secretary of War James McHenry, who pressed for conflict with France and openly or discreetly accused Adams of softness; and staunch Republicans who loved France, hated England, and accused Adams at every turn of leading an imperial presidency bent on making war. As he walked this tightrope, an increasingly bitter Adams felt Benjamin Bache and other Republicans always jimmying the line, trying to get him to fall. They were not just making his life and his job difficult; they were directly impeding his ability to govern the country through a precarious time.

Never mind that this "wartime measure" lacked one crucial component: a war. The Sedition Act, Adams and others suggested, was an emergency procedure akin to martial law, a curfew imposed in extraordinary times to maintain order in the streets. But this is refuted by the overtly political nature of the law. Nowhere does the Sedition Act refer to any emergency. Nowhere does it suggest that the bill was necessary only to get the nation through a time of peril. True, the bill came with a time limit—but that was determined not by the nature of tensions with France, but by the dates during which Federalists were guaranteed to remain in office. These were, indeed, times of tension and fear, but the offenses the government identified in the Sedition Act were not the true crimes of espionage, or selling secrets to the enemy, or organizing armed insurrection; they were about making government officials look bad in the eyes of other Americans.

There were other factors that no doubt contributed to Adams's decision. Among these was his wife, Abigail, whose opinions and advice he valued perhaps above all. Abigail was incensed by attacks in the press against her husband, and believed that a sedition bill was the only way to stop them. Bache, in particular, infuriated her. When the *Aurora* mocked the first couple as provincial rubes from Quincy, Abigail wrote in private letters that Bache's beloved grandfather, with his "illegitimate ofspring," was nothing to be proud of.[10] The barrage of assaults on her husband made her fear for his physical safety. Other countries would not allow such outrages, she protested. To her, Republican editors were "vipers" who should be forced to "cease to hiss." In the end, though, Abigail was a protective spouse. As historian Edith B. Gelles notes, Abigail didn't sign the Sedition Act into law. "John did."[11]

The questions linger: How could Adams and the Federalists so clearly and resoundingly repudiate the ideas they themselves had recently embraced as inviolable in the First Amendment? What sort of malevolence overtook these men? What special aberration made them so thoroughly disavow their principles?

Perhaps it is our surprise that is misplaced. Given the course of human history leading up to the Sedition Act, the most surprising thing might have been if they recognized the need for restraint. In justifying their actions, to the world and to themselves, they had only to look for their model at thousands of years of history. Freedom, as framed so ambitiously in the founding documents, had yet to be tried.

If anything, Federalists had good reason to consider themselves magnanimous. Compared with the swift and unequivocal punishments that even supposedly enlightened governments routinely dealt to nettlesome dissenters, the Sedition Act and its limited punishments seem positively mild—a point Federalists made frequently when Republicans decried the injustice of the law.

In England in the late seventeenth century, for example, nearly five hundred years after the Magna Carta and on the very cusp of the age of reason, writing anything critical of the Crown was considered high treason. Here was one way the Crown dealt with high treason: The condemned would be strapped to a hurdle, dragged to the place of execution, and hanged by the neck for a period long enough to cause excruciating suffering but not death. While still conscious, the prisoner would be cut down and forced to witness having his "privy-members" cut off and burned before his eyes. By which time the next step, beheading, came almost as an act of mercy. The body would then be quartered, and the four parts disposed of "at the king's pleasure."[12]

Against this monument to cruel and unusual punishment, it's hard to imagine how anyone summoned the courage to question the king's authority. But some people did and one case bears telling because of its impact on the course of American freedom. On June 26, 1683, Colonel Algernon Sidney was enjoying his afternoon meal when a magistrate named Philip Lloyd burst into his London home. He presented a search warrant, arrested Sidney, and seized stacks of papers from a writing desk and from an old trunk in his study.[13]

At his arraignment, Sidney was charged with high treason against King Charles II. Though prosecutors would weave a tangled conspiracy of subversive plots, secret meetings, and envoys supposedly sent by Sidney to Scotland to drum up an insurrection, the only real evidence against Sidney was the cache of papers found in his study. Sidney had written a discourse on the proper relationship between kings and their subjects. A king, Sidney wrote, serves at the consent of the people, and therefore "must be content to submit his interest unto theirs." And then came the words that sealed Sidney's fate. Any king who does not wish to serve under these circumstances may renounce his crown, he wrote. But a king who accepts his oath and fails to honor it must expect to have "revenge taken by those he hath betrayed." Sidney carefully avoided any reference to Charles II, professing instead to discuss royals of antiquity. But nobody was fooled. For this suggestion, Sidney was charged with "compassing and imagining the death of the king."

His trial transcript reads like a pre-Kafkaesque legal nightmare. After being read a rambling, invective-filled indictment at his preliminary hearing, Sidney was denied legal counsel and given two weeks to prepare his own defense in his cell. Presiding judge George Jeffreys refused to provide Sidney with a copy of the indictment or even to name the statute under which he was to be tried. Once the trial started, when Sidney attempted to object to testimony from prosecution witnesses, Jeffreys warned him not to interrupt. When Sidney made points in his own defense, Jeffreys interrupted and silenced him.

At the close of the trial, Jeffreys instructed jury members that they were to decide only whether Sidney had written the papers, not to make any judgments about whether the content of the papers amounted to treason. The court had already determined the writings to be treasonous, Jeffreys reasoned. Therefore, if Sidney wrote them, he was guilty of treason. The jury retired for half an hour before returning a verdict of guilty.

Hearing the decision, Sidney said: "My lord, I humbly conceive, I have had no trial . . ."

Jeffreys explained in precise detail to a horrified Sidney what was to become of his "privy-members" and other bodily parts, adding, solemnly, "And the God of infinite mercy have mercy upon your soul." King Charles II took pity—sort of. He restricted the punishment to beheading. On December 7, 1683, Algernon Sidney, age sixty-one, was led to a scaffold on Tower Hill in London. Before meeting his fate, he said, "We live in an age that maketh truth pass for treason."

Sidney was posthumously exonerated after the Glorious Revolution of 1688. His offending papers were finally published in 1698 as *Discourses Concerning Government*. So while Sidney died, his ideas lived on, eventually making their way across the Atlantic Ocean. Although *Discourses*, like its author, has fallen into relative obscurity, eclipsed by the works of the more celebrated John Locke, it directly influenced the thinking of American founders. Thomas Jefferson drew on Sidney's ideas when drafting the Declaration of Independence. In 1804, while president, Jefferson wrote to a publisher who had asked his advice on issuing a collected works of Sidney. Jefferson responded: "The world has so long and so generally sounded the praises of his Discourses on government, that it seems superfluous, and even presumptuous, for an individual to add his feeble breath to the gale." He called Sidney's work "probably the best elementary book of the principles of government, as founded in natural right which has ever been published in any language."[14]

# Chapter Twelve

The notion of European liberty seekers condemned in their own lands finding fertile soil for their ideas in the New World is particularly pleasing to Americans, affirming as it does the nation's self-image as the land of the free. This impression has a strong foundation in truth, but it can also be misleading. The better part of a century passed between the publication of Sidney's *Discourses* and Jefferson's Declaration. In the intervening years the colonies were anything but swift in embracing ideas of free speech. As historian Leonard W. Levy wrote in his landmark book from the early 1960s, *Legacy of Suppression*, "The persistent image of colonial America as a society in which freedom of expression was cherished is an hallucination of sentiment that ignores history. The evidence provides little comfort for the notion that the colonies hospitably received advocates of obnoxious or detestable ideas on matters that counted."[1]

Had Levy laid the blame for intolerance on the usual suspects—Puritan fanatics or British tyrants—he would not have caused such a fuss. But Levy's exhaustive study of colonial attitudes toward free speech found everyday citizens right up through the revolution and Constitutional Convention and beyond to be deeply conflicted and often hypocritical on the subject. "The American people," he wrote, "simply did not understand that freedom of thought and expression means equal freedom for the other fellow, especially the one with hated ideas."[2]

Levy's book was controversial because his thesis directly challenged long-standing assumptions that the Founders had a robust understanding of, and desire for, widespread free speech when they penned and approved the seminal words in the First Amendment. Levy suggested that the First Amendment's enshrinement of free speech should be looked upon as "in large measure a lucky political accident."[3]

Through much of the eighteenth century leading up to the revolution, American common law regarding free speech drew from the same source that shaped English thinking: Blackstone's *Commentaries on the Laws of England*. Sir William Blackstone, a prominent English jurist, politician, and Oxford professor, wrote the *Commentaries* between 1765 and 1769. More than any other single document, this resource provided the foundation for modern English law. By extension, *Commentaries* also played a large role in the development of the legal system in the United States. "The liberty of the press is indeed essential to the nature of a free state," Blackstone stated promisingly.[4]

To Blackstone, that meant "laying no *previous* restraints upon publications." Removing prior restraint represented a huge leap forward for personal liberty. It meant, essentially, that the government could not regulate presses by determining in advance, through licensure or other means, who was permitted to speak and who was not. But Blackstone was also quick to add that freedom to print in no way implied freedom from punishment once something was published. Anyone who puts his ideas before the public "must take the consequences of his own temerity." Actionable offense might include anything that upset "the preservation of peace and good order, of government and religion." Blackstone added, "Thus the will of individuals is still left free; the abuse only of that free will is the object of legal punishment."[5]

But the lack of prior restraints does nothing to protect the printer from powerful people who don't like what's been printed.

Indeed, Blackstone considered it a crime to write things that "make discord between the king and nobility, or concerning any great man of the realm." Also forbidden were "*False* and *pretended prophecies*, with intent to disturb the peace." Such prophecies "raise enthusiastic jealousies in the people and terrify them with imaginary fears." As for libel, Blackstone forbade "any writings, pictures, or the like, of an immoral or illegal tendency" when directed toward another person. In the American colonies, accordingly, printers were routinely hauled before juries and made to answer for the charge of "seditious libel."[6]

In comparison with Blackstone's itemized exceptions and qualifications, the language of the First Amendment is clear, sweeping, and unequivocal in its protection of speech: "Congress shall make no law respecting an establishment of religion, or prohibiting the free exercise thereof; or abridging the freedom of speech, or of the press; or the right of the people peaceably to assemble, and to petition the Government for a redress of grievances."

But was the First Amendment, as Leonard Levy suggests, an accident? While Levy was a libertarian on speech, the "First Amendment as accident" proposition raises serious questions for free speech and freedom of the press. For if it can be said that the Founders were not committed to such freedoms, then those rights might be negotiable, with each generation free to expand or limit the right according to its own desires.

The Bill of Rights today figures so closely into the American discussion on everything from hate speech to the relationship between church and state to gun control that it's difficult to imagine the nation settling a serious debate without resorting first and last to that document. Yet original passage was by no means a certainty, and many Founders felt a bill of rights would actually be dangerous to the country. The debate was intense and often heated. It would drive a wedge between two close friends, Alexander Hamilton and James Madison, who had collaborated on the Federalist Papers, the eighty-five essays in 1787 and 1788 that formed the single most persuasive argument in favor of a strong federal government.

Hamilton was one of the most vocal opponents of a bill of rights. Among that elite circle of leading Founders, Hamilton was the great pragmatist, the man who above all others relished the *process* of government, a bureaucratic genius who viewed a powerful federal government as the only way to prevent petty tyrants in each state from pursuing their own selfish agendas. We must not forget, he warned, "that men are ambitious, vindictive and rapacious."[7] He spoke of the Constitution as a document so strong as to require no additional amendments outlining freedoms. Indeed, Hamilton insisted, "The truth is, after all the declamation we have heard, that the constitution is itself in every rational sense, and to every useful purpose, A BILL OF RIGHTS." By closely defining the federal government's duties and powers, the document would effectively prevent the government from seeking or exercising any powers not specifically mentioned. Any further elaboration of rights would thus be counterproductive, even "dangerous," he insisted. "Why for instance, should it be said, that the liberty of the press shall not be restrained, when no power is given by which restrictions may be imposed?"[8]

Yet even Hamilton, the progenitor of "big government" and the fundamental pessimist when it came to human behavior and motivations, declared individual rights as sacred. Rather than being a replacement for individual rights, he saw a strong federal government as the only means to ensure them. As Hamilton biographer Ron Chernow observes, "Hamilton was as quick to applaud checks on powers as those powers themselves, as he continued his lifelong effort to balance freedom and order. In the final analysis, he thought that the federal government, not the states, would be the best guarantee of individual liberty."[9]

Indeed, most of those who opposed a bill of rights did so on the grounds that it would limit freedom. Enumerating rights in a series of specific amendments, critics argued, might actually embolden the government to usurp other rights under the presumption that what was not mentioned was open to regulation. As one Federalist put it, a bill of rights "would be at best useless, and if one right were to be omitted, it might injuriously grant by implication, what was intended to be reserved."[10]

Other opponents derived their opposition from the fact that the United States would not be ruled by a king, but by the people. Since the people would control the government, the only threats to liberty were if the people themselves proved to be unworthy of maintaining it. A Virginian writing as "Civis Rusticus" argued that "the liberties of the people never can be lost, until they are lost to themselves, in a vicious disregard of their dearest interests, a sottish indolence, a wild licentiousness, a dissoluteness of morals, and a contempt of all virtue."[11] North Carolina Federalist James Iredell argued that unless the country decided to establish a monarchy, the very idea of protecting the people's rights from the people themselves would be "nugatory and ridiculous."[12]

Some opposition was practical rather than philosophical. A group of Boston tradesmen including Paul Revere worried that bickering over "pretended amendments, or alterations," would slow down adoption of a document they considered crucial to reviving a slumped economy.[13]

One of the most consistent voices against the Bill of Rights was Noah Webster, which may surprise modern readers, since Webster's name is still synonymous in America with dictionaries and the use of words. Webster was one of the progenitors of an idea that would become known as the elastic Constitution—the idea that the document should be open to broad reinterpretation from one generation to the next, and that no generation could rightly assign moral absolutes for those to come. Writing as "Giles Hickory" in the *American Magazine* in 1787, Webster called the very idea of a bill of rights "ridiculous" in a nation where political power derived directly from the will of the people. "The present generation have indeed a right to declare what *they* deem a *privilege*," he wrote; "but they have no right to say what the *next* generation shall deem a privilege."[14]

In the end, the search for the "Founders' intent" amounts to a sort of quest for a holy grail. The intents of the figures involved were so varied that parsing their pre-constitutional writings and speeches for specific intentions behind this or that phrase in the Bill of Rights becomes a game of postcolonial Whac-A-Mole. But, in fact, there was broad consensus on the most important point of all. While they wrestled and haggled over specifics, all or most agreed that they wanted to found a country based on liberty. They wanted to be free.

The yearning for liberty comes through in everything they said and wrote. In 1788, Samuel Bryan, a twenty-nine-year-old Pennsylvania state official and editor who opposed adoption of the Constitution without a bill of rights, wrote with youthful ebullience and optimism about his country, a land where "happy equality and independency pervades." He declared, "It is here that human nature may be viewed in all its glory . . . The unfortunate and oppressed of all nations, fly to this grand asylum, where liberty is ever protected, and industry crowned with success."[15]

Thomas Jefferson, watching the constitutional debates unfold from afar in Paris as minister to France, wrote home to James Madison in December 1787 his conviction that "a bill of rights is what the people are entitled to against every government on earth, general or particular, & what no just government should refuse, or rest on inferences."[16] A few weeks later he wrote to his friend Alexander Donald of the necessity of a bill stipulating freedom of religion, press, and other rights as "fetters against doing evil, which no honest government should decline."[17]

That revolutionary idea, that it was government, rather than the people, that needed fettering, was by no means limited to advocates of a bill of rights, or to Republicans versus Federalists. Having so recently cast off one oppressive government, they were terrified of replacing the tyrannies of King George III with a homegrown variety. They recognized the need for government to preserve order and protect liberty, but they also recognized inherently that any government, as a product of man, would be flawed and subject to the flaws of human nature.

The Founders, in their deliberations, wanted their freedom, demanded their freedom, and recognized unequivocally and absolutely that they would not be free unless they were free to speak their minds. The fact that they did not always (or even often) agree on the specific implementation of these principles in no way undermines their conviction that individual liberty was to be the essence of the new country.

Leonard Levy seemed to acknowledge as much in a revised and expanded version of *Legacy of Suppression*, published in the 1980s with the more optimistic title *Emergence of a Free Press*. Though he held on to many of his earlier arguments, including the idea of the First Amendment as a "lucky political accident," a closer reading of fractious, chaotic early American newspapers had convinced him that "the American experience with a free press was as broad as the theoretical inheritance was narrow."[18] In other words, the theory of free speech in America had yet to catch up with its practice. But how could it be otherwise? How could the Founders have fully understood political consequences of formally enshrining a broader level of individual rights than any country had ever attempted? The essential gift the Founders gave to themselves and to us was not a specific, unified theory behind the words contained in the First Amendment, but the words themselves.

A Connecticut Yankee knew the importance of freedom in his own life, but he hardly anticipated that such would also mean the rights of an uneducated Irish immigrant to rise up, get himself elected to office, and start offending everyone. John Adams appreciated the rights of journalists to hurl insults at the British authorities, but he hardly anticipated Benjamin Franklin Bache and James T. Callender unleashing daily invective on *him*.

By affixing his name to the Sedition Act, by betraying his better self, John Adams did more than create a mechanism for silencing political enemies. He set in motion a great national test of whether this first generation of independent Americans would understand, appreciate, and live up to the words they had adopted. Some modern scholars suggest that the very passage of the Sedition Act offers evidence that early Americans didn't much value speech and press freedoms,[19] or that Americans didn't take the First Amendment seriously until the great Supreme Court cases of the twentieth century—prior to which those words "were essentially dead letters."[20]

But they weren't dead letters to the Republicans in 1798. The intended targets of the Sedition Act knew precisely what was at stake in the new law. Their objections—in newspaper articles, on the floor of Congress, in stump speeches, letters, and diary entries—reflected a vivid understanding of what free speech meant to them, and a clear conviction that their First Amendment rights were being torn asunder. They backed their arguments with constitutional principles.

"'*Congress shall made no law abridging the freedom of speech or of the press*,'" one New Yorker wrote to the U.S. House and Senate shortly after the act was passed. "A prohibition more express can scarcely be devised." The author was General John Armstrong, a Revolutionary War veteran and convert from Federalist to Republican. Armstrong wondered how "the most enlightened nation upon earth" could have come to a point that a man with reservations about the president "must also conceal them with care; to hint them to a neighbour, exposes you to *fine*; to breathe them to a brother subjects you to *imprisonment*."[21]

Armstrong's long, thoughtful letter also criticized the Alien Acts, but it was the Sedition Act that filled him with special foreboding. "The former assails the *few*, the latter attacks the *many*. The former is directed at *foreigners*; the latter is levelled at *ourselves*. The former tyrannizes over men, who in general have been born and bred under *oppression*. But it is the superlative wickedness of the latter, to convert freemen into slaves."

# PART II

# THE JAWS OF POWER

# CHAPTER THIRTEEN

Despite his own looming court case and the new "gag law," as he called it, Benjamin Franklin Bache vowed to fight his enemies with everything he had. On July 23, the *Aurora* chided the president over news of Alexander Hamilton's adulterous affair. "'*Thou shalt not commit adultery*,' is one of the commandments of the Deity himself," the article stated. Although President Adams "wishes us to believe that he is a true believer and a very pious man," his appointment of a confessed adulterer as inspector general of the army proves otherwise, it continued. "Mr. Adams ought hereafter to be silent about *French* principles."[1]

This insinuation of loose morals by association must have been particularly galling to Adams. He and Hamilton intensely disliked and mistrusted each other.

Amid the XYZ Affair and continued French harassment of U.S. shipping, some Federalist members of Congress were calling for an immediate declaration of war against France. Adams had chosen a more restrained approach of preparing for conflict by building the military.[2] Congress in July responded to Adams's requests for funding by approving $2 million in property taxes and authorizing the president to borrow an additional $5 million to expand the nation's paltry complement of ships and soldiers.[3]

Adams added symbolic weight to the military buildup by luring George Washington from his Mount Vernon retirement to serve as commander of the armed forces. But the decision backfired on Adams when Washington asked him to name Hamilton, his former Treasury secretary and Revolutionary War aide, as second-in-command. Adams wanted nothing more than to be rid of the arrogant, cocksure Hamilton. Hamilton, for his part, considered Adams to be a weak leader, especially on military matters. And because Washington was sixty-six years old and unlikely to lead forces in the field, Hamilton's appointment would make him, for all practical purposes, the leader of the army. Though Adams at first balked at the request, Washington had thrown the weight of his enormous prestige behind Hamilton. Hamilton had been out of government for three years, building his law practice in New York, and was eager to return to public life. He and his friends, including members of Adams's own cabinet, began a letter-writing campaign to build support for Hamilton's nomination. When Washington made clear that without Hamilton he would refuse to serve, Adams, feeling boxed in, had bitterly complied.[4] It was a humiliating capitulation; and now, thanks to Bache, Adams was being publicly stained by Hamilton's marital infidelities.

But two days after Bache's invective, when Adams left Philadelphia by carriage with Abigail for their farm in Massachusetts, it was to escape a danger more menacing than political battles or poison pens. Yellow fever killed with nonpartisan relish. The summer of 1798 would prove to be the worst outbreak of the disease in Philadelphia since 1793. Adams and many others who fled the city had vivid memories of the earlier epidemic, which killed more than one in ten of the city's residents.

Presidential travel in the 1790s bore no relation to the cocooned comfort to which modern-day presidents are accustomed. The carriage journey from Philadelphia to the Adams farm outside of Boston—a distance of more than three hundred miles—took the better of two weeks, assuming things went well. Often, they did not. Weather and washed-out roads could slow a journey to a crawl, particularly in rural areas. Horses had to be changed about every twelve miles. Travelers endured endless bumps and the discomforts of extreme heat or cold, depending on the season—not to mention the ever-present danger of food poisoning from even the best hotel kitchens and roadside taverns along the way.[5] On top of these difficulties was a reality of presidential travel that both John and Abigail Adams despised: endless rounds of salutes and fetes at every city, town, and wide spot in the road through which they passed.

Unlike kings, these early presidents were expected to be accessible. Being honored and toasted and, worse, having to return each toast or speech with a toast or speech of his own was something that Adams's predecessor, the private and reserved George Washington, accepted with at best grim forbearance.[6] Adams, though not the iconic figure that Washington had been, nevertheless drew his full share of attention wherever he went. This journey was no exception. "At every point along the way enthusiastic crowds cheered them. There were dinners and addresses and replies by the president."[7] But the most significant salute they would receive during this particular journey was one that neither John nor Abigail noticed at the time—and it was anything but fawning.

On the morning of July 27, two days after leaving Philadelphia, the president's carriage approached the bustling riverfront town of Newark, New Jersey. Although Federalists held sway in many New Jersey towns, including Trenton, Newark was sharply divided. That only made local Federalists more eager to show their support to the president. Members of a local militia called the Association of Young Men stood at the flagpole on Broad Street, preparing to fire an artillery salute.

Earlier that spring, the Young Men had sent Adams a proclamation full of bravado, promising their "lives and fortunes" to their country should a war with France arise. Adams had stoked the flames with his response: "You prefer war, with all its concomitant evils, rather than to be tributary, and you judge well—tribute is an evil without end . . ."[8] Adams had responded in similar fashion to several militias around the country. Alarmed by these exchanges, Vice President Jefferson excused the militias' "indiscreet declarations," but not Adams's. "We cannot expect a foreign nation to shew that apathy to the answers of the President . . . ," he wrote to Madison. "Whatever chance for peace might have been left us . . . is completely lost by these answers."[9] Anonymous Republicans, referring to themselves as "Several Young Men of Newark," matched Adams's bravado and belligerence with a warning, published in newspapers, not to use the possibility of war with France as an excuse to trample liberty at home. They vowed that if U.S. officials were to use the threat of war with France as a pretext to install a monarchy or subvert liberty at home "we will, with equal readiness, rally round our constitution, and oppose with all our energy, the first strides towards domestic tyranny and oppression."[10]

The atmosphere was thus politically charged on both sides as the presidential carriage turned onto lower Broad Street in Newark at around 11 A.M. Into this scene wandered forty-six-year-old Luther Baldwin, weaving unsteadily through the crowd. Already feeling "a little merry" after a morning of drinking, Baldwin and his two companions had little interest in the parade.[11] Baldwin was not an admirer of the president, or of any Federalist, for that matter. What the three men wanted was another drink. Just as they approached John Burnet's dram shop on Broad Street, the Adams supporters let loose their artillery, filled with harmless wadding but plenty loud enough to let everyone know that the president's carriage had arrived. Bells from the local Episcopal and Presbyterian churches rang and a chorus sang out, "Behold the Chief who now commands!"[12]

An onlooker—probably Baldwin's friend Brown Clark—cracked, "They are firing at his arse."

Baldwin replied, "I don't care if they fire *through* his arse."

John Burnet had stepped outside to see Adams's carriage and overheard the exchange. Clearly, news of the president's newly minted Sedition Act had arrived in advance of the president himself, for Burnet turned to Baldwin and uttered three fateful words:

"That is sedition."

A crowd quickly gathered around Baldwin and Burnet. As the Republican *Centinel of Freedom* recounted, "the pretended federalists, being much disappointed that the President had not stopped that they might have had the honor of kissing his hand, bent their malice on poor Luther, and the cry was, that he must be punished, he must be punished."[13]

The carriage rolled on, the president and first lady unaware of the commotion. The crowd's passions cooled and it seemed the fracas would end right there. Burnet and others had expressed their anger. Baldwin's joke, while tasteless, could not in any sense have been seen as an actual threat to the president's safety. All concerned had had their say. Burnet went back to his dram shop, and Baldwin and his friends wandered off in search of a more congenial watering hole or a bed in which to sleep it off. Baldwin could not know that his drunken joke would soon make him the unlikeliest folk hero in the nation's first great crisis over the freedom of speech.

Not everyone who deserted Philadelphia in the summer of 1798 did so to escape yellow fever. Matthew Lyon departed for Vermont to fight for his political life. During his own journey north Lyon traveled by stage, following much the same route as Adams. But whereas Adams had seen mostly respectful crowds (Luther Baldwin notwithstanding), Lyon faced open hostility, derision, and abuse. The XYZ Affair had been a public relations disaster for the Republicans, stirring waves of Federalist and nationalist pride. According to William Cobbett's *Porcupine's Gazette*, Trenton residents had followed Lyon when he exited his stage, banging drums and serenading him with sarcastic chants about the wooden sword. Crowds in Brunswick, New Jersey, treated him much the same.[14]

When Lyon stopped in New York City, he shared lodgings with fellow Republicans Albert Gallatin and Edward Livingston. The three politicians got a taste of what it meant to be the opposition at a time of turmoil. About 10 P.M., a raucous crowd of youths gathered outside, shouting "Jacobins!" and singing English patriotic songs.[15] As sitting members of Congress, the legislators were, according to the wording of the Federalists' own Sedition Act, supposed to have been immune to such abuse, for clearly the crowd's antics were intended to "defame" them, to bring them "into contempt or disrepute," and to "excite against them . . . the hatred of the good people of the United States." Yet there's no evidence that anyone pointed a finger into the crowd and said, "That is sedition."

The *Aurora* reported the abuse Lyon had faced on his way home, noting ruefully, "Were a posse of people to meet President Adams on the public highway and insult him for his public opinions and in a manner that would disgrace *even an English mob*, we should never hear the end of it."[16] But greater challenges awaited Lyon when he finally reached Vermont. It was a treacherous time to be seeking reelection. In addition to the XYZ Affair, Lyon had his own personal public relations crisis to contend with, thanks to his feud with Roger Griswold. And beyond these political considerations, Lyon had good reason to fear for his own freedom. In the Sedition Act, the Federalists had a powerful new weapon to silence their foes by force.

A few weeks before leaving Philadelphia, Lyon had written a letter to the editor of a Vermont newspaper, excoriating the president. The letter, published in *Spooner's Vermont Journal*, was a response to an unsigned article that had attacked him. Lyon cited the president's "unbounded thirst for ridiculous pomp, foolish adulation, and selfish avarice."[17]

Now, in a series of stump speeches in towns and villages around his district, Lyon went on the offensive against the "aristocrats" in Vermont and in Philadelphia. In the charged political atmosphere of 1798, his speeches sometimes led to brawls between his supporters and detractors.[18] Lyon pressed on. As a standard feature of his speeches that summer, Lyon would read aloud a quote by Joel Barlow, a Connecticut poet and activist.[19] Like Thomas Paine, Barlow, a fiery rhetorician, had transformed from beloved bard of the revolution into a hated Jacobin because of his support for France. The letter from which Lyon quoted accused Adams of lifting arguments wholesale from the Irish conservative Edmund Burke, and of fomenting hostilities with France in order to justify an arms buildup. The letter suggested that Adams belonged in a "madhouse."[20]

As Lyon pressed on, Nathaniel Chipman and the Federalists bided their time, content to let him fit the noose securely around his own neck. In their minds, Lyon's article, and the quotes from Barlow, had given them the evidence they needed to put Lyon in his place once and for all.

Some journalists, too, found it prudent to beat a hasty retreat from Philadelphia in that fetid summer of 1798. In June, James T. Callender had officially become a U.S. citizen, thus avoiding by one month a potential deportation or imprisonment under the newly minted Alien Acts. But with Bache under indictment and Lyon fighting for his political life, Callender knew his name couldn't be far down on the list of targets for the Sedition Act. In addition to his fears of persecution at the hands of Federalists, Callender had been hurt when Republicans turned on him for defending William Cobbett in Cobbett's libel case. "I am entirely sick even of the Republicans," he wrote, "for some of them have used me so dishonestly . . . that I have the Strongest inclination, as well as the best reason, for wishing to Shift the Scene."[21]

Callender figured to hide out in Virginia. There were a number of reasons why he expected to find a more congenial home there than in Philadelphia. For one thing, Virginia was the land of Jefferson. The vice president had been impressed with Callender's writings. Recognizing the value of a forceful pen against political opponents such as Hamilton and Adams, Jefferson subscribed to Callender's books and pamphlets, and sent him periodic checks, usually for fifty dollars, to keep him going. Another reason for Virginia was that a sympathetic Republican senator, Stevens Thomson Mason (one of the six who had voted against the Sedition Act), invited Callender to stay at his plantation near Leesburg through the following winter.

Like Jefferson, Mason recognized Callender's skills. He gave the journalist use of his home and extensive library.[22] But however congenial Virginia promised to be, Callender could never outrun his troubles, which were so often self-inflicted. Within a few weeks of his arrival in Leesburg, Callender mortified his host by getting drunk and winding up in a local prison. The news quickly made its way back to Philadelphia, where John Fenno's *Gazette of the United States* reported the details: "On the second of August, a little dirty toper, with a shaved head and greasy jacket, nankeen pantaloons, and woolen stockings, was arrested at a whiskey distillery near Leesburgh, [*sic*] Virginia, under the vagrant act." The report called Callender "the notorious Scotch fugitive, the calumniator of Washington, Adams, law, order, government, God."[23] When Callender was released, the accommodating Mason let his guest stay on, but Callender's troubles in the Old Dominion were only starting.

# CHAPTER FOURTEEN

As the summer of 1798 deepened, Philadelphia was coming to resemble a ghost town. One English visitor noted, "[O]ut of fifty thousand inhabitants being the computation of the population of Philadelphia, not above ten thousand are said to have remained in the city."[1] At the direction of Secretary of State Timothy Pickering, the entire Department of State, from records to furniture, was transported to Trenton, New Jersey, to temporary offices in the New Jersey State House.[2]

Many Philadelphians who stayed behind were simply too poor to go anywhere else; they waited out the fever in densely packed neighborhoods where on some streets virtually no home was spared from disease or death. "The miseries of the poor are great," wrote Samuel Powel Griffitts, a Philadelphia physician who stayed throughout the summer.[3] Sixteen local volunteers appointed by the health board distributed money to the poor. From Quincy, President Adams sent an anonymous donation of $500 to help relieve the suffering.[4] Dr. Benjamin Rush, the famed physician, educator, and signer of the Declaration of Independence, slept outside the city but returned each day to treat patients. The 1798 epidemic was, he pronounced, "much more malignant" than the 1793 outbreak. At the city hospital, "I witness more suffering in one hour than I have been accustomed to see in common times in a year."[5]

Because of the prevalence of the disease in port cities, doctors had drawn a connection between yellow fever and ships arriving from the tropics. They believed the culprit was bad air belched from holds and clinging to the clothing of arriving passengers. The Academy of Medicine of Philadelphia cited a spoiled coffee shipment from Jamaica in July as one source of the city's "putrid exhalations of alleys and gutters, and docks."[6]

Bad air was a reasonable guess but it was, of course, wrong. In his diary of the summer, Dr. Griffitts came tantalizingly close to the true cause when he noted, "Musketoes torminting—mortality greatest amongst women, children & old people."[7] It would take another century for researchers to establish that yellow fever is spread by the *Aedes aegypti* mosquito, a native of Africa that migrated to the New World with the slave trade.[8] *Aedes aegypti* flourished in the warm, moist climate of the Caribbean and South America. By the late eighteenth century ships from the tropics landing in Philadelphia, New York, and other port cities unloaded infected mosquitoes along with cargo. The insects quickly multiplied in abundant pools of stagnant water on the streets and alleys.

The true villain in yellow fever isn't the mosquito at all, but an RNA virus approximately a thousandth the width of a human hair. With one bite, an infected female mosquito injects up to one hundred thousand virus particles into the skin of a human victim. The virus reproduces rapidly at the point of the bite and spreads to the lymph nodes and through the lymphatic system to the kidneys, liver, and other organs, and then into the bloodstream. Though the disease can't be coughed, sneezed, or excreted from one human to the next, an uninfected mosquito that bites an infected person when the virus is present in the person's bloodstream (known as the viremic phase) may subsequently transmit the virus to any other human on which it feeds—hence the rapid spread of yellow fever in crowded cities.[9]

It's easy to see why the disease caused such panic in Philadelphia in the summer of 1798. Yellow fever seemed to take perverse pleasure in taunting its victims, killing capriciously and by all appearances at random. Three to six days after a bite, victims developed a sudden fever and headache, often accompanied by chills, back pain, body aches, nausea, vomiting, and weakness. After that came a round of viral Russian roulette, during which the symptoms disappeared and the victim emerged into a wonderful, albeit depleted, post-fever euphoria. For many, that stage signaled the start of full recovery and lifelong immunity from recurrence. In other cases, after a few hours or perhaps a day of relief, the symptoms roared back with renewed vengeance.[10]

Victims unfortunate enough to enter this next and more serious phase had only a 50 percent chance of survival.[11] Dr. Griffitts described a husband and wife in the city who nursed their eight-year-old daughter through the first round of fever, experiencing the nervous joy of an apparent recovery as the girl smiled and asked for food, only to watch, heartbroken, as she relapsed and died a few hours later. She was the fourth and last of the couple's children. All had died that summer in precisely the same manner.[12]

Given the ravages of yellow fever, it's a testament to the durability of the human body that anyone survived. And while physicians such as Dr. Griffitts were courageous in the extreme, the treatments they used were at best (blister patches on the wrists) unhelpful and at worst (frequent bleedings, calomel and other purgatives) simply hastened dehydration and death.[13]

As the death toll mounted, health officer William Allen kept the city's health office open day and night, trying to keep up with the sick who needed conveying to the hospital, and the dead who needed burial. Soon, even physicians were fleeing the city. After watching a faithful servant die of the disease, Dr. Griffitts reached a moment of despair toward the end of August, noting in his diary: "*I feel indeed alone.*"[14]

One of the few prominent Philadelphians who remained behind by choice was Benjamin Franklin Bache. Facing trial in the fall, he would not give up the one powerful weapon in his arsenal: his press.

The *Aurora* tracked the progress of the disease, noting ruefully its disproportionate impact on the poor and helpless. In August, the newspaper published recommendations of the Philadelphia Academy of Medicine that ships and their cargoes be removed from city wharves, that families be relocated away from the docks, and that docks, dockyards, and city gutters be scrupulously cleaned.[15] But the recommendations were ignored. As shipping continued unabated, Bache wrote that wealthy shipowners had left town with their families, noting the irony that "the laboring poor should almost exclusively be the victims of the disease introduced by that commerce, which, in prosperous times, is a source of misery to them, by the inequality of wealth which it introduces."[16]

Through the summer, as Bache and his wife, Margaret, remained in their home above the *Aurora* office, the newspaper's primary focus was politics, cranking out belligerent, defiant articles condemning President Adams and the Federalist government. Staying behind, while courageous, was also reckless, not just for Bache but for his family. For Margaret, the summer of 1798 involved so many stresses that it's difficult to imagine which one she worried about first, or how she continued to function. It fell upon Margaret to hold her family of three young sons together, as the lone steadying influence through weeks when residents died all around them and her husband waged his mad crusade. Now, financial difficulties mounted as advertisers, afraid of angering the Federalist leadership, withdrew from the pages of the *Aurora*. Amid all of these pressures, Margaret was in the late stages of pregnancy with the couple's fourth child. This could not have been the life she imagined a decade earlier, when she met the sensitive, intellectual boy with the impressive lineage and bright future. But she never wavered in her loyalty to Bache.

On August 3, the *Aurora* charged that gangs of young men were roving the streets at night and harassing Republicans—certain evidence that "it is the intention of the federalists to introduce into this country the system of [terror]."[17] A few days later, Bache intimated that the Sedition Act was but the first step in a campaign intended to wipe out opposition through actual violence: "*Gagging*, though it be really an act of violence in itself, is more to be dreaded as being a prelude to greater and more atrocious villainy—after the victim is gagged appears the *stiletto* and *bow-string*."[18]

Though several Philadelphia newspapers had shut down for the summer to avoid the fever, one that stayed as stubbornly in print as the *Aurora* was the *Gazette of the United States*, published by John Fenno. Fenno's Federalist wrath and sharp pen matched Bache jab for jab. The feud between the two men escalated on the pages of their newspapers. Fenno responded to Bache's adultery article on Adams by noting the peccadilloes of the man Bache most admired: "One Bache, printer of the *Aurora*, not long since held forth in vehement terms against *adultery*. Is this the same villain . . . who is also the grandson of old *Ben Franklin*?" To which Bache responded: "The memory of Dr. Franklin must be odious to the adherents of England, as he was hated and envied by them when living."[19]

The feud culminated in early August when Bache published an item accusing Fenno of being in cahoots with a Federalist swindler named Joseph Thomas, who had fled the city to escape prosecution for forgery.[20]

Fenno's son, Jack Ward Fenno, appeared at the *Aurora* office to demand that Bache publish an apology. When Bache brushed him aside, claiming to be too busy with deadlines to speak, Jack approached him the next day on the street, fists flying. Bache responded by smacking young Fenno with a cane before onlookers separated the pair. In the next issue of the *Aurora*, Bache insinuated that Jack ("the little miss") had soiled himself out of fright. *Porcupine's Gazette* countered that Jack's fists had proven "that Bache's skull was even more penetrable than could have been supposed."[21]

On September 3, amid all the turmoil and strife, Margaret gave birth to a fourth son, Hartman Bache.[22] The joy that this event brought the family was short-lived. Bache was working on the next issue of the *Aurora* when he felt the first telltale symptoms, headache and fever. As Bache's symptoms progressed, a physician prescribed frequent baths for the weakened editor. Margaret, despite having so recently delivered, managed to drag herself from bed to fill the tub for her husband. The tub leaked and water sloshed onto the floor. Margaret kept it filled. Like other yellow fever victims, Bache must have experienced his remission, perhaps even feeling well enough to think about his next issue of the *Aurora*. But he had seen enough of the fever over the course of the summer to know he wasn't safe yet. Given his tortured, combative life, perhaps it was ordained that the fever would return. By September 7, he was composing his will, leaving everything he owned, including the *Aurora*, to Margaret. Beyond the tragedy of leaving a wife and four small children behind, Bache would never have his day in court—something he must have relished. He died on September 10.[23]

The same fever also took the life of Bache's nemesis John Fenno. Nevertheless, Federalists saw the disease as well-deserved punishment for wayward Republicans. Wrote one: "Bile is the basis of the yellow fever. Is it surprising that it killed Bache?"[24] Secretary of State Timothy Pickering noted with satisfaction that the disease had killed not just Bache but one of his employees, "an old man who furnished, as I am informed, much of the matter his mischievous paper contained." Pickering added, "I am happy to hear this."[25]

Even nine years later, President Adams could barely contain his satisfaction at Bache's death. Adams had grappled with Bache's famous grandfather when both were serving diplomatic missions in France during revolutionary days. Adams wrote that Bache "became of course one of the most malicious Libellers of me. But the Yellow Fever arrested him in his detestable Career and sent him to his grandfather from whom he inherited a dirty, envious, jealous, and revengefull Spight against me for no other cause under heaven than because I was too honest a Man to favour or connive at his selfish schemes of ambition and Avarice."[26]

Indeed, for a short time the fever, however ghastly, seemed to the Federalists to spread on a divine wind dedicated to ridding the country of the Republican pestilence. As the fever made its way through one port city after another, from Philadelphia to New York to New London to Boston, Charles Holt, the publisher of the *New London Bee*, temporarily closed his newspaper after one of his staff succumbed. The *Bee* was a rare Republican newspaper in Connecticut. On September 10 (the same day that Bache died in Philadelphia) the Federalist *Courant* in Hartford reprinted the *Bee*'s suspension notice with this comment: "It seems by the above paragraph, that the Yellow Fever does some good, among the immense mischief it causes. It can kill the Bee, at least for a little while. The probability is, that it never will rise again."[27]

But if Adams, Pickering, and other Federalists thought that the fever would bring an end to the unfavorable press or to the hated *Aurora*, they were mistaken. Margaret, still mourning and ill herself from stress and grief and childbirth, served notice to Federalists about what they could expect from the *Aurora* and from its new publisher. At 1 A.M. on September 11, just hours after Bache's death, Margaret published a handbill that read:

> The friends of civil liberty and patrons of the *Aurora*, are informed, that the editor, BENJAMIN FRANKLIN BACHE, has fallen a victim to the plague that ravages this devoted city. In ordinary times, the loss of such a man would be a source of public sorrow—in these times, men who see, and think, and feel for their country and their posterity, can alone appreciate the loss—the loss of a man inflexible in virtue, unappalled by power or persecution—and who, in dying, knew no anxieties but what were excited by his apprehensions for his country—and for his young family.

And Margaret vowed:

> This calamity necessarily suspends the Aurora—*but for a few days* only—when such arrangements shall have been made as are necessary to ensure its wonted character of intelligence and energy—it will *re-appear under the direction of* HIS WIDOW.[28]

# CHAPTER FIFTEEN

Now that Mother Nature had laid Bache in the grave, Federalists concentrated on vanquishing their second great foe, Matthew Lyon, in Vermont's congressional race. In the eastern part of the state, Federalist Lewis R. Morris was a lock to win his congressional race and return to Philadelphia. But dislodging Matthew Lyon in the west was proving to be more of a challenge than Federalists had hoped. In a summer of tenacious campaigning, Lyon was drawing crowds, gaining momentum. With September's election rapidly approaching, and with no candidate strong enough to beat him, they settled instead on a divide and conquer strategy.

Vermont law required that the winning candidate receive a majority of the votes rather than simply more than his opponents. If nobody took more than half the total, the top three contenders would face one another in a runoff election. Since there was as yet no formal recognition of political parties, and hence no primary system, ballots were open to multiple candidates, whether they called themselves Republicans or Federalists or anything else. In 1798, the Western District of Vermont included no fewer than ten candidates vying for Lyon's seat, among them Nathaniel Chipman's thirty-two-year-old brother, Daniel, an attorney.[1]

When the polls opened in September, the Federalist tactic worked by the barest of margins. Out of 6,985 ballots cast, Lyon drew 3,482 votes, or 49.8 percent of the total. He finished almost two thousand votes ahead of his nearest rival, Samuel Williams, but eight thin votes shy of a majority.[2] The runoff was scheduled for December, leaving Federalists more than enough time to implement part two of their plan, involving their newest and as-yet-untested weapon, the Sedition Act. Forcing Lyon to fight for his freedom in a criminal case would clearly disrupt his campaign; there would be no time for fiery stump speeches inciting the rabble. Better still, a guilty verdict—whatever the penalty—would brand Lyon a convicted criminal, which might convince even the wild voters of western Vermont to find another representative.

On October 1, Lyon launched a magazine called the *Scourge of Aristocracy, and Repository of Important Political Truths.* Edited by his eldest son, James, the publication promised "to strengthen the cause of Republicanism and truth, against aristocracy and falsehood."[3]

Beyond the usual attacks on "villainous" "tory" "prostitutes" of the Federalist press, *Scourge* contained some of Lyon's most careful thinking on government and liberty, laid out in the fashion of a man eager to have his say while he still could. In a sort of backwoods Socratic dialogue with an unnamed neighbor, Lyon answered some of the Federalists' most familiar charges against him, starting with the assertion that he and other Republicans were antigovernment for opposing the Federalist way of doing things. "I do not understand what people can mean by opposition to Government, applied to the Representatives of the people, in that capacity," Lyon wrote. Representatives are elected to vote according to their own conscience, and to advance the beliefs of their constituents. While a representative may disagree with the president on matters of policy, how can it be said that such a figure duly elected to serve in the government is antigovernment? Lyon wondered. While not seeking fights with the president, he explained, "I am bound by oath, as well as by every consideration of duty, to oppose" wrongheaded policies.[4]

According to *Scourge*, President Adams deserved full blame for the Sedition Act, and the publication didn't mince words about what

Adams's support for the bill represented, in its conspiracy of executive, legislative, and judicial power to silence critics: "Its provisions are a refinement upon Despotism, and present an image of the most fearful Tyranny."[5]

These words might well have formed the basis of a sedition charge against Lyon. But his enemies already had what they needed. On October 5, Lyon learned that a grand jury had been called at Rutland, about fifteen miles from his home. Lyon later remembered the grand jury as being "composed of men who had been accustomed to speak ill of me." When a friend urged him to flee, "My answer to all this was, it could not be honourable to run away—I felt conscious that I had done no wrong, and my enemies should never have it to say, that I ran away from them."[6]

On October 6, a deputy marshal appeared at Lyon's home in Fair Haven with an arrest warrant in hand. Lyon promised to appear the next day at the federal court in Rutland. On October 7 he was formally indicted, thus becoming the first defendant in a Sedition Act case. The indictment contained three counts, each supporting the government's contention that the congressman intended to "bring the President and government of the United States into contempt."[7]

The first pertained to the letter Lyon had written to *Spooner's Vermont Journal* in June. Beyond the question of whether the Sedition Act itself was just or unjust, this first charge presented what should have been a serious problem for the prosecution. Lyon had written and postmarked his letter in June, weeks before Adams signed the Sedition Act into law. In other words, Lyon was being charged for violating a law that did not exist when he violated it.

The other two parts of the indictment pertained to the Barlow letter that Lyon had been quoting publicly all summer long. The offending sections stated that Adams had pilfered ideas from Edmund Burke, and that the president belonged in a madhouse. Though Lyon had not written the passages himself, the Sedition Act had made it a crime to "assist" in spreading seditious words.

Lyon was permitted to post bail pending his appearance at trial the following Monday. In a state as sparsely populated as Vermont, it would probably have been impossible to conduct a high-profile trial free from conflicts arising from personal or professional friendships and animosities. Yet the court made no effort to apply even a veneer of impartiality to Lyon's trial.

The presiding judge was to be U.S. Supreme Court associate justice William Paterson, a former senator from New Jersey, a reliable Federalist, and a friend and sometime dining companion of President Adams. Today the Supreme Court's role as the court of last appeals is firmly established. Justices hear only those cases that have passed up through various layers of the federal judicial system, and an appointment as associate justice of the Supreme Court is the signature and rarest honor of a distinguished legal career.

But in the 1790s, an appointment to the high court was generally considered "neither a great honor, nor a post of great influence, nor a particularly good living."[8] Compared with the Constitution's lengthy Articles I and II detailing the roles of Congress and the president, Article III, calling for the formation of the Supreme Court, is relatively brief and mentions nothing about determining the constitutionality or unconstitutionality of laws. Not until 1803 and *Marbury v. Madison*—a complex dispute over political appointments—would Chief Justice John Marshall firmly establish the court's essential role of judicial review, by declaring portions of a federal law passed several years earlier to be unconstitutional.

In the late eighteenth century, the Supreme Court met only twice a year in Philadelphia, and heard few cases as a body. Instead, the chief justice and five associates (expanded to nine justices in the late nineteenth century) were required to ride the circuit twice a year, hearing cases in federal courts convened around the country. Long-distance carriage travel was arduous and frequently dangerous. Associate Justice Samuel Chase, who would figure notoriously in pursuing Sedition Act trials, nearly drowned one winter day when trying to cross the frozen

Patapsco River in Maryland on his way to a case. The ice cracked beneath his feet and only quick work by his son saved his life.[9] When John Jay, the first chief justice, threatened to resign over the travel requirement, circuit riding was reduced from twice each year to once—but still the difficulties of travel encouraged some candidates to decline to serve.[10, 11]

In each court case involving a Supreme Court justice, a federal circuit court judge from that state also presided. In the Lyon case, U.S. district judge Samuel Hitchcock presided with Paterson. Hitchcock had personal reasons to settle a score: Lyon had beat Hitchcock in the congressional election of 1796. Meanwhile, the federal district attorney prosecuting the case, Charles Marsh, was a close friend of Lyon's principal enemy, Nathaniel Chipman. John Allen, the Connecticut congressman who had vocally supported both the Sedition Act and Lyon's ouster from Congress following the Griswold affair, made the long trek to Vermont just for the opportunity to witness the trial.

Both sides challenged some jurors. Marsh challenged and dismissed one who had been overheard saying he didn't think Lyon would or should be convicted. Lyon succeeded in removing a juror who had written articles critical of him, yet he would insist several times throughout the proceedings that the jury had been hand selected and custom packed to produce a guilty verdict. Judge Paterson waved off Lyon's objections, saying the jurors had been called from a pool selected long before anyone knew on what case they would serve.

As the case sped toward trial, Lyon did his best to assemble a defense. Asked by Paterson if he was ready, Lyon replied that he was ready to pronounce himself not guilty. But he didn't trust any of the attorneys in Rutland, and needed time to send for two lawyers from Bennington. Unfortunately, neither proved to be available. Lyon next turned to Israel Smith, a Republican politician and judge.

Smith and Lyon had a long, competitive history together. Smith had defeated Lyon in his first two attempts at the congressional seat, in 1792 and 1794, and Lyon had defeated Smith in 1796. Most recently, Smith, who would later go on to become governor of Vermont, had been one of the ten candidates on the ballot in the September voting, but had garnered just 3.4 percent of the vote. Still, Smith and Lyon shared a bond since they were both Republicans, and Lyon trusted him. Because he had had no time to prepare a case, Smith agreed only to sit next to Lyon at the trial and offer advice insofar as he could.[12]

Paterson offered to postpone the trial until the next court session in May. But here the geographical imperative of Vermont came into play. The court customarily traveled from town to town, and the next session would be held over the mountain, in Windsor, far to the east and staunchly Federalist. Lyon recalled, "This I could not wish for." Faced with a number of bad choices, Lyon chose a speedy trial acting as his own counsel.[13]

Lyon's first act was to move to dismiss the case on the grounds that the Sedition Act was unconstitutional. Paterson immediately rejected his motion and, moreover, specifically instructed the jury that it could not consider the constitutionality of the law. When Lyon attempted during the course of his brief trial to raise the constitutionality question, Paterson told the jury directly: "You have nothing whatever to do with the constitutionality or unconstitutionality of the sedition law. Congress has said that the author and publisher of seditious libels is to be punished; and until this law is declared null and void by a tribunal competent for the purpose, its validity cannot be disputed."[14]

Thus, the central argument against the Sedition Act, that it had no business existing in a country whose citizens were protected by the First Amendment, was effectively off the table. This ruling, which would emerge as a standard feature of the sedition trials, set a perfect trap for the defendant. Among the few remaining issues for the jury to consider was whether the defendant had, indeed, written or published the offending item or items. Lyon openly conceded he had written the anti-Adams letter and quoted from Joel Barlow. How could he claim otherwise?

The other two factors given to Lyon's jury to consider, while seeming to offer a possible defense, were every bit as constraining. The first concerned whether, in so publishing, the defendant had the intention (in the words of Judge Paterson) of "making odious or contemptible the President and government, and bringing them both into disrepute. If you find such is the case, the offence is made out, and you must render a verdict of guilty." Yet what is the purpose of political attack if not to bring the opposition "into disrepute"? By that standard virtually any writer or public speaker engaged in vigorous debate might be guilty of sedition. Thus free speech inevitably transforms from an unalienable right to a privilege granted by the powerful for approved opinions.

Prosecutor Marsh summoned witnesses who reported having read Lyon's printed materials and heard him in person quoting from Barlow's letter on such and such occasion, in a manner that "had frequently made use of language highly disrespectful to the administration."[15] Lyon halfheartedly countered that on at least one occasion he had attempted to prevent publication of an offending document. But in the end there was no disputing that Lyon had written and said critical things about the president. Wasn't that the point of dissent? Marsh also claimed that Lyon had created a threat to public safety and peace with his fiery campaign speeches. He called two Federalist witnesses who said they had attended a speech in Middletown, where Lyon's reading of the Barlow letter caused a "tumult," one said. On cross-examination by Lyon, both witnesses had to concede that if they had not appeared at the rally, looking for an argument, no tumult would have occurred.[16]

In the end, the prosecutor was no more than a bit actor in the drama, his part rendered insignificant because it was so easy to play. As would become a pattern in Sedition Act cases to follow, the prosecutor had merely to prove that the defendant had written or said something that everybody already knew he had written or said. When defending the Sedition Act for its supposed mildness and leniency, Federalists made much of the fact that writers or speakers could only be convicted for spreading falsehoods. Yet according to judges who tried the cases, the burden of proof rested not on the prosecutor, but on the defendant. This represented a vastly more onerous and vexing burden than a defendant today would face on charges of libel or slander. In a modern defamation case, the burden is on the plaintiff to prove the statement or statements false. Moreover, the law today offers special latitude to defendants when the plaintiff is a public figure, such as a politician. By contrast, Matthew Lyon, for criticizing the president, found himself in the position of proving to the court that his opinions were "true."

When Marsh rested, Lyon laid his defense on three arguments. First, in spite of Judge Paterson's instructions, Lyon persisted in calling the act unconstitutional. Second, he repeated the argument put forth in his recent article in *Scourge of Aristocracy*—that his statements were made in the spirit of vigorous debate rather than *malice*—another key word contained in the act. Third, he claimed that his opinions were true. To make his case, he called his one and only witness: the presiding judge, William Paterson. Since Paterson knew Adams personally, Lyon said he needed the justice's testimony to prove that Adams was a pompous man.

Paterson reluctantly agreed to testify.

Lyon asked whether, during his dinners with Adams, the president "displayed ridiculous pomp and parade?"

Paterson responded that he had seen only "plainness and simplicity."[17]

Lyon asked the judge whether he had seen more pomp on display when dining with Adams, or when dining with Rutland residents at the tavern where he was currently staying. Paterson declined to answer. After a perfunctory summation by Marsh, Lyon explained at length to the jury why he believed the Sedition Act to be unconstitutional, hoping that they would look beyond Paterson's warning to ignore the question.[18]

But Paterson had the last word in his instructions to the jury before it retired. He sternly reminded members that no justice system can survive with juries questioning the constitutionality of every law in every case. "The only question you are to determine is that which the record submits to you. Did Mr. Lyon publish the writing given in the indictment? Did he do so seditiously?" Paterson then helpfully answered the first question himself: "The evidence is undisputed, and in fact, he himself concedes the fact of publication as to a large portion of libellous matter." The only thing left for the jury was to consider whether Lyon's words were issued with the intention of "making odious or contemptible the President and government, and bringing them both into disrepute." If so, "you must render a verdict of guilty."[19]

Eleven of the twelve jurors were prepared to find Lyon guilty immediately. A twelfth held out for a while but ultimately relented. "It was impossible to acquit him," he later reported.[20] The entire trial had occupied a single long day. By 8 P.M., after less than an hour of deliberation, the jury returned its unanimous verdict of guilty.

Given that he believed from the start that the jury was packed with handpicked Federalists, Lyon could not have been surprised by the verdict. But as a sitting U.S. congressman, he expected at most to be dealt some small fine and warned against further writings. The reality broke over him the next morning when Judge Paterson made clear from his opening words that he intended to make an example of Lyon. A member of Congress, of all people, "must be well acquainted with the mischiefs which flow from an unlicensed abuse of government," Paterson said. He went on to say, "Your position, so far from making the case one which might slip with a nominal fine through the hands of the court, would make impunity conspicuous should such a fine alone be imposed." With that, Paterson slapped Lyon with a fine of $1,000 and four months in jail.[21] Even for a man of means, $1,000 was serious money in 1798, when the median value of a house in U.S. cities was just $614.[22] Lyon had explained to Paterson prior to sentencing that he had suffered business reversals of late that would make it difficult to pay a substantial fine. Nor was four months in jail the slap on the wrist it might appear to modern eyes. At a time when the average life span for an American was fewer than forty years and death was an ever-present factor in life, four months in a dank jail cell was a prospect to be met with foreboding.[23] Jails were notoriously dirty and cold, and between atrocious food and the spread of disease in cramped quarters, even a short stretch behind bars could very well amount to a death sentence. Lyon could hardly believe his ears. "No one," he wrote later, "expected imprisonment."[24]

But the worst was yet to come. No sooner had Lyon been sentenced than he found himself in the hands of one Jabez Fitch, a district marshal and his avowed enemy.[25] A small-minded sadist, Fitch had long harbored bad feelings toward Lyon, based on some business dealings from years earlier in which Fitch felt he had come up short. Whatever transpired in those dealings, the feeling was mutual. "I have ever since most heartily despised him," Lyon wrote: "this he has no doubt seen and felt." From the moment the sentence was handed down, Fitch treated Lyon like a violent criminal. When Lyon asked if he could stop by his lodgings in Rutland to retrieve some of his papers before heading to jail, Fitch refused.[26]

Instead of jailing Lyon near his home in Rutland, Fitch— granted full jurisdiction—chose to transport the convict forty-four miles north to the town of Vergennes. Vergennes was Fitch's hometown and a rare Federalist stronghold in western Vermont. Although Lyon promised no resistance, Fitch enlisted two armed deputies to accompany them. Throughout the journey, Lyon rode in front with the deputies just behind, guns at the ready, as if guarding a murderer.

Instead of taking the most direct route from Rutland to Vergennes, Fitch took his time, parading his prisoner like a circus animal in every village. Along the way, Lyon asked for and was refused a pen and paper. Vergennes was, at the time, the only official "city" in Vermont, though that was a big word for a hamlet comprising some sixty businesses and homes. The *Vergennes Gazette* assured its readers that despite Lyon's claims to the contrary, justice had been served, saying, "there seemed to be an unanimous approbation of the Court, the Attorney, and the Jury."[27]

Fitch led the prisoner to a cell at the corner of Main and Green Streets. Although the prison had empty cells, Fitch placed Lyon in a common cell where, depending on the prisoner haul for the day, he shared quarters with "horse-thieves, money-makers, runaway negroes, or any kind of felons," as he wrote to a friend. "There is a half-moon hole through the door, sufficient to receive a plate through, and for my friends to look through and speak to me." The cell was just sixteen feet long and twelve feet wide, Lyon reported, with "a necessary in one corner, which affords a stench about equal to the Philadelphia docks in the month of August." Moreover, there was no heat. He stayed warm by wearing a coat and marching back and forth. Eventually, Lyon's friends took up a collection to buy him a stove.[28]

Federalists in the Vermont General Assembly rejoiced at Lyon's imprisonment. On October 20 they sent a formal address to President Adams, affirming the right of "the honest, the pious, and the peaceable, to protect themselves from the wickedness of the dishonest, the impious, and the unruly."[29]

The Federalist press hailed the assembly's address as proof that Lyon was finished, once and for all. Adams, for his part, couldn't resist a sort of symbolic victory dance, not to mention self-flattery, citing the leniency of a law that contained seditious wickedness without spilling blood.[30] The law at last gave righteous, upstanding leaders the means by which to silence those who wanted to destroy the country from within, and a compliant legal system was committed to doing its part.

After a few days in prison, Lyon again pressed Fitch for pen and paper. Fitch replied that he could have the materials, but that he would personally review any writings that left the prison. Should Lyon violate this rule, Fitch assured him, he would be clapped in irons to physically prevent him from writing. Fitch added a threat to send Lyon, should he misbehave, to a still more remote prison in Woodstock.

One of Lyon's earliest letters from prison was to Stevens Thomson Mason, the thirty-eight-year-old Republican senator from Loudoun County, Virginia. The scion of an old Virginia plantation family, Mason had been a brigadier general in the Virginia militia and an aide to General Washington at the decisive Siege of Yorktown during the Revolutionary War.[31] By breeding, wealth, and circumstance he was far more aristocratic than the northeastern "aristocrats" such as Nathaniel Chipman and John Adams whom Lyon so heartily despised. But then, as now, political alliances made strange bedfellows, and the upper-crust Mason and roughneck Irish immigrant had become friends in Philadelphia. Lyon's letter laid out in exhaustive detail the trial and the prison conditions.

"My friends, and the friends of Liberty, sensibly feel the injustice and indignity done to me and themselves," Lyon noted defiantly, adding, "They will be neither idle nor bashful in the next election."[32] But then his thoughts turned melancholy. Weary, cold, and for one of the few times in his life perhaps a little afraid, Lyon thought of his old comrade in spirit, Benjamin Franklin Bache. "I mourn with you the death of our good friend Bache," he wrote. "He was too good a man to be tortured with the Sedition law—God saw in that light, and took him to himself."[33]

# CHAPTER SIXTEEN

One October morning the town of Dedham, Massachusetts, awoke to a mystery. A large wooden pole, erected during the night, loomed over the Hartford Road, a main highway running through Dedham's Second District. A sign atop the pole contained a hand-painted message:

No Stamp act; no sedition; no alien bill; no land tax. Downfall to the tyrants of America; peace and retirement to the President; long live the vice President and the minority.[1]

During revolutionary days such displays had sprouted like instant trees on town squares and roadsides from Concord, Massachusetts, to Savannah, Georgia. Liberty poles, they were called. Each time British authorities chopped one down, two seemed to spring up in its place. Liberty poles helped galvanize revolutionary spirit and served as an important communication device. A red flag hoisted atop a liberty pole might signal a secret meeting that night.[2] In 1780, when twenty-three-year-old Lieutenant Colonel Alexander Hamilton of the American revolutionary forces, already forming his conception of a powerful federal government, wrote a long letter outlining the defects of the Continental Congress, he datelined the letter with the name of General Washington's temporary headquarters: Liberty Pole, New Jersey.[3]

But now that liberty poles were being aimed at the U.S. government rather than the British, Federalist enthusiasm for this form of free speech had cooled. The *Columbian Centinel* of Boston suggested that those who put up liberty poles to protest government policies "were certainly born to be slaves or to be hanged."[4] Another Boston newspaper, *Massachusetts Mercury*, called liberty poles "a rallying point for the enemies of a Free Government."[5] When the Dedham pole appeared, nobody was more incensed than the town's most famous son, Fisher Ames.

While Massachusetts as a whole was solidly Federalist, Dedham was divided and contentious. Within a day or two of the pole's appearance, Ames's friend, circuit court judge John Lowell, dispatched a federal marshal from Boston, Sam Bradford, to destroy it. But by the time Bradford arrived at the scene, locals had already taken matters into their own hands, dismantling the pole and removing the handwritten sign as evidence.[6] Ames had fretted that Federalists would be too gentle, too slow to embrace the priceless opportunity the Sedition Act offered to any leader with the moral strength to push the country back from the edge of populist chaos. Cast in the mold of Alexander Hamilton, he fundamentally doubted the competence of average Americans to run a country. He believed in a meritocracy, if not aristocracy, to keep the republic on its course. And he lived his entire life in fear of populist bogeymen lurking in every dark corner of the republic, including, now, his own hometown. He wrote to a friend, "There is at least the appearance of tardiness and apathy on the part of government in avenging this insult on law."[7] Somebody had to pay for this affront.

The first arrested was Benjamin Fairbanks, a prosperous local farmer who was one of about forty people said to have helped erect the pole. An impressionable, rather excitable man descended from one of Dedham's original founding families, Fairbanks was allowed to post bond. His case was bound over to the next circuit court, scheduled for June in Boston.[8]

But Fairbanks was never the main target of the investigation. Inevitably, the Federalists focused their blame on that ever-reliable villain, the outside agitator. A Boston newspaper, *Russell's Gazette*, was certain that the ringleader was "a vagabond *Irishman*, or *Scotchman* . . . who has sturred up a few ignorant people to erect a liberty pole . . ."[9] In the end the primary suspect was indeed an outsider, though neither Scotch nor Irish. He was David Brown, a native of Bethlehem, Connecticut. Brown had lately been seen around town. Described in newspaper accounts as being somewhere between forty and fifty years old and a veteran of the Revolutionary War, Brown was an inveterate traveler and homespun political activist.[10]

Prior to arriving in Dedham in October 1798, he had spent two years traveling from one Massachusetts community to the next, eighty in all, by his own estimate. He preached politics to anyone who would listen, drumming up subscribers for a series of crudely written pamphlets. That fall, Brown had stopped at the home of James Foard, in the town of Milton, hoping to convince Foard to edit some of his manuscripts for publication. Foard declined, and later offered a succinct assessment of Brown's writing and spelling skills: "bad."[11]

A sample of Brown's writing confirms the diagnosis. It is a rambling, disjointed attack on government covering everything from the Jay Treaty to government land policies:

> The land tax, stamp act, and treason-law, and the exorbitant taxes Britain were about to fetch on us without representation, are now brought on us by representatives of speculators, and not of the people; which it is to be feared that the majority of the house of Congress are at this day, and have been for a number of years; who have represented the new lands into their hands, the soldier's pay, and are determined to represent the stock and farms of the yeomanry, to bring the country into lord's tenents and boroughs. The first stratagem

which the fiends of darkness made use of, was to make a new treaty with Britain, to overturn the republican government of America.[12]

Little is known about David Brown's personal life, or what real or perceived wrongs he suffered that led him to so thoroughly mistrust his new government. Perhaps, after the privations of the revolution and the subsequent promise of the newly free United States, he found his pursuit of happiness led only to reversals and frustrations. Many revolutionary soldiers had been paid in war bonds that they subsequently sold to speculators for pennies on the dollar. Perhaps Brown was one of those soldiers who watched bitterly as the federal government stabilized and speculators made a killing by cashing those bonds in at par value. Or perhaps as a farmer he had been stung by land taxes that had led to Shays's Rebellion several years earlier. Maybe he was just a crank. Whatever the reason, Brown harbored a deep and abiding mistrust of government, particularly of John Adams and Fisher Ames.

Brown made up for his lack of rhetorical elegance with a passion and zeal that others found inspiring. Stopping one day at a store in the town of Medfield, Massachusetts, Brown attracted a small crowd with his message that the government's primary occupation was "to plunder and steal the business of the people, [and] to secrete their property by fraud." He quoted a passage from Joel Barlow, the same thinker whose words had led to the arrest of Matthew Lyon. Horatio Townsend, a Medfield resident, noted that Brown's oratory seemed "to make impressions on several of the bystanders."[13]

Brown carried his message to Dedham in October, drawing enough adherents to help him put up the liberty pole. He paid a local sign painter named Amariah Chapin to paint the message on a board. A witness, Luther Ellis, later testified that Brown held a ladder while another man (presumably Benjamin Fairbanks) affixed the board to the top of the pole.[14]

By the time Fairbanks was arrested, Brown had moved on from Dedham. With the pole torn down and the ringleader departed to places unknown, one might have assumed the authorities would stand down. Surely, the message affixed to the top of the pole was mild by any standards of insult and invective. Had they simply let the matter drop, Dedham officials probably would never have seen or heard from David Brown again. In some seventy-nine other towns he had simply spread his message and departed, leaving the town and its citizens none the worse for wear. But he stepped into this, his eightieth town, like a blind man into a minefield.

Fisher Ames saw Brown not as a harmless malcontent but as the embodiment of what he presumed to be hordes of riotous, ignorant insurgents ready to tear the republic apart. "One David Brown, a vagabond ragged fellow, has lurked about in Dedham, telling everybody the sins and enormities of the government," Ames reported in a letter to a friend. In another he wrote to a friend that Republicans "abound in Dedham, though the liberty-pole is down." He added, "The devil of sedition is immortal, and we, the saints, have an endless struggle to maintain with him."[15]

Adding to the intrigue over the liberty pole (and, surely, to Fisher's anger) was the high probability that his brother, Nathaniel, had taken an active role in seeing the pole erected. Nathaniel, town physician and legendary curmudgeon, was as ardent a Republican as his brother was a Federalist. Some historians have suggested that Nathaniel, with a gift for writing superior to Brown's, actually penned the words on the sign atop the pole.

In a life as private as his brother's was public, Nathaniel avoided giving speeches and seldom wrote for publication. Instead, he poured his thoughts, emotions, and observations into the cramped pages of a diary that he maintained for more than sixty-four of his nearly eighty-two years. His unedited take on life in the late eighteenth and early nineteenth centuries offers an extraordinary window on the period, its weather, medicine, commerce, and politics. He avidly followed

Matthew Lyon's case, noting of the Sedition Act, "The traitors that passed it ought to be hung up by their tongues."[16]

For anyone aware of the tortured relationship between the Ames brothers, there's no mistaking the fraternal hostility embedded in those words. Nathaniel knew perfectly well that except for his forced retirement, Fisher Ames would not just have been one of those Federalist "traitors" passing the Sedition Act; he would have led the charge.

Nathaniel was the oldest and Fisher the youngest of five children raised by a widowed mother. Of this oddly matched set of bookends, Fisher was the more precociously brilliant. Born in 1758, he began studying Latin at age six, entered Harvard at twelve, and graduated in 1774 at sixteen. He taught school for several years while studying law, but seemed predestined for politics. He was gregarious and socially and politically ambitious. He loved the give-and-take of policy making and longed to be at the center of important affairs, among people who mattered. He was good at making social and political connections.

As first son, Nathaniel, born in 1742, had inherited both the name and profession of his doctor father. Nathaniel Ames Sr. had founded *Ames' Almanack* in 1726, predating Benjamin Franklin's *Poor Richard's Almanack* by seven years. Between the brothers there was always friction. For a while after passing the bar exam in 1781, Fisher operated a law office out of a room on the first floor of Nathaniel's home, but this was a difficult arrangement at best and did not last.[17] The relationship degenerated into outright hostility in 1787, regarding a dispute over the property left by their father. Fisher, who was ambitious, organized, and business-like, hoped to buy up most of the property. But first he had to get past his unambitious, disorganized, and unbusiness-like brother who, as oldest sibling, was trustee. When Nathaniel failed to reply to Fisher's letters of intent, Fisher wrote an arch, stiff letter to "Doctor Ames," threatening a lawsuit. When Nathaniel refused to respond, Fisher wrote a still more threatening letter. Nathaniel at last replied but promised nothing and pointed out that his "embers of Affection" for his brother were burning low. Fisher made good on his threat, with a summons to appear at the probate office in Boston. By the time the case wound down at the end of May, with Fisher getting his way, the relationship had been thoroughly soured.[18]

The brothers' disdain for each other's politics hardened along with their personal battles. As early as 1786 and 1787, they took opposite views of Shays's Rebellion, when farmers in western Massachusetts, led by former Revolutionary War captain Daniel Shays, rebelled against land taxes, shut down courts, and rioted against state government. In his diary, Nathaniel sided with the rebels, calling taxes that ran as high as 50 percent as "extortion and usury." When state militia suppressed the rebellion by force, Nathaniel bitterly accused authorities of "staining their hands with human blood needlessly."[19] Fisher Ames heartily approved the show of force, noting, "No sooner is the standard of rebellion displayed, than men of desperate principles and fortunes resort to it; the pillars of government are shaken; the edifice totters from its centre, the foot of a child may overthrow it; the hands of giants cannot rebuild it."[20]

Elected to the Massachusetts House of Representatives at age thirty, Fisher was part of the Massachusetts convention called in 1788 to ratify the Constitution. A year later he headed to Philadelphia as a member of the First Congress. During four terms, despite chronic ill health, he became a pillar of the Federalist party, culminating in his stirring speech to save the Jay Treaty for President Washington.

If Nathaniel felt any pride in his brother's pivotal role in such a major event, such did not find its way into his diary. Months earlier, when Washington first approved the treaty, Nathaniel had recorded his dismay: "Better his hand had been cut off when his Glory was at its height before he blasted all his Laurels!"[21] Following House approval, he called the treaty "the highest insult on the feelings of Americans of anything that has happened this long time."[22]

Nathaniel admired Jefferson and hated Adams. "The first party strive for John Adams, who favors the Britons our enemies," he wrote; "the second party strive for Thomas Jefferson, who is a friend to the French, who are friends to the Human Race, and helped us out of the paws of the British Government."[23] He subscribed to Republican newspapers and corresponded personally with editors such as Charles Holt of the *New London Bee*, a rare Republican newspaper in Federalist Connecticut.

Nathaniel was an acerbic, hard-bitten Yankee who could spare only this cryptic reference to describe his own wedding in 1775: "Connub'o junctus" ("joined in marriage").[24] He grumbled about his extended family, in particular an ungrateful niece, Betsy Shuttleworth, who lived with him and his wife, Meletiah, for years and seems to have given them no end of trouble. He betrayed a sense of alienation from all of his relatives—"My family combine against me worse & worse, must dismiss some as every day the contempt increases"— and despite a long and apparently faithful marriage, was not above observing: "Of all the foolish things you ever do let marriage be the last, is one of my favorite sayings."[25]

Despite these rough edges (or perhaps because of them), Nathaniel comes off as an oddly endearing character. He rarely traveled far from home, yet he was endlessly intrigued by new ideas. His diary is ornamented with passages in Latin and French, and reflects careful perusal of national and international events. At the same time, it offers a fascinating glimpse of small-town New England life from the mid-eighteenth through early nineteenth centuries, during which time the doctor presided over innumerable local births and deaths and recorded weather patterns, sleighing and road conditions, the cost of labor for work done to his house, local gossip, floods in his meadows, the price of nails, and any number of other details.

His brother, by contrast, traveled widely and lived and moved among the most celebrated figures of his time. Yet for all of his worldly experiences he seems to have suffered an acute provincialism of the spirit. Fisher was so convinced of his rectitude that he never so much as peeked over the hedge at the other side of life, or an opposing opinion, except to frown. He was a hardworking, highly disciplined teetotaler who counted among his favorite sayings "He who holds parley with vice and dishonor is sure to become their slave and victim." Fisher seems to have skipped from prodigal son to productive, sober adult without sowing so much as a single wild oat. "Happily, he did not need the smart of guilt to make him virtuous, nor the regret of folly to make him wise," his friends recalled in a memoir published several years after his death.[26]

His friends were overgenerous. The absence of personal guilt and folly didn't necessarily make Fisher Ames strong and wise; beneath his worldly, self-assured exterior he was brittle and intransigent. Fisher seems to have lived with the express purpose of painting himself into an oil portrait over the fireplace, that proverbial long-dead ancestor staring with disapproval upon the living. As Dedham historian Robert Brand Hanson, editor of the Nathaniel Ames diary, observes, "Both the brothers were brilliant, but Nathaniel somehow seems more human."[27]

Fisher Ames had returned to Dedham in 1797, still shy of forty, an exalted figure, famous and respected enough to have sat for portraits by not one but two of the era's most famous portrait painters, Gilbert Stuart and John Trumbull. He moved into a fine new home built two years earlier on family property, next door to his brother, and resumed his law practice. "His hospitable mansion was the resort of friends at home and abroad, who gathered around him to enjoy the surpassing beauty and richness of his conversation," a nineteenth-century Dedham historian gushed.[28]

The brothers carefully avoided direct confrontation with each other, venting instead against alternative targets. The *Dedham Minerva*, a newspaper rare in its day for striving for nonpartisan reporting on local and national events, found itself in the crosshairs of the Ames's fraternal fractiousness. Although the editor, Herman

Mann, had pledged to publish an equal number of articles sympathetic to Republicans and Federalists, Nathaniel believed the paper to be "wholly dictated by F.A. [Fisher Ames] to smother political enquiry & make public Servants, Lords." In February 1798, Nathaniel had angrily canceled his subscription, advising Mann that he should "go to England to print."[29] This cold relationship was probably the only sensible approach to avoid a more public and unseemly feud. But it created an odd situation—as though Fisher and Nathaniel, with their fiery and divergent views, were fighting on separate planes rather than in the same town.

As the search for David Brown expanded around Massachusetts, Fisher's agitation grew. In December he wrote to his friend Christopher Gore, an American diplomat serving in England, betraying how deeply Brown had gotten under his skin. He promised revenge "not to preserve my reputation, but to disarm his [Brown's] wickedness." The only way to deal with such characters, Ames added, was "*in terrorem*."[30]

# CHAPTER SEVENTEEN

The *Philadelphia Aurora*, still recovering from the death of its founder, Benjamin Franklin Bache, decried the irony that planting a liberty pole—that precious symbol of righteous rebellion against tyranny—could be considered a crime. "Who would have believed it, had it been foretold, that the People of America, after having fought seven long years to obtain their Independence, would, at this early day, have been seized and dragged into confinement by their own government . . ."[1]

Bache had left all of his possessions, including the *Aurora*, to his wife, Margaret. And he had named his chief pressman, William Duane, to serve as its editor. Nine years older than Bache, Duane had been born in the American colonies in 1760 but moved to Ireland as a boy. As a young man he had worked as a printer and publisher in London, then lived for a number of years in India, where he edited a newspaper called the *World*. Duane first ran afoul of the British government by attacking its colonial policies in India. Authorities deported him to London, where his support for the French Revolution left him in perpetual danger of arrest. He fled England in 1796 and landed in Philadelphia. With Margaret's blessing, Duane was to carry on as the voice of the *Aurora*. On November 1, 1798, with the yellow fever finally lifting, the newspaper leaped back to life.

"Under the guidance of *BENJAMIN FRANKLIN BACHE*, this paper has for eight years maintained a character of freedom and intelligence, unrivaled . . . until calamity for a while arrested its career and deprived society of the Editor," the paper boldly stated in its new inaugural issue.[2]

Margaret's assumption of the reins as publisher of the *Aurora* cheered beleaguered Republicans who thought they had lost their most consistent and strident voice. The *Farmers' Register*, of Chambersburg, Pennsylvania, noted, "We feel ourselves happy in congratulating the friends of civil liberty on the re-appearance of the Aurora, under the direction of Mrs. Bache."[3]

Some Federalist editors assumed that Margaret, as a woman, was merely a figurehead for Duane and other Republicans. An open letter in the Federalist *New-York Gazette and General Advertiser* instructed her in the realities of hard-nosed journalism as practiced in a man's world: "I consider it a duty to warn you of the censures you are exposed to from various classes of *our Fellow-Citizens*—whose esteem is essential to the well-being of your children."[4]

William Cobbett, who, as editor of *Porcupine's Gazette*, had been one of the fiercest critics of Benjamin Bache, did Bache's widow the honor of treating her as a worthy rival, refusing to attribute the reincarnated *Aurora* just to its hired printer, William Duane. "The proprietor of the paper, the person whose name it bears, who causes it to be published, is the only one who is responsible for its contents, either in the eye of reason or the eye of the law. That person, therefore, whether bearded or not bearded, whether dressed in breeches or petticoats, whether a male or female sans culotte, shall receive no quarter from me."[5]

Cobbett didn't make threats idly, and he was a formidable enemy, both because of his hard-nosed style and his direct line of communication with the Sedition Act's most eager enforcer, Secretary of State Timothy Pickering. Pickering relied on Cobbett as well as editors of newspapers in other towns around the country to keep him informed of articles in rival Republican newspapers that might be open to prosecution under the Sedition Act. And he kept U.S. attorneys busy with "suggestions" to investigate suspicious characters.

In New Jersey, an ambitious thirty-three-year-old U.S. attorney named Lucius Horatio Stockton needed no such prompting. He was eager to demonstrate his loyalty to the man who had appointed him only a few months earlier, John Adams. Stockton was the well-connected scion of an old New Jersey family. His father, Richard Stockton, had signed the Declaration of Independence. His brother, Richard Jr., though just a year older than Horatio, was already a U.S. senator. As such, he had been one of the eighteen who the previous July 4 had approved the Senate's draconian version of the Sedition Act. The younger Stockton had graduated eleven years earlier from the College of New Jersey, where he finished first in his class of twenty-three and delivered a valedictory address devoted to "the qualities of a true Republican."[6] By now that word had taken on a new and incendiary meaning. All Stockton needed was the right opportunity to make a name for himself by taking down a seditious Republican.[7]

Stockton found his opportunity in a complaint filed several months earlier by the local marshal. It seems that John Burnet, the tavern owner who had tangled with Luther Baldwin on the street back in July, had not been so quick to forgive and forget Baldwin's drunken joke about the cannon salute and president's rear end. Burnet was more than just a tavern owner; he was also the town's postmaster, and hence politically connected.[8]

By now Baldwin had probably forgotten all about the incident. Considering his condition when it occurred, he may not have remembered it the next morning. Regardless, he had long since gone back to his customary trade, plying the waters in and around Newark in his boat. From a logical perspective, Stockton faced enormous obstacles in presenting any kind of coherent case. The only witnesses were bystanders who would have to recall what they may or may not have overheard several months earlier, on a crowded street, with ears that had just been rattled by artillery blasts, in an incident in which nobody had been hurt.

But Stockton pressed, and on November 6, the local *Centinel of Freedom* reported the arrest of Luther Baldwin, whom Stockton's indictment described as "a pernicious and seditious man."[9] Stockton spared no adverbs in framing Luther as a Republican monster:

> [The defendant] maliciously, diabolically, seditiously, wickedly and scandalously in the presence and hearing of divers faithful citizens of the United States, then and there present did utter and with a loud voice pronounce assert and affirm, that the President (meaning the President of the United States) was a *damned rascal* and ought to have his arse kicked, and one of the cannon shot thro' it (meaning the President of the United States ought to have his arse kicked) and ought to have one of the cannon (then and there firing as aforesaid shot though his arse:) to the great scandal and contempt of the President of the United States and government thereof, to the evil example of all others in the like case offending, and against the peace of the United States the government and dignity of the same.[10]

Modern historians have seized on the comic elements of Baldwin's story and handed down an image of an oaf, a simpleton, "a hapless New Jersey Republican of absolutely no repute,"[11] and his entire episode a mere "comic footnote"[12] to the weightier intellectual, political, and legal dramas surrounding the Sedition Act. Baldwin was not, after all, a politician, editor, or thinker trading in big ideas, but instead a common man who got drunk and opened his mouth at the wrong time.

Though Baldwin was by no means a leading figure of his time, his life was marked by colorful adventures, and, despite his apparent fondness for drink, he was a resourceful businessman. Born in Newark in 1752, Baldwin spent his life in and around the water. In his twenties when the Revolutionary War began, Baldwin joined up with a band of coastal spies and raiders led by Captain Baker Hendricks. Hendricks and his brother, John, were important members of George Washington's extensive spy network that ran up and down the East Coast.[13] Hendricks and his men plied the waters between New Jersey and New York in a pair of whaleboats colorfully named *Flying Squirrel* and *Charming Betsy*, gathering intelligence to send back to General Washington and "attacking whenever opportunity presented itself," according to one nineteenth-century historian.[14]

One Friday night in 1782, Hendricks, Baldwin, and a small party of raiders slipped their whaleboat to a quiet landing on enemy shores. They surprised the crew of a British sloop. Unable to make off with the vessel itself, because of the small size of their party, the raiders took a pair of three-pound guns, two blunderbusses, and other arms, along with the sloop's sails, rigging, cable, anchor, and long boat. They stealthily moved on and stripped two more sloops before the night was done.[15]

Baldwin's service ended on a sour note when, a year after the war ended, Samuel Hayes, an agent for Essex County, New Jersey, listed him among more than 115 men ordered to forfeit their property for disloyalty to the American cause. The notice offered no details about the nature of the supposed offenses of any of the men.[16] Much later, after Baldwin had become an accidental celebrity courtesy of the Sedition Act, Federalists resurrected the charge to discredit him, much as they had with Matthew Lyon and his wooden sword. Republican defenders argued just as strongly that Baldwin's posting on the list was a mistake. As a spy for Washington, they said, Baldwin had sold chicken, eggs, and other provisions to British forces, but only as a means of gaining valuable information on the movements of enemy troops—for which he was even imprisoned when the British became suspicious. He had masked his loyalty for the American cause to maintain his cover, defenders insisted. And they denied he had ever had his property confiscated by Americans.[17]

Whatever the case, Baldwin had little trouble reentering the mainstream of civilian life in Newark in the years following the war. Though he never made a fortune, Baldwin showed entrepreneurial flair for using his boat and his knowledge of the waterways to turn a profit. Advertisements he placed in local newspapers suggest that Baldwin plied an intracoastal trade route between Newark and Albany, New York. He promised Newark farmers top dollar in cash for English hay,[18] then sailed up the long trough of the Hudson River to Albany, a distance of approximately 140 miles, where he sold or traded the hay and loaded up on New York lumber. Sailing back downriver with his heavily laden vessel, he offered boards and planks on the Newark town dock in exchange for money or "Good, Strong Shoes," the latter presumably for sale at the end of yet another voyage.[19] When winter ice made the rivers impassable, Baldwin stowed his sloop in favor of sleds, ferrying travelers across the frozen Passaic and Hackensack Rivers at half the fare charged on local toll bridges.[20]

Outside of the obvious distaste for President Adams that Baldwin displayed on that day in July 1798, the only clue to his Republican leanings is that he chose to advertise in the strongly Republican *Centinel of Freedom*. He wasn't a vocal force in local or national politics, and, indeed, seems to have expected even after the confrontation with John Burnet that life would go back to normal and stay that way.

Certainly, no one could confuse Luther Baldwin as a political mind on the order of Benjamin Bache or Matthew Lyon, let alone Jefferson or Adams. Those men clamored for their place in the sun. Yet it is precisely because Baldwin was a rather average example of late eighteenth-century American humanity that his arrest deeply alarmed Republican editors of his day, and they, rather than history, seem to have gotten it right about Luther. They understood that beneath the drunken high jinks lay a deadly serious matter. His arrest showed how quickly and ominously such a law could reach its icy fingers into the general population, and how quickly and arbitrarily rights can disappear with the unleashing of coercive powers to punish dissent.

One editor, while acknowledging that Baldwin's comments were "highly improper and unbecoming," argued that rendering rudeness toward elected officials a crime amounted to "placing them, who are servants or agents of the people, above the people themselves. Here's *liberty* for you!"[21]

Federalists, too, saw little humor in the Baldwin case. As descriptions of the incident made their way around the country in papers from Albany, New York, to Georgetown, South Carolina, the message was condensed and evolved into a sincere wish "that the president of the United States was dead."[22] The *Northern Centinel* of Salem, New York, declared that, "Sedition, by all the laws of God and man, is, and ever has been criminal."[23]

Because the ceremonial artillery discharged powder and wadding rather than actual cannonballs, one might reasonably argue (as some Republicans did) that the worst Baldwin wished upon the president was a singed bottom. But even accepting the worst, that Luther Baldwin had truly wished for the president's demise, was expressing such a wish a crime?

Recall the political philosopher Algernon Sidney, who in 1683 had gone to the executioner's block for *imagining* the death of Charles II. The *Centinel of Freedom*, Baldwin's strongest defender, harkened back still further, to the sixteenth century: "In the days of Harry the Eighth, when arbitrary power was much in vogue, it was high treason to *predict* the death of the King; in the twenty-third year of American Independence, it is deemed sedition to wish the death of the chief magistrate."[24]

Baldwin pleaded not guilty. His drinking companions, Brown Clark and a man named Lespenard, also were charged. Clark pleaded not guilty and Lespenard, despite initially doing the same, changed his mind and his plea. Lespenard was fined forty dollars plus court costs. Baldwin's case was postponed. His ordeal was just beginning. To be sure, there was a wide difference between Algernon Sidney's destiny with an executioner's blade and whatever awaited Luther Baldwin. Baldwin would wait out his trial on bail through the winter of 1798–1799, still earning his living ferrying passengers across frozen waterways.[25] Yet Republican editors were sincere and reasonable in wondering: If Baldwin's flippant remark was prosecutable, how could anyone feel safe? What had the struggle for liberty been about?

# Chapter Eighteen

As the gray autumn of northern Vermont descended toward winter, Matthew Lyon's discomforts intensified. Jabez Fitch continued to hold him in a communal cell with transient prisoners, including one man being held for four days and nights over nonpayment of a twenty-dollar debt. "He had such a terrible dysentery as caused the room to smell worse than any hospital I was ever in," Lyon reported to a friend. "He slept but little, and I less. This, I was almost sure would sicken me, and throw me into a fever, as I was in an ill state of health before I came here, but contrary to all expectation, I am at present pretty well."[1]

Considering Lyon's history of hotheaded reaction to the slightest provocations, Federalists who sent him to jail had assumed he would immediately lose his composure and attempt to escape. At the very least, Nathaniel Chipman and other Federalists clearly hoped that the man they had always framed as a wild, untamed beast would, as a "caged Lyon," prove himself unfit to resume his role as a political figure.

Instead, his jailers found themselves with custody of the last thing they expected or wanted: a model prisoner. He complied with all the rules and put up with any indignity. When he wanted something, he asked politely, and acquiesced when his requests were denied. His quiet forbearance under trying circumstances lent a new and surprising element to Lyon's reputation as a fighter and a hothead who responded with his fists to the slightest provocation. Escape, Lyon declared in a letter to a friend, was out of the question. "If I wished to come out, they could not hold me; and as I do not, if my limits were marked by a simple thread, I would not overstep it."[2] By jailing Lyon, Federalists would manage to do what Lyon himself had never been able to accomplish on his own—turn him into a sympathetic character.

But there was one thing Lyon refused to do: admit any wrong-doing. While he sat placidly in jail, Lyon let his new magazine, the *Scourge of Aristocracy*, edited by his son, do the attacking. In a letter to his friend, Virginia Republican senator Stevens Thomson Mason, written from jail and reprinted in the *Scourge*, Lyon claimed that Adams was hoping for him to break out of jail, or, better yet, that a mob of Lyon supporters would descend on Vergennes and release him by force. Such would give the president cause to do something he was as yet too timid to do, but desperately wanted to: call up and commission a standing army. Lyon wrote, "The appearance of an insurrection of 1000 men to break this gaol, I dare say they [the administration] think would be cause for issuing 500 commissions."[3]

Three weeks into Lyon's confinement, Jabez Fitch at last affixed a glass pane over the empty window, keeping out the draft and some of the chill. Still, Lyon was denied a private room, despite offering Fitch a $100,000 surety, backed by his friends, that he would not escape. As Mason began to circulate Lyon's letter from jail, Republicans who had winced at Lyon's antics in the House, and recoiled in embarrassment from his fights with Griswold, now saw him as a man willing to suffer for his own cause and for theirs.

The *Aurora* printed Lyon's letter in Philadelphia, and other newspapers around the country quickly picked it up. Republicans expressed outrage that one of their own, and a sitting congressman, no less, was being treated like a common criminal for engaging in spirited debate. In Virginia, he was emerging as a symbolic figure for freedom, and everyday citizens were beginning to arouse to the dangers of tyranny. "People had been told that the Sedition Bill was harmless, was only meant as a bug-bear and would not be enforced," Mason wrote. "But when they see it so speedily carried into execution, and its first victim one of the Representatives of the People, every considerate man shudders at the danger with which civil liberty is threatened, and considers you as a martyr in its cause."

Mason recalled the days of the constitutional debates, and the assurances from anti–Bill of Rights forces that there was no need to explicitly declare rights, since the Constitution gave the government no authority to deny them. "We were told that personal liberty never could be endangered under the Constitution," he wrote. He closed with a note of encouragement that Lyon and his cause were growing larger and more symbolically important by the day. Lyon's martyrdom would awaken the American people before "the foundations of their liberty, are sapped, all the barriers of the Constitution broke down, and themselves reduced to a state of vassalage."[4]

A poet identified only as Z. Porter of Coventry, Vermont, published a pocm on November 10, 1798, in the voice of Matthew Lyon sitting in his cell. Crudely spelled and none too subtle, it nevertheless captured the spirit of rising indignation, with such lines as:

> *Our Ruler can feast on six dollars pr day*
> *the poor Must be taxt their extorsion to pay*
> *And if I Should unto them any Thing say*
> *they would trump up a Bill of Sedition*[5]

Despite his compromised circumstances, Lyon remained, after all, a sitting U.S. congressman—and one with a reelection bid coming up. Of all the twists and turns of his extraordinary life, the most unusual chapter was yet to come. With the runoff election scheduled for December, he would have to campaign for reelection from prison. His inability to hit the campaign trail with fiery speeches, far from hurting his chances, became his greatest advantage. Voters inflamed by his treatment surged to the polls. Almost two thousand more turned out this time than had done so in September. Lyon's margin of victory was even more impressive (4,576 for Lyon, versus 2,444 for his nearest competitor), giving him the clear majority he needed for another term in Philadelphia.[6]

From jail, Lyon wrote an open letter to his constituents, thanking them for doing what a stacked jury would not: declaring him not guilty of "pretended crimes." He wrote, "With a heart truly overflowing with gratitude have I, in this dismal prison, received the intelligence that you have again considered me entitled to your confidence and worthy of your suffrages, as your representative in the Congress of the United States."[7]

Lyon still had two months remaining on his sentence, and his captors weren't about to let him out simply because he had won the popular vote. The Reverend John Cosens Ogden, an Episcopal minister from New Hampshire, carried a petition with several thousand Vermont signatures four hundred miles to Philadelphia asking the president to waive Lyon's $1,000 fine. Adams agreed to meet with Ogden, but denied the request when Ogden conceded that Lyon had not personally begged the president's pardon. Adams was in no mood to forgive and forget. He told Ogden that "penitence must precede pardon."[8]

Among Lyon's most steadfast defenders throughout his ordeal was Anthony Haswell, publisher of the *Vermont Gazette* in Bennington. A native of Portsmouth, England, who immigrated to Boston at age twelve with his widowed father, Haswell had his political views shaped and cured by the revolutionary spirit of his adopted hometown. Having apprenticed as a printer, Haswell set out for Bennington, in the southwestern corner of Vermont, where he founded the *Vermont Gazette* in 1783. Within two years, Haswell enraged the religious establishment by printing Ethan Allen's book of deist religious philosophy, *Reason, the Only Oracle of Man*. Deism espoused a belief in God as experienced through reason and observable nature.

As such, the book criticized organized religion with its bureaucratic hierarchies and its emphasis on miracles and other supernatural occurrences. The Reverend Timothy Dwight IV, who would go on to serve as president of Yale and become a leading Federalist, blasted Allen's book as "contemptible plagiarism of every hackneyed, worn-out, half-rotten dogma of the English deistical writers."[9]

As the divisions deepened between Federalists and Republicans, Haswell's newspaper, the first regularly published newspaper on the western side of the mountains, struck a consistent note for the Republican party. Haswell supported Lyon as representative and frequently printed his letters. As Lyon sat in prison, Haswell printed advertisements for a lottery to raise money to pay off his fine. The repeated advertisements were pugnaciously addressed "To the enemies of political persecution in the western district of Vermont." They described Jabez Fitch, Lyon's jailer, as "a hard-hearted savage, who has, to the disgrace of Federalism, been elevated to a station where he can satiate his barbarity on the misery of his victims."[10]

Lyon's sentence expired at last in February 1799. If a convicted, bedraggled, downbeat Matthew Lyon had entered the prison at Vergennes, it was something on the order of a conquering hero who emerged into the cold winter sunlight. Hundreds of supporters descended on Vergennes to welcome Lyon back to life among the free. In addition to the lottery plan, a wealthy Vermonter, Apollos Austin, organized a group of friends who came up with $1,000.

In the end, though, it was a savior on horseback from Philadelphia who had the privilege of securing Lyon from his fine. His old friend, Senator Mason, bore $1,060 in gold coins in his saddlebags. He had collected the money from wealthy Republicans around the country—including Thomas Jefferson, James Madison, and Albert Gallatin—and traveled all the way to northern Vermont to deliver the money himself.[11]

The supporters who appeared in Vergennes had more on their minds than simply cheering Lyon. They were there as a show of force. Lyon's writings from prison, which had so stoked Republican sympathies, had in equal measure inflamed Federalists. Lyon now faced the very real threat that his nemesis Fitch would rearrest him moments after his release, under fresh charges of sedition based on those jailhouse letters or his articles in the *Scourge of Aristocracy*.

Yet it was not protesters but the Constitution that saved Lyon from a second arrest. To prevent senators and members of Congress from being waylaid and missing crucial votes, the framers included a provision in Article I, Section 6 protecting members of Congress from arrest while traveling to or from sessions. Immediately upon leaving his cell, Lyon proclaimed his intention to proceed to Philadelphia to take up his seat. He boarded a coach drawn by four horses and brandishing an American flag. Friendly crowds lined the road virtually the entire eleven-mile journey south to Middlebury, toasting his health.[12] At the town of Tinmouth, schoolchildren stood in line to watch Lyon pass. One child offered a salute to "Our brave Representative, who has been suffering for us under an unjust sentence" and who "this day rises superior to despotism."[13] Lyon's enemies could only look on in consternation. As one Daniel Church grumbled to a friend in Brattleboro, "No doubt you have heard that Lyon went out of prison with great *Pomp*."[14]

Even as Lyon journeyed southward across the frozen landscape, rumblings of rebellion against the Sedition Act were bubbling up in Congress. On February 13, Andrew Gregg, a Republican, presented 270 signatures from his district in central Pennsylvania, demanding repeal of the Sedition Act and the Alien Acts. A day earlier, Edward Livingston of New York had introduced a similar petition on behalf of a group of Irish-born citizens. Federalists, insulted by the idea of outsiders questioning the constitutionality of their bill, said in no uncertain terms that they would not waste time on such a petition when there were pressing concerns of "our citizens" to be tended to. Gregg avowed that the signers of his petition were reputable, hardworking, law-abiding American citizens, many of whom had served their country during the revolution. For most, it was the first time in their lives they had petitioned the government with a complaint. These were not political people spoiling for a fight, he said. They were average folks content to go about the business of their lives, and to leave the debating and legislating to others. But they knew right from wrong, Gregg believed, and that the government had overstepped its authority.[15]

The following Wednesday, February 20, the Annals of Congress noted, simply: "Matthew Lyon, from Vermont, appeared and took his seat in the House."[16]

Those few sedate words belied the fact that Lyon had lost none of his ability to inflame passions in the People's House. Yet this time, Republicans were more eager to directly embrace the Vermonter. He was no longer the party's wild, unpredictable poor relation, but a champion. After Lyon took his seat, Livingston announced that he had received a number of petitions from Vermont residents, "praying for a repeal of the alien and sedition laws."

While Republicans celebrated Lyon's reelection, Federalists greeted his return to Congress as an affront, and one more example that foreign influences and Republicans were destroying the American experiment in self-government. William Cobbett saw in Lyon's reelection proof positive that the rabble was too ignorant to be entrusted with the vote. "Happy must the nation be where it is but a single step from the *dungeon* to the *Legislature!*"[17]

Throughout Lyon's first day back Federalists in Congress bided their time through a lengthy discussion of a report by the Committee of the Whole, encouraging the capture of French privateering vessels by U.S. ships by offering a bounty on guns taken. Then, just prior to the session closing for the day, James Bayard, a Delaware Federalist, rose and introduced a motion to expel Lyon for "having been convicted of being a notorious and seditious person, and of a depraved mind, and wicked and diabolical disposition; and of wickedly, deceitfully, and maliciously, contriving to defame the Government of the United States."[18]

Of course, calling a sitting U.S. congressman "wicked and diabolical" might in its own right be seen as a violation of the Sedition Act. Anticipating that charge, Bayard brought with him the record of Lyon's Vermont trial as proof that his description of Lyon was "true." "Will any one say that a man who does not keep the laws ought to be allowed to make them?" Bayard asked.[19] Republican John Nicholas responded by reading aloud the entire Joel Barlow letter over which Lyon had in part been tried. The Virginian challenged his fellow members to cite a "fact" that could be proved or disproved. Lyon was not only within his rights to express opinions against the administration; it was his duty to do so, Nicholas continued. "If the people of Vermont choose to have a person possessing these opinions to represent them, who have a right to say they shall not?"[20] Lyon, largely subdued during the discussion, offered only the assessment that he had received "an unjust trial and a hard sentence."[21]

When at last the expulsion came down to a vote, the count fell strictly on party lines, 49 in favor, 45 opposed. Once again, a simple majority wanted Matthew Lyon out, yet once again, his enemies failed to muster the required two-thirds. Lyon remained a member of the House of Representatives.[22]

# CHAPTER NINETEEN

Among those keeping a close eye on the resurrection of Matthew Lyon was Vice President Thomas Jefferson, who sensed in the results an incipient shift in the political winds. "Lyon is rechosen in Vermont by a vast majority," he wrote excitedly to James Monroe. "It seems agreed that the republican sentiment is gaining ground fast in this state & in Massachusetts."[1] Republicans had long looked to Jefferson as their philosophical leader. Certainly, he was the highest-ranking Republican in the land, even though as an opposition vice president his practical power was nil. Despite his professed dislike for politics and suspicion of federal government, Jefferson was a consummate politician with long-term ambitions for higher national office. And he possessed the skilled politician's most valuable asset: an acute sense of timing.

From the early debates on the Sedition Act through the first several months of its implementation, Jefferson confined his deep misgivings to letters to friends. Though he quietly supported opposition journalists, publicly he had remained neutral on the bill.[2] But by late 1798, Jefferson was growing alarmed. He wrote to John Taylor, a member of the Virginia House of Delegates, "Our general government has, in the rapid course of 9 or 10 years, become more arbitrary, and has swallowed more of the public liberty than even that of England." The time was right for a declaration of the power of individual states, Jefferson believed. He envisioned strongly worded resolutions that might be adopted by state governments, declaring "the alien & sedition laws to be against the constitution & merely void."[3]

With Federalists in control in most states, the two likeliest choices for Jefferson's plan were Kentucky and Virginia. Jefferson decided to write the Kentucky Resolutions himself. Though he would not acknowledge authorship until decades later, putting pen to paper in such a way represented a real risk, especially by Jefferson's careful, cautious standards. Should he be discovered as the author, essentially suggesting that states could repudiate federal law, he might be opening himself to charges of sedition. To write the Virginia Resolutions, Jefferson tapped his old friend James Madison.

Madison had been even more withdrawn than Jefferson from the Sedition Act drama. As Federalists consolidated power in the capital, Madison had left the House in 1796 and retreated to self-imposed retirement on his plantation in Montpelier, Virginia. He concerned himself with the management of his estate, running the farm, worrying about his crops, and declaring himself to be through with the political life.[4] Only the cajoling of his good friend Jefferson was enough to finally convince him to rejoin the battle.

Although both the Kentucky and Virginia Resolutions aimed at the same general purpose of undermining the Alien and Sedition Acts, the two documents were markedly different. Jefferson's, written in September and October and passed by the Kentucky legislature in November, was notably darker and more petulant.[5] Constructed as a series of nine resolutions, it opened in the negative, with an ominous, almost combative note: "*Resolved*, That the several States composing the United States of America, are not united on the principle of unlimited submission to their General Government . . ." Rather, the states created the federal government "for special purposes" and gave the government "certain definite powers." Much of the rest of the document was devoted to a careful explanation of why the federal government lacked the specified authority to punish any crimes outside of a narrow, well-defined spectrum including such offenses as counterfeiting and treason; and that if any limits needed to be placed on speech and the press, the right to do so belonged to the states.[6]

Allowing these acts to stand would, Jefferson warned, open the door to innumerable federal abuses in the future, by allowing the government to punish any behavior it disapproved of.[7]

Compared with Jefferson's reflections on human liberty in the Declaration of Independence, his draft of the Kentucky Resolutions was rather limited in scope, focusing on the *processes* of government and the relationship between one governmental body and another. Moreover, while the document extended a friendly hand to the other states, offering assurances that Kentucky valued the "esteem of their friendship and union," it suggested an affiliation of independent states rather than a single, inviolable nation. The message running just below the surface was of the reserved right of any state to leave the union if its rights were to be violated.[8]

Madison's Virginia Resolutions, adopted by the Virginia General Assembly in late December, strove toward the same end—declaring the Alien and Sedition Acts unconstitutional—but did so in a way that was at once more expansive, optimistic, and hopeful about the future of a united republic. Madison had been a compatriot of Hamilton's and his coauthor in the seminal Federalist Papers. He had argued forcefully for a strong union and helped recalcitrant Virginians to overcome their doubts. And while he had broken with what he perceived to be the excessive nature of Federalist ambitions, he still believed strongly in the necessity of a powerful federal government. Indeed, just a few days after introducing his Virginia Resolutions, Madison wrote to Jefferson, worried that his fellow Virginians might overreact. "It is to be feared their zeal may forget some considerations which ought to temper their proceedings," he fretted.

Madison concurred with Jefferson that Congress had overstepped its bounds. But if states had the right to guard against federal overreach, where did it say that state *legislatures* per se had the authority to make such determinations? Where did that authority come from? This distinction was pure Madison, evidence of his overriding belief that the founding documents, if they were to have any staying power, must be respected most carefully in times of crisis. What would be the advantage in having state legislators, in their zeal to correct an unconstitutional power grab by Congress, assume an unconstitutional authority in order to do so?[9] With this question Madison was of course raising the broader issue of the proper system of constitutional oversight and review. If not the state legislatures, then who should be in charge of determining whether a given law was unconstitutional? That question would be established during the 1803 lawsuit bearing Madison's name, *Marbury v. Madison*.

Madison's ambivalence and hesitation, far from weakening his Virginia Resolutions, made the document stronger, more resilient, and more forward-looking than Jefferson's Kentucky counterpart. Instead of opening with wronged states declaring a right to reject federal legislation (and, by implication, rejecting the very underpinnings of federal authority), Madison described states as fervently interested in preserving and jealously protecting the sanctity of the union. It's no accident that the document opens with a resolution by the Virginia General Assembly "to maintain and defend the constitution of the United States." Because of their reverence for the union and the Constitution, Madison continued, Virginians believed it to be "their duty, to watch over and oppose every infraction of those principles, which constitute the only basis of that union, because a faithful observance of them, can alone secure its existence, and the public happiness."[10]

By positioning the Virginia Assembly not as potential mutineers on the American ship but rather as ardent protectors, Madison skirted the dangers implicit in the Kentucky Resolutions. Jefferson's document, in its insistence of framing the argument around states' rights, raised as many troubling questions as it answered. Were states so uninterested in union that they might up and leave at any provocation? Indeed, Jefferson's resolutions would be used in decades to come

as providing intellectual cover for secessionists in the years leading
to the Civil War. If Hamilton placed too much faith in the capacity
of a centralized national government to guide a nation in need of
rulers, Jefferson suffered from the opposite extreme, an overcharged
certainty that state and local governments would automatically do
a better job of protecting liberty. One assumes that Jefferson, had
he lived to see the Civil War, would have been deeply disturbed
at the uses to which secessionists put his doctrine of states' rights.
Yet there's no denying that Jefferson bears some intellectual blame
for the tragedies that states would inflict in seeking to preserve an
economic system and a way of life that denied unalienable rights to
millions of people. After Jefferson's death Madison, who outlived him
by a decade, would jealously defend Jefferson's legacy, insisting that
Jefferson did not intend the Kentucky Resolutions as a manifesto
for secession, and sharply criticizing "the nullifiers who would make
the name of Mr. Jefferson the pedestal for their colossal heresy."[11]

Federalists, though, weren't to be bothered with the subtle distinctions between the Kentucky and Virginia rebellions against over-
reaching federal authority. To them, both documents were seditious.
New York State's *Albany Centinel* declared the Virginia document
"Virginian Folly and Impudence,"[12] and the *New York Daily Advertiser* noted, "[I]t appears more and more evident, that the Kentucky
resolutions, are part of a concerted plan to embarrass the measures
of Government, and dismember the Union."[13]

While the Federalist *Gazette of the United States* accused Kentucky of being a puppet for the French, Cobbett's *Porcupine's Gazette*
struck a note of metropolitan snobbery by framing Kentuckians
as semiliterate hicks who "doe beeleev that our leebeerte es in
daingur." [14, 15]

The U.S. House of Representatives, alarmed by the resolutions,
ordered extra copies of the Sedition Act to be printed and distributed around the country. Robert Goodloe Harper, the Maryland
Federalist, believed that Virginia legislators had the more draconian

Senate version of the act rather than the toned-down final version. Harper believed the Kentucky and Virginia legislatures had made their votes based on "gross errors." Anybody who actually read the measures, he reasoned, must surely be "convinced of their wisdom and propriety."[16]

Nor did the Virginia and Kentucky Resolutions find a warm reception in the other state legislatures. Virginia and Kentucky had sent official copies to each of the state governments. The rebukes came one after another. By a majority of 58 to 14, the New York State legislature declared the documents "unwarranted" and "highly improper." Assemblies in Maryland, Delaware, Rhode Island, Massachusetts, New Hampshire, and even Matthew Lyon's Vermont issued rebukes. Virginia's neighbor Maryland attacked the Virginia Resolutions on two fronts, reaching the opinion that "no state government by a legislative act is competent to declare an act of the federal government unconstitutional and void, it being an improper interference with that jurisdiction which is exclusively vested in the courts of the United States." The Maryland response did not address how courts whose judges were actively hearing Sedition Act cases and passing judgment on defendants would be capable of determining the same law unconstitutional.

No matter, the Maryland politicians also specifically addressed the laws themselves, arguing that "viewing the present crisis of affairs," any effort to repeal the laws would be "unwise and impolitic."[17] A few months later, the Connecticut Assembly declared that it "views with deep regret, and explicitly disavows the principles" of resolutions it believed were "calculated to subvert the Constitution and to introduce discord and anarchy." The assembly sent copies of its rebukes to the assemblies of Virginia and Kentucky.[18]

Despite such strong rhetoric, Republicans leaders were beginning to get their backs up. Madison, energized by his involvement with Jefferson in the Kentucky and Virginia Resolutions, had emerged from his plantation in Montpelier and was out of retirement for good. In February 1799, the same month that Lyon returned from his Vermont prison cell, Madison published a long article in the *Aurora* offering a bold defense of France. Signed only "A Citizen of the United States," the article charged that most news of France "is brought to this Country chiefly from England and Germany, and is consequently adulterated with all the exaggerations & perversions which the most raging hostility can infuse."[19] A month earlier, in the same newspaper, Madison (writing as "Enemy to Foreign Influence") turned the table on France's critics by laying out step-by-step why England, not France, "ought to be dreaded and watched, as most likely to gain an undue and pernicious ascendency in our country." In particular, he wrote, England sought to strangle U.S. manufacturing in order to preserve the former colonies as a market for its own manufactured goods, and to restrict the growth of U.S. shipping in order to maintain mastery of the seas. Most particularly, Madison added, England feared and wished to stifle American republicanism, before its influence spread to its own shores and threatened the monarchy with popular revolt.[20]

Even stronger than the defense of France were the article's warnings about the corrupting and liberty-destroying potential of war. "*The fetters imposed on liberty at home have ever been forged out of the weapons provided for defence against real, pretended, or imaginary dangers from abroad,*" he wrote. And in a clear jab at Adams, he added that the greatest threats came in the way that war concentrated power in the executive branch of the government.[21]

Even as the Sedition Act shook James Madison from his Montpelier retirement, it provoked lesser-known Americans into reflecting on the meaning of freedom. Freedom, of course, had been at the forefront of the American mind since before the Revolutionary War. But now the conversation was changing from bold declarations against a ruling foreign power to subtler reflections on what liberty means

in a functioning society, whether it can survive, and why objectionable voices must be permitted to speak. In January 1799, a Virginian
named George Hay published *An Essay on the Liberty of the Press*. Hay,
a thirty-four-year-old attorney with a private practice in Petersburg,
south of Richmond, addressed his essay to the Republican printers
of the United States.

It was divided into two parts, the first comprising a precise,
detailed analysis of why he believed the Sedition Act was unconstitutional. Drawing a distinction between speech and action, Hay
readily acknowledged the power of Congress to punish "insurrection
or *actual* opposition" to government measures, "because the best
laws would be of no avail, unless Congress possessed a power to
punish those, who opposed their execution."[22] Hay then argued the
case of constitutional limitations on federal power, pointing out that
Congress had authority only over those areas specifically described
in the Constitution. Thus even without the First Amendment, Congress lacked the specific authority to regulate speech and press, since
those powers aren't granted in the Constitution. But, of course, the
First Amendment *did* exist, and this, in Hay's view, eliminated any
reasonable argument on the matter.

If his essay had ended with part one, the best that might be
said of George Hay is that he added a logical if not terribly inspiring argument in favor of a strict interpretation of the Constitution
and the Bill of Rights. But the genius of Hay's *Essay on the Liberty of
the Press* lay in part two, where he anticipated and began to address
such questions with a new American conception of liberty, one that
needed some repressive test such as the Sedition Act in order to be
fully galvanized. "The words, 'freedom of the press,' like most other
words, have a meaning, a clear, precise, and definite meaning, which
the times require, should be unequivocally ascertained," Hay wrote.
"That this has not been done before, is a wonderful and melancholy
evidence of the imbecility of the human mind . . ."[23]

The Bill of Rights is perhaps the single most beautiful and vital document ever produced by a government—you can get goose bumps just thinking what it meant, against the long, grisly train of human tyranny through the ages, for a government to set about declaring the limits of its own power. Still, the Bill of Rights is not the source of our rights but a reflection of them, a mechanism for protecting them. This is of course what the Founders meant by unalienable rights being derived from nature or the Creator, as distinct from privileges, which can be granted (or revoked) by men. What George Hay and others were awakening to was what that meant on a practical level, in the daily life of an often chaotic, dissonant society.

Hay drew a distinction between "absolute freedom which belongs to man, previous to any social institution; and the other, that qualified or abridged freedom, which he is content to enjoy, for the sake of government."[24] Speech, Hay asserted, belonged firmly in the former category. "If this definition of freedom be applied to the press, as surely it ought to be, the press, if I may personify it, may do whatever it pleases to do, uncontrouled by any law, *taking care to do no injury to any individual*. This injury can only be by slander or defamation, and reparation should be made for it in a state of nature as well as in society."[25] Should the press be ascribed to the abridged category, it would cease to be true freedom at all, Hay observed. "It will amount precisely to the privilege of publishing, as far as the legislative power shall say, the public good requires: that is to say, the freedom of the press will be regulated by law."

Hay continued: "This argument may be summed up in a few words. The word 'freedom' has meaning. It is either absolute, that is exempt from all law, or it is qualified, that is, regulated by law. If it be exempt from the controul of law, the Sedition Bill which controuls the 'freedom of the press' is unconstitutional. But if it is to be regulated by law, the amendment which declares that Congress shall make no law to abridge the freedom of the press, which freedom however may be regulated by law, is the grossest absurdity that ever was conceived by the human mind."

If Federalists sought to emulate British society, with its love of orderliness and social strata in which every member knew his place and function, Hay argued for a more wide-open society in the United States, even at the price of disorder. "In Britain, a legislative controul over the press, is, perhaps essential to the preservation of the 'present order of things;' but it does not follow, that such controul is essential here." Equating a free press to freedom of religion, he argued that even hateful ideas must be permitted in any society that wishes to live in freedom. "The evils arising from the toleration of heresy and atheism, are less, infinitely less, than the evils of perse-cution," Hay wrote. Likewise, "if the words freedom of the press, have any meaning at all, they mean a total exemption from any law making any publication whatever criminal," since the only way to stifle objectionable voices would be to exercise "a power fatal to the liberty of the people."

Indeed, for a society to remain free, "A man may say every thing which his passion can suggest; he may employ all his time, and all his talents, if he is wicked enough to do so, in *speaking* against the government matters that are false, scandalous, and malicious." The best way to counter such maliciousness is with truth, as discerned by free, reasoning minds, Hay added. "The truth cannot be impressed upon the human mind by power."

# Chapter Twenty

The course of the Sedition Act, whether it would presage similar actions defining the relationship between citizens and their government, or be recognized as a colossal blunder, would in the end have to be determined not by professional thinkers but by everyday people. Would Americans wake up in time to recognize what they stood to lose before they lost it?

Republicans had taken to collecting signatures of average Americans opposed to the Alien and Sedition Acts. At first a trickle, the signatures grew into streams and torrents flooding the floor of Congress to the great annoyance of Federalist leadership. On February 21, 1799, Albert Gallatin presented a petition containing 755 signatures from residents of Chester, Pennsylvania, and 78 more from Washington County. Robert Brown, another Pennsylvania Republican, presented petitions containing 1,940 signatures from Montgomery County and 1,100 from Northampton County. From the Northern Liberties neighborhood of Philadelphia came 587, courtesy of Representative Blair McClenachan. To that single-day total of 4,460 Pennsylvania signatures, David Bard the next morning added nearly 1,487 from Franklin County—for a grand total of 5,947. On February 25, there were 2,500 signatures from New York, more than 700 from Delaware, and an additional 2,676 from around Pennsylvania.

Had the Federalists been more astute politically they might have caught the message contained in such an outpouring. The combined 8,623 Pennsylvania signatures, for example, equaled 12.3 percent of the voters who would turn out for the state's gubernatorial election that year, and more than 1.4 percent of Pennsylvania's entire population of 600,000—proportionately the same as if a congressman marched into Congress today and dropped 180,000 Pennsylvanian signatures on lawmakers' desks.[1]

At first, Federalists called the petitions an "atrocious libel" against the courts and juries, in the words of Robert Goodloe Harper. Harper blamed Republican members for spreading poisonous lies and inciting an uninformed population. Gallatin, the even-spoken voice of reason among the Republican party, asked whether, as part of their assault on liberty, Harper and the Federalists intended to thwart the right of people to petition the government as well.

The right to petition the government for redress of grievances was an English tradition dating to the Magna Carta and before. American colonial assemblies had recognized petitioning as a legitimate way for all members of society to voice concerns about government action.[2] The Massachusetts *Body of Liberties*, adopted in 1641 and viewed as an early precedent to the Bill of Rights,[3] included petitioning among its essential rights. With independence, Delaware and Pennsylvania included the right to petition in their state constitutions, and the new federal government followed suit by guaranteeing the right to petition as part of the First Amendment. The Constitution does not stipulate how, if at all, the government must respond to such petitions. Yet to the early Americans, petitions were, according to legal historian Gregory A. Mark, a cherished and sacrosanct part of the political process, carrying more force than they do today.[4]

Gallatin brought forth yet another petition, from 678 more Pennsylvanians demanding repeal. The tide of signatures began at last to draw the Federalists' attention. House leaders appointed a special committee to review the petitions. Having passed the Sedition Act with an air of imperial arrogance, Federalists felt, for the first time, the need to officially explain themselves. Their resulting report was by far their most cohesive, complete, and thoughtful argument on behalf of the Sedition Act. In contrast to the smug assuredness of their arguments in passing the bill, this time the Federalists honored their opponents by treating objections to the Sedition Act seriously rather than dismissing them as the ramblings of un-American misfits. And they did posterity (the rest of us) the honor of finally laying out their most cogent arguments for why a government must control malicious and angry speech if it is to maintain security and order.

Petitioners had claimed that Congress had no authority to pass such a law, since no such powers were granted in the Constitution. The Federalists responded that without such a law they could have no hope of "carrying into effect the power vested by the Constitution in the Government of the United States."[5] Recall that in 1799 the idea that opposing parties would compete, conflict with, and undermine one another had yet to take hold. George Washington's parting words, warning of "the alternate domination of one faction over another, sharpened by the spirit of revenge natural to party dissention," still rang loud in Federalist ears.[6]

As for the First Amendment's unequivocal prohibition on abridging free speech, "To this it is answered, in the first place, that the liberty of the press consists not in a license for every man to publish what he pleases without being liable to punishment, if he should abuse this license to the injury of others." Echoing Blackstone's *Commentaries*, the committee argued liberty of the press implies only a lack of previous restraint on publication. The writer may use his own judgment in deciding what to publish, but "being answerable to the public and individuals, for any abuse of this permission to their prejudice." They continued: "Liberty of speech does not authorize a man to speak malicious slanders against his neighbor, nor the liberty of action justify him in going, by violence, into another man's house, or in assaulting any person whom he may meet in the streets."[7]

The Federalists fell back on historical precedent, stating, "liberty of the press did never extend, according to the laws of any State, or of the United States, or of England, from whence our laws are derived, to the publication of false, scandalous, and malicious writings against the Government." How, then, could the law be deemed unconstitutional, when "it makes nothing penal that was not penal before, and gives no new powers to the court, but is merely declaratory of the common law"? True, previous liberties had never been so broadly interpreted by a government. But this was the very essence of the American experiment. What was this new government, after all, but a test of the limits of freedom?

The final argument of the committee was the shakiest. Instead of reading the prohibition on abridging freedom of speech and the press as strong and decisive, it claimed the language was deliberately weak and vague, in comparison to the affirmative against meddling in religion. The First Amendment stipulates, "Congress shall make no law respecting an establishment of religion, or prohibiting the free exercise thereof; or abridging the freedom of speech, or of the press." According to the committee, that means Congress has no business "legislating at all on the subject of religious establishments."[8]

But because the press and speech provisions carried different language, Congress was not in fact prohibited from passing laws in those areas, only from "abridging" the liberty of the press. After this round of hairsplitting, the committee fell back on Blackstone's *Commentaries*, the English common-law authority stating that legislators were restricted only from placing prior restraints on the press, but were free to punish anyone who abused his freedom by printing "improper publications."[9] After all, "Our safety consists in the wisdom of the public councils; a co-operation on the part of the people with the Government, by supporting the measures provided for repelling aggressions, and an obedience to the social laws." Repealing the law, the committee concluded, would be "inexpedient." The full House, hearing the report, voted 52–48 in favor of upholding the Sedition Act.[10]

# CHAPTER TWENTY-ONE

Secretary of State Timothy Pickering found new and ever more creative ways to ferret out troublemakers. He asked Robert Wharton, Philadelphia's mayor, to investigate a seamstress in the city who was rumored to be making military uniforms "in the French fashion." In a note marked "Confidential," Pickering wrote, "It is not easy to conjecture what can be the destination of such cloathing: Certainly none of the kind is providing [*sic*] by the Government of the U. States. You will render a very acceptable service by tracing the matter to its source; I beg you to do it."[1]

Having thus struck a blow against seditious tailoring, Pickering next instructed William Rawle, the U.S. attorney for Pennsylvania, to scrutinize a German-language newspaper "printed in Reading by one Schneider." A friend of Pickering's had sent him the newspaper, containing a translation into German of a recent speech addressed to German immigrants living in Cumberland County. Fearful that Germans might be spreading anti-American messages, Pickering asked Rawle, "If any passages in the address do in your opinion make the printer liable to a prosecution, I pray you to direct its being commenced."[2]

For Fisher Ames, stewing away in Dedham, Massachusetts, only one sedition case really mattered: finding and prosecuting David Brown, the fugitive who had led the liberty pole brigade. To Ames's delight, Brown was at last apprehended in March 1799, in Andover,

Massachusetts, about twenty-eight miles north of Dedham. At the time of his arrest, authorities also seized some of his writings, including a poem entitled "A Dagger for Tyrants."[3]

Brown was taken to Boston, where he and Benjamin Fairbanks, the Dedham farmer who had been arrested as his accomplice, were scheduled for June trials at the U.S. Circuit Court in Boston. The treatment they received was markedly unequal. Fairbanks descended from a fine old Dedham family, predating even the Ames family. Town records list one Jonathan Farebancke as an original land grantee of twelve acres when Dedham was founded in 1636.[4] Fairbanks posted bond and was permitted to await trial from the comfort of home.

David Brown was hauled to a jail in Salem, north of Boston, the hometown of Timothy Pickering and site of the original American witch hunt. Bond was set at $4,000, twice the maximum allowable fine were he to be convicted of sedition. By conservative estimates, $4,000 in 1799 would be equivalent to well over $73,000 today.[5] The fine would have been well beyond the means of most Americans, let alone the itinerant David Brown. So he sat alone in jail, awaiting trial.

Powerful forces were arrayed against the defendants. Supreme Court associate justice Samuel Chase, a Federalist, would hear the case. As the trial date approached, Benjamin Fairbanks's rebellious spirit withered along with his confidence and his desire to fight the charges. He switched his plea and began apologizing to anyone who would listen. "It is true that I was present when the liberty pole was set up," he wrote. "But it was not then known by me, nor perhaps by others concerned, how heinous an offense it was." Fairbanks claimed that he had initially refused to take part, then had been "misled" into doing so. "I am now fully sensible of my offense," Fairbanks noted. "I am in my heart a friend to my country, its liberty and independence, and will try to conduct so in the future, as to shew my sincerity and duty as a good citizen, in support of the laws and government of the United States."[6]

To help his case, Fairbanks had asked Fisher Ames to serve as his counsel. Though Ames declined, he did appear as a witness on Fairbanks's behalf—one Dedham townsman to another. "His character, I really think has not been blemished in private life, and I do not know that he is less a man of integrity and benevolence than others," Ames told the court, adding that Fairbanks had served as a town selectman, and was known as a respectable citizen with "a family and a good estate."[7]

Ames attributed Fairbanks's misjudgment to a quick temper and the narcotic influence of dangerous minds. "He is a man of rather a warm and irritable temperament, too credulous and too sudden in his impressions; and, unfortunately, the scene he lives in and the persons in whom he misplaced his confidence, has exposed him, and many others like him, *to delusion*, and in consequence to *guilt*," Ames said. "Such bold falsehoods, and such artful and inflammatory sophistry as that wandering apostle of sedition disseminated for many weeks, no doubt misled many pretty well informed and well disposed citizens in that quarter."[8]

Judge Chase was duly impressed by Fairbanks's apology and Ames's appeal. "One object of punishment, *reformation*," had been accomplished, he said. Chase sentenced Fairbanks to six hours in prison and a fine of five dollars, plus court costs.[9] It was to be the single lightest sentence handed down to any of the Sedition Act defendants. Chase urged critics of the law to take note of the court's leniency. The decision proved that "The Government of the United States was not, as they might have conceived, arbitrary and unfeeling, but mild, dispassionate, and considerate, and exercised its authority with humane and liberal views."[10]

Now it was David Brown's turn to face justice. He appeared before the court on June 8, a day after Fairbanks. After three lonely months in his Salem jail cell, he, too, was having second thoughts. Perhaps encouraged by the leniency shown to Fairbanks, Brown pleaded guilty. But this "wandering apostle of sedition" could expect no warm character references from Fisher Ames, nor mercy from Judge Chase.

Chase had once been a rebel, a revolutionary, and a radical for freedom. Born in Maryland in 1741, he had by 1765 joined the Sons of Liberty, inciting mobs to destroy British buildings in protest of the Stamp Act. In March 1776 he risked hanging for treason by joining Benjamin Franklin and Charles Carroll on a mission to Canada to try to persuade Canadians to join the struggle for independence. A few months later, in July, he compounded his risk by affixing his signature to the Declaration of Independence.[11]

In the early days of independence, Chase was an ardent Anti-Federalist, arguing against the Constitution and for states' rights. But under the new government Chase had undergone a change. A series of government positions culminated in an appointment by President Washington to the Supreme Court in 1796. By the time he stared down at David Brown in Dedham, he was as fiery a Federalist as he had been a rebel. His ruddy complexion, which gave rise to the nickname "Old Bacon Face," intensified when he was angry.[12] He now viewed protest as a form of societal cancer, writing that "If a man attempts to destroy the confidence of the people in their officers, their supreme magistrate, and their legislature, he effectually saps the foundation of the government."[13]

While Fairbanks's light punishment was designed to symbolize the government's capacity to forgive, Judge Chase had clearly decided that David Brown would serve as an example to all seditious Republicans of the government's capacity for righteous wrath. There is no other way to explain the court's extraordinary next move. Chase allowed Brown to plead guilty, accepted the plea—and then insisted on trying the case anyway.

Chase wasn't about to let the prosecution's carefully assembled roster of witnesses go to waste. The evidence against Brown must be heard, he insisted, in order that "the degree of his guilt might be duly ascertained."[14]

The hapless defendant, without the benefit of counsel, watched as one chastened Dedham resident after another sheepishly took the stand, each adding a few more brushstrokes to the prosecution's portrait of sedition. Jeremiah Baker recalled hearing Brown preach about government fraud in public land sales. Amariah Chapin recalled painting the liberty pole sign at Brown's direction. Luther Ellis told of watching it go up on that October evening. Next, the prosecutor read a selection of Brown's "seditious writings," including his "A Dagger for Tyrants" that "contained the most virulent invective against the President and Government of the United States." Joseph Kingsbury admitted to hosting a gathering at his home, during which Brown had discussed Thomas Paine's *The Age of Reason*.[15]

During the Revolutionary War, Paine's *Common Sense* and *The Crisis* had captured in plain, emphatic prose the fighting spirit of the America cause. General Washington had sought out Paine as a friend and ally. On the eve of his triumphant crossing of the Delaware River and assault on Hessian troops at Trenton in December 1776, Washington revived the spirits of his shivering troops with Paine's immortal words, "These are the times that try men's souls."[16] In later years, though, Paine had supported the French Revolution and, in the wake of the Jay Treaty, attacked Washington's presidency. And now, the act of holding a discussion on the works of Thomas Paine became one more damning piece of evidence of sedition.

There was one Dedham witness who refused to take part in the circus. On June 8, after noting Brown's guilty plea in his diary, Nathaniel Ames added succinctly that he himself had "Rec'd two illegal summons to the High Fed Circ't Court."[17] It's unclear what, precisely, the prosecution hoped he would reveal, and the diary offers no clues. But clearly the doctor had more than a passing interest in the case and in David Brown—perhaps, as some have suggested, composing the offending words that appeared on the liberty pole.[18] Whether he hosted or attended any of Brown's appearances in town, or met privately with him, is unknown.

In any case, Nathaniel was made of sterner stuff than his fellow townsmen, and the prospect of being hauled into court to testify under the watchful eyes of his younger brother and Samuel Chase was more than he could bear. He ignored the summonses. The following October, Nathaniel would be arrested and brought before a Boston judge under charges of contempt for failing to appear. Apparently, nothing came of the charges.[19]

Nathaniel's refusal to testify was courageous, but could only have angered Fisher Ames and brought the weight of Samuel Chase's court down that much harder on Brown. With the testimony phase complete, Chase told Brown he could demonstrate the sincerity of his repentance by providing the court with names of everyone who had helped him in his "mischievous and dangerous pursuits," along with the names of all those who had subscribed to his pamphlets.

The following Monday, having been given several days to consider the gravity of his situation, Brown appeared again before Judge Chase. He apologized once more for his political opinions, "more especially in the way and manner I did utter them." He promised to reform his conduct. He knew he would serve time in prison, he said, and requested only that his punishment be in the form of jail rather than fines. After all, he was a poor man with no way to pay a fine from behind bars.

But there was one line that David Brown would not cross. He refused to name any of his associates or subscribers. Considering how many Dedham residents had testified against him, Brown's refusal seems all the more moving. He offered this simple explanation: "I shall lose all my friends."[20]

Unimpressed, Chase resolved to give the defendant a taste of justice that was anything but "mild, dispassionate, and considerate." The judge had seen "no satisfactory indication of a change of disposition, or amelioration of temper," and no reason to mitigate "the punishment which his very pernicious and dangerous practice demanded."

After handing down the most lenient sentence to Benjamin Fairbanks, Chase imposed on David Brown what would be the harshest punishment of any Sedition Act defendant: eighteen months in prison and a $480 fine.[21] Earning that sum would have been difficult or impossible even if Brown were free. In jail he would have no way of earning money. Since he could be held until making good on the fine, the eighteen-month sentence became merely a number—he would remain a guest of the federal government until the government decided to set him free.

# CHAPTER TWENTY-TWO

In the early years of the republic, while Americans fretted that their experiment in self-government was dissolving into chaos, rancor, and possible civil war, often the most steadfastly romantic believers in the promise of the United States were Europeans. To them, America's troubles seemed quaint and small and the physical space in which to roam indescribably large.

Today, the town of Northumberland emerges from the endless rolling hills of rural Pennsylvania like a mid-Atlantic Brigadoon, with neat blocks of brick and stone homes and parks nestled snugly into a fork of the Susquehanna River. The isolation is charming, but in the 1790s it was stark. Northumberland comprised just a hundred or so houses, most of them crudely built of logs rather than brick or stone. The town was more than one hundred miles west and north of Philadelphia, five arduous days of travel. Diversions were few and rudimentary, and even in the better of the town's two inns, rain seeped through gaps in the roof and drenched guests as they lay in bed.[1]

From this modest hamlet of rough-hewn buildings rose one house altogether out of place in its elegance, size, and craftsmanship. It was a white Georgian estate meticulously built not from logs but from thousands of straight boards painstakingly sawed and planed from local timber, then kiln dried in trenches for two weeks. The house, which gazed down on the North Branch of the Susquehanna, featured a spacious hallway, elegant dining room, and a library capable of holding hundreds of volumes devoted to science, theology, history, and politics. But the most important feature was the addition to the north side of the house: a spacious laboratory outfitted with the latest scientific equipment and two furnaces for conducting chemical experiments.[2]

The owner of this house was as unlikely to the location as the house itself. He was the famous English scientist Joseph Priestley, one of the most important thinkers of his age. A polymath on the scale of his close friend, the late Benjamin Franklin, Priestley had made major contributions to science, theology, and political theory in England—contributions that are still felt today. He was also a freethinker and a political and religious radical. When his views made him a pariah in his home country, he looked for the farthest place he could find from Europe's crowded cities, repressive monarchies, rigid class structures, and intellectual intolerance. He envisioned a sort of utopia for fellow European intellectuals on the run.

By all rights his native England should have lionized him. Born near Leeds, in West Yorkshire, Priestley is best known by the label "discoverer of oxygen."[3] In fact, he identified no fewer than ten distinct gases, but even that barely begins to describe his accomplishments. Experimenting with mice and mint plants in sealed glass containers, he was first to notice and describe the exchange of oxygen and carbon dioxide between plants and animals—the fundamental relationship for sustaining life on earth. His electrical experiments with oscillatory discharge were vital to the much later developments of radio and television. And the next time you crack open a soft drink, thank Joseph Priestley. Standing over steaming vats at the Jakes and Nell Brewery in Leeds, he found that plain water exposed to carbon dioxide developed a "delightful" fizz, leading the way for today's multibillion-dollar carbonated beverage industry. Priestley is even credited (though perhaps apocryphally) with noting how effectively the dried latex of certain South American plants rubbed away pencil markings, and giving the substance its everlasting name, "rubber."[4, 5]

Rare among scientists, Priestley shared with Franklin an ability to communicate engagingly with mass audiences. It may be said that in addition to all of his other accomplishments he was a principal founder of the field of science journalism. His *History and Present State of Electricity, with Original Experiments*, published in England in 1767 when he was thirty-four years old, helped popularize scientific discovery. Without Priestley's book, the world might never have known the iconic tale of Franklin flying his kite in a thunderstorm and harnessing electricity. Franklin had described the event to Priestley but never written about it himself.[6]

Had he confined himself to performing and writing about scientific experiments, Priestley might have lived comfortably amid his laboratory equipment and enhanced his legacy as a great English scientist. Yet for all of his breakthroughs, Priestley thought of himself first and foremost as a minister, theologian, and political philosopher. And it was his views in these areas, rather than his science, that made him one of England's most controversial figures. A religious freethinker, he espoused the supremacy of the material over the spiritual world. He and other materialists questioned the existence of souls and the divinity of Jesus Christ, whom they saw not as the Son of God but as a prophet.

In 1774, Priestley helped his friend Theophilus Lindsey found the Unitarian Church in England. At a time when religious dissenters (that is, anyone not a member of the Church of England) had only limited rights, and Catholics and Jews practically no rights at all, Priestley argued that members of all religions should be able to participate equally in the public life of England. He was fully aware how incendiary his comments were. He and other dissenters were, he wrote, "laying gunpowder, grain by grain, under the old building of error and suspicion." Powerful enemies in the religious establishment took to calling Priestley "Gunpowder Joe."[7]

He was just as strident in taking on entrenched political powers. Starting in the early 1770s, he began to see independence of the colonies as necessary for global freedom. His 1774 essay, "An Address to Protestant Dissenters of All Denominations," warning England of the dangers of trying to keep the colonies in chains, deeply angered conservatives. The essay had been published with the encourage-ment of Franklin, his philosophical as well as scientific compatriot. Priestley and Franklin met frequently in London coffeehouses until the time Franklin sailed home for Philadelphia in 1775. But Franklin was expected to hold these views; in England and on the Continent he was the rustic Yankee, the outsider, and he knew how to play the part well. Priestley, on the other hand, not only lacked Franklin's sense of humor and showmanship, but as an Englishman espousing such views he could be considered a traitor.[8]

Priestley's life in England grew precarious with his support of the French Revolution. In 1791, a group calling itself the Constitu-tional Society planned a dinner at a Birmingham hotel to celebrate the second anniversary of Bastille Day. A mob stormed the hotel, and then trashed the group's regular meetinghouse. Priestley hadn't attended the dinner. But as one of the groups more celebrated mem-bers, he was a natural target. The mob made its way to Priestley's home, Fair Hill, and burned it to the ground. Priestley and his wife, Mary, managed to escape, but Priestley lost most of his scientific equipment, rare tools, and, most precious, thousands of pages of writings.[9]

It was about then that Priestley began to imagine a settlement in the United States. In 1793 he sent two of his sons, as well as his friend and fellow radical Thomas Cooper, to scout likely locations. Cooper had good reasons of his own for wanting to put an ocean between himself and Europe. Born in 1759 into a prosperous fam-ily, Cooper, like Priestley, had a long history of rubbing those in power the wrong way. At Oxford University Cooper studied law, medicine, and philosophy, but was denied a degree for refusing to sign the Thirty-Nine Articles, the official doctrine of the Church of England—at least that's how Cooper's family explained things.[10]

Cooper believed that people act appropriately out of enlightened self-interest, and chafed at the idea of one person asserting authority over another. Influenced from a young age by the thinking of Priestley and other materialists, Cooper adhered to a rational, scientific approach to religion and rejected out of hand any aspect of Christianity that he considered mystical or opaque. He believed that everything from a tree crashing in the woods to the more psychic realms of human experience answered to physical, observable laws of nature. Like Priestley, he therefore believed it impossible for a human soul to exist after the body died. While he prudently accommodated a Supreme Being into his beliefs (the alternative could be hazardous), religion "probably meant very little to Thomas Cooper," his biographer observed. "The God he worshipped was Truth and his creed was Freedom."[11]

Like many intellectuals on both sides of the Atlantic, Cooper had been enthralled at first with the French Revolution. But a visit to France in 1792 gave him a firsthand view of "liberty by the bayonet" and "freedom by the guillotine."[12] Thus for Cooper, as for Priestley, America represented the last best hope for freethinkers.

In 1794, Priestley, his wife, and their grown children, as well as Cooper and his family, set off for their Pennsylvania paradise. Although the intellectual commune they envisioned founding there never panned out, Priestley, now in his early sixties, went about designing and building his fine home on the river.[13] He preached Unitarian principles to curious local residents, identified carbon monoxide as a distinct gas, and wrote a multivolume history of the Christian faith. Cooper took up editorship of a local newspaper, the *Sunbury and Northumberland Gazette*. In no time, these two men who had caused uproars everywhere they went would find themselves doing the same in the United States. Even from this remote outpost in the hills, they found their way into America's crisis of ideas, at the forefront of the battle over free speech.

Both Cooper and Priestley were dismayed by what they saw as Federalist attempts to impose the same sort of order and oppression on the United States that they themselves had come so far to get away from. Cooper could not resist weighing in on American politics. In England, Cooper had been, in addition to a political agitator, an industrialist with a fabric printing and dyeing company, a chemist, an attorney, and an aspiring physician. He was a man of striking physical appearance. According to his biographer, "It was said that he was less than five feet tall, and that his massive head dominated a tapering figure, making him look like nothing so much as a wedge with a head on it. Another way of saying that in him, the intellectual was supreme."[14]

When President Adams declared Thursday, April 25, as a "National Day of Humiliation, Fasting, and Prayer," businesses in Northumberland and elsewhere around the country dutifully shut down in observance. Where others saw a leader trying to unite a nation in uncontroversial thanks, Cooper the individualist and constitutional idealist saw a politician crossing the boundary separating church and state. Where in the Constitution, he asked, was the president granted authority to declare a day of fasting and prayer? A politician, he reasoned, should have no more power than any other citizen to declare a national day of fasting and prayer—less in fact, because when an elected official makes such declarations, "it has more than a semblance of uniting two subjects that ought never to be joined together, politics and religion."[15]

While the day of prayer irritated Cooper, he viewed the Sedition Act as a direct threat to the liberty of thought and expression that he had crossed an ocean to experience. It had been passed, he declared, "in defiance of the plain and obvious meaning of the words of the constitution." Not only did the Sedition Act open the door for any subsequent law that Congress might wish to pass in violation of the Constitution, it threatened the foundations of sound government by denying people "the right of investigating the characters of public men."

Yet to Cooper, freedom of speech had a deeper meaning and purpose than just ensuring open government. At stake was the right of each individual to his own life, to form his thoughts and express them as he pleased. The most insidious aspect of the Sedition Act, he believed, was its direct transferal of rights from the speaker or writer to a faceless, unaccountable mob. Cooper saw in the law an invitation to tyranny in which unaccountable ignorant men would pass judgment on "the most elegant writer." Cooper added, "They may find him guilty of what they cannot understand."[16]

It's no leap to suggest that Cooper had himself in mind when describing that unnamed writer of prose too refined and elegant for the rabble to comprehend. Never one to underestimate his own intellectual powers, Cooper moved through his combative life with the assumption that he was always the smartest man in the room. Self-confidence was his strongest asset but also his greatest liability, since he lacked any balancing humility. The closest he could come was a sort of studied, patronizing deference that seemed to say, *I sincerely apologize for the fact that you lack the intelligence to agree with me*. As off-putting as this may have been back in England, it would prove positively toxic to American ears. In any case, Cooper, who attracted controversy wherever he went, might have sensed that he would inevitably shift from being a Sedition Act critic to a defendant.

The catalyst was an article in the *Sunbury and Northumberland Gazette* of June 29, 1799. The article was, in fact, Cooper's swan song for his brief tenure as editor. After writing innocuously that he planned to fill up a few "vacant columns," Cooper launched into a detailed dismantling of the Adams presidency, accusing Adams of abusing his authority and seeking to impose tyranny on an unsuspecting nation.[17]

Without ever mentioning Adams by name, Cooper adopted the conceit of himself as a president bent on increasing his own power at the expense of the people. "My first business would be to undermine that Constitution, and render it useless, by claiming authority which, though not given by the express words of it, might be edged in under the cover of general expression or implied powers—by stretching the meaning of the words used to their utmost latitude,—by taking advantage of every ambiguity—and by quibbling upon distinctions to explain away the plain and obvious meaning."

Next, he would restrict the press, ignore the rights of man, advance tyranny and despotism, support large banks and merchants over farmers, build standing armies and navies to intimidate the people into submission, and engage in unnecessary wars—charges he believed fit Adams to a tee.

This article caught the eye of a Sunbury resident named Charles Hall. Adams had appointed Hall in 1797 to a position arbitrating disputes over British and American debts. As one of Timothy Pickering's trusted informers, Hall mailed the article to the secretary.[18] Pickering thanked Hall for exposing "Mr. Cooper's mischievous address." Pickering set out to punish both Cooper and Priestley, whose role in mentoring Cooper was "unpardonable." "I once thought of him as a persecuted Christian," Pickering wrote. "But I am now satisfied that ambition influences him." Pickering decided that deportation would be the best way to deal with Priestley, who had yet to apply for U.S. citizenship. Cooper was a different matter, since he had recently become an American citizen. To Pickering, such was a mere technicality; Cooper was still a foreigner "meddling with our government." The idea that becoming a citizen made Cooper an American had clearly not entered the secretary's mind.[19]

# CHAPTER TWENTY-THREE

Timothy Pickering could hardly wait to tell the president. And he could barely contain his own excitement. Thanks to Charles Hall, here was a real case—not some suspicious seamstress, German printer, or obscure hack, but one worthy of passing along directly to the commander in chief. Here were two of the most controversial agitators on the international stage—one a world-famous scientist and philosopher; the other a leading intellectual—practically hand delivered into their grasp. Pickering fired off a note to Adams marked "(Private)," describing the offending publication written by "a connection of Dr. Priestley." Like Priestley, Cooper was "a warm opposition man." Such characters, Pickering added, "will never be quiet under the freest government."[1]

Adams read Cooper's article and was incensed. "A meaner, a more artful, or a more malicious libel has not appeared," the president wrote to Pickering.[2] To Adams, the insult was personal as well as professional. As a younger man, Adams had deeply admired Priestley's political writings. When Priestley had first arrived in the United States several years earlier, the two had dined together in Philadelphia. At the outset of the Adams presidency in 1797, Priestley had written to him from Northumberland, in hopes of securing an appointment for Cooper as a claims agent, a government job helping negotiate disputes between American and British officials over debts—the job that ultimately went to Charles Hall.

Cooper had followed with a letter of his own, stating his qualifications. Both letters—particularly Cooper's—had irritated Adams. He never responded to what he viewed as a naked bid for patronage. Now, Adams was convinced that Cooper's criticisms of his presidency amounted to nothing more than spiteful revenge. Despite Pickering's urgings, he didn't have the heart to go after his old acquaintance Priestley. Describing Priestley as a harmless old man on the decline, Adams noted that the scientist's "influence is not an atom in the world." But Cooper was another story. "As far as it alludes to me I despise it," Adams wrote of Cooper's article. "But I have no doubt it is a libel against the whole government, and as such it ought to be prosecuted."[3]

First, though, Adams and Pickering would launch a counterassault in the court of public opinion. In October, the Federalist *Reading Advertiser* published an anonymous rebuttal to Cooper's article, detailing his earlier bid for the political appointment. Though the item was unsigned, Adams clearly had a personal hand in the process. Only Adams would have been able to describe how, after receiving it "with disdain," the president had thrown the letter on the table and said, "Does he think I would appoint any Englishman to that important office in preference to an American?"[4]

Cooper responded a few days later with a fresh pamphlet in his own defense. In the end, it was this pamphlet rather than his original article that formed the basis of the Sedition Act case against him. The pamphlet contained his original application letter, Priestley's letter, and a new essay even more vigorous than his previous article. Branding the anonymous *Reading Advertiser* correspondent a "cowardly propagator of anonymous falsehoods," Cooper claimed that his own article had been born not out of revenge fantasies but deep and sincere disappointment with Adams's record as president.

At the time he applied for the job, Cooper wrote, he had entertained high hopes for Adams. The president "had not yet sanctioned the abolition of trial by jury in the alien law, or entrenched his public character behind the legal barriers of the sedition law. *Nor were we yet saddled with the expence of a permanent navy, or threatened under his auspices with the existence of a standing army. Our credit was not yet reduced so low as to borrow money at 8 per cent in time of peace, while the unnecessary violence of official expressions might justly have provoked a war.*"

The reference to Adams dismantling the idea of trial by jury referred to a recent case in which the United States, bowing to diplomatic pressure, had turned an American sailor named Jonathan Robbins, accused of killing a British naval officer, over to British authorities.[5, 6]

William Rawle, Pennsylvania's U.S. attorney, sprung into action, ordering Cooper's arrest on November 2, 1799, as "a person of wicked and turbulent disposition."[7] Cooper was released on bail, after he and his attorney, Israel Israel, each posted $1,000 bond. The trial was set for the following April.

The Federalist press applauded Cooper's arrest and approaching trial. The *Philadelphia Gazette* called him a hypocrite for demanding protection for his own rights while denying the right of the government to protect itself from "the unbounded licentiousness of private citizens."[8] True freedom, the *Gazette* argued, comes from the security provided by a strong government. "If a state has a government and laws, every *citizen* is a *subject* of the Constitution and laws. There is no middle way . . . the *freedom of citizens* consists in *their subjugation* to the constitution and laws."

This article laid out with absolute clarity the dangers that Federalists perceived in allowing citizens to freely criticize those in power. Such freedoms place citizens above their rulers, the *Gazette* warned, an arrangement that "has made France, for ten years past, a great slaughter house of human victims—and which is upon the verge of commencing the same horrible scenes in this country."

Cooper had no intention of playing the meek or repentant defendant—something in this diminutive man relished the opportunity to stand up tall. It's not hard to see why Federalists found

Cooper infuriating, with his Oxford accent, polished rhetoric, and self-assured manner. The more Federalists got to know this imported expert, the less they liked him. To ensure his place at center stage, he decided to represent himself. His defense would be precise, logical, and impeccable—and only deepen Federalist determination to see him punished.

As Cooper set about preparing his defense for a trial scheduled for the next spring, the case of Luther Baldwin and his drunken joke was at long last to be resolved. Baldwin's day in court was set for October 1799—some fifteen months after he announced he didn't care if the ceremonial cannon fire hit John Adams in the rear end. But alas, Lucius Horatio Stockton, the prosecutor so eager to display his loyalty to the administration, would never get the show trial he clearly relished. Luther Baldwin had had enough. He reversed his original stance and pleaded guilty. The court fined him $150. His friend, Brown Clark, the one who had likely incited Baldwin's comment, did likewise and was fined $50.[9] There's no record of whether he or Clark spent any time in jail while coming up with the payment, but the total of $200 in fines collected from the two defendants cost the Federalists much more in terms of derision and abuse from the Republican press.

To Republicans, Baldwin's year-plus legal ordeal over a harmless remark harkened chillingly back to Old World lèse-majesté (injured majesty) laws that for centuries had dictated harsh punishment for any utterance thought to insult the dignity of a monarch. Years earlier, during the debates over the Constitution, opponents of the new national government had feared it would spawn a ruling elite, immune to criticism by a general population permitted only, in the words of one satirist, to "lick the feet of our well born masters."[10] With the persecution of Luther Baldwin, the king of England could take solace that the spirit of lèse-majesté had taken firm root in the United States, according to *Greenleaf's New York Journal*. As if to challenge that assumption, the article took its own swipe at the president's dignity, suggesting that not even the most partisan Republican would find much pleasure or gratification "in firing at such a disgusting target as the —— of J.A."[11]

For every Republican the Federalists arrested for sedition, it seemed, four or five were ready to take his place condemning the Adams administration and the Sedition Act. On October 16, Charles Holt, editor of the *New London Bee* in Connecticut, reprinted a widely disseminated article recounting the Baldwin case and pointing an accusatory finger at the tavern keeper John Burnet, who had shown such eagerness to see his fellow citizen charged: "Of what material must a man be composed, that will become a voluntary informer against another for a mere expression, drawn from him when in liquor, that did not injure any one's person or property . . ."[12]

In Philadelphia, a reinvigorated *Aurora* had resumed its place as the leading critic of the party in power. If Republicans of the period are to be believed, the campaign to silence Margaret Bache went all the way up to the intellectual leader of the Federalist party, the most forceful architect of centralized government and the Republicans' greatest enemy. A blunt letter from Philadelphia, an extract of which appeared in the *New York Argus* and other Republican papers around the country, directly accused Alexander Hamilton of being the mastermind of an elaborate scheme to silence the *Aurora*.[13]

According to the letter, Bache was offered $6,000 as a down payment for agreeing to stop publishing, with an additional sum to be paid when she formally gave up the paper. Bache "pointedly refused it, and declared she would not dishonor her husband's memory, nor her children's future by such baseness," the letter stated. If she decided to sell the *Aurora*, it would be to Republicans only. But what came next truly enraged Hamilton. The article hinted at two possible sources of money to meet Hamilton's nefarious aims: an unnamed group of "orderly federalists" bankrolling him, and "British secret service money."[14]

Hamilton, whatever his failings as a husband in the Reynolds affair, took his standing as an honest leader with the utmost seriousness. He fired off a letter to Josiah Ogden Hoffman, New York's attorney general, declaring himself the victim of "malignant calumnies," and demanding that the publishers of the *Argus* be brought to justice. Like Fisher Ames, John Adams, and others who responded to attacks by summoning the law, Hamilton claimed that personal honor had nothing to do with his desire to bring charges. "But public motives now compel me to a different conduct," he said. "The design of that faction to overturn our government, and with it the great pillars of social security and happiness, in this country, become every day more manifest."[15]

The attorney general dutifully targeted the *Argus* and its publisher for arrest. As with Margaret Bache and the *Aurora*, the publisher of the *Argus* was a woman, Anne Greenleaf, who had inherited the paper after her husband, editor Thomas Greenleaf, died of yellow fever. Eventually, Hoffman transferred the blame to Greenleaf's head pressman, David Frothingham. When Greenleaf and Frothingham argued that the offending letter, including the commentary linking Hamilton to British secret service money, had first appeared in a Boston newspaper, and merely been reprinted in the *Argus*, Hoffman was unmoved.[16] Because the state attorney general had no power to press charges regarding violation of federal law, Frothingham was charged under New York common law. The law made no exception for whether an item was published as an original or reprinted. Moreover, under the state law, more stringent than the federal Sedition Act, the truth or falsehood of the printed matter was not to enter into the case.[17]

The charges were that Frothingham acted "with a design to injure the fame and reputation of general Hamilton, and to expose him to public hatred and contempt, and to cause it to be believed, that he was hostile and opposed to the republican government of the United States."[18] Though Frothingham's defense attorney, B. Livingston, argued that Greenleaf, not Frothingham, should be the defendant, the cards were clearly stacked against Frothingham. Hamilton himself sat in the courtroom during the brief trial, and at one point testified in the case. The jury required just two hours to return a verdict of guilt. Frothingham was sentenced to four months in jail and fined $100.[19]

Although David Frothingham and the *Argus* weren't charged under the federal Sedition Act, the prosecution and conviction were directed at the same goal—silencing the voice of the opposition. Within months Greenleaf had sold the paper, and David Frothingham, once released from jail, was scarcely heard from again. Margaret Bache, William Duane, and the *Aurora* stuck by the *Argus* throughout its ordeal. When Hamilton testified, the *Aurora*, by way of needling the "*amorous*" general, expressed mock surprise at his testimony. "He was then asked whether he considered the *Aurora* as *hostile* to the government of the United States? And he replied in the *affirmative!*"[20]

Together, Duane and Margaret Bache held fast throughout the ordeal. It was perhaps only natural that in their joint effort to carry on Bache's traditions, the two would eventually become joined in the fullest sense. On June 28, 1800, a Saturday, Margaret Bache and William Duane were married by the Reverend Bishop White. The *Aurora* marked the occasion with a simple straightforward announcement two days after the fact. A few days later, the Federalist *Gazette of the United States* mocked the wedding with this bawdy observation: "Since the late auspicious nuptials of a happy Editor, his paper has been observed to be more than usually spiritless and vapid. A grave philosopher of my acquaintance supposes that those animal spirits which used to slash in petulance, aflame in anger, are now *flowing in a new channel!*"[21]

# CHAPTER TWENTY-FOUR

Federalists had set out to establish order and rid their country of the Republican menace. What they discovered instead was a remarkable facility for creating martyrs. With Matthew Lyon unshakably installed back in his congressional seat, Federalists set their sights on one of his defenders, Anthony Haswell of the *Vermont Gazette*. The charges stemmed from an advertisement Haswell had printed in his Bennington newspaper during Lyon's imprisonment in 1798, for a lottery to pay off Lyon's $1,000 fine.[1]

Marshals rousted Haswell from his home on a cold, rainy night and forced him to ride by horseback more than fifty miles to Rutland, where he was tossed into a cold prison cell to await formal charges. Haswell's jailer was the same notorious Jabez Fitch who had guarded Matthew Lyon. The lottery advertisement in Haswell's newspaper had pointed out Fitch's sadistic behavior, and now Fitch set out to prove Haswell correct. Deprived of heat and decent food, the inmate contracted a chronic illness that he claimed impaired his health for the rest of his life.[2] In the spring of 1800 he was convicted after a brief trial and sentenced to two months in jail and a $200 fine. Despite the short sentence, his sufferings were real. Poignantly, Haswell was unable to comfort or attend the funeral of his twelve-year-old daughter, Mary, who fell suddenly ill during his sentence and died.[3]

Haswell remained deeply bitter about the experience for the rest of his life. But news of his sufferings turned him from a journeyman printer into a state hero. The entire town of Bennington delayed celebrating the Fourth of July that year, pending Haswell's release from jail a few days later. When he arrived home the town erupted in raucous celebration of independence—the nation's and Anthony Haswell's.[4]

Thomas Cooper, likewise, found himself transformed through his ordeal from an annoying know-it-all into an "able and admirable" man who, one Republican editor predicted as the trial approached, "will pass through the fiery ordeal of persecution with the resolute spirit which has at different times rendered the persecuted asserters of civil rights, the saviours of freedom."[5]

Cooper had decided to represent himself. The case may have been stacked against him but at least he would go down fighting. Shortly before his trial began in Philadelphia on April 16, 1800, he requested that the court clerk issue subpoenas to Timothy Pickering, Jacob Wagner (a clerk in Pickering's office), and assorted members of Congress, plus one other witness: President John Adams. After all, Cooper reasoned, President Adams was responsible for leaking the contents of Cooper's 1797 job application to the Reading correspondent, which in turn prompted Cooper to write his offending pamphlet. How could Cooper hope to defend himself in court without the opportunity to examine a man so materially involved in the events?

On the opening day of his trial Cooper found himself face-to-face with Supreme Court justice Samuel Chase, the same hard-nosed judge who had presided over the liberty pole case of David Brown in Dedham. Cooper asked if his subpoenas had been served. No, the judge responded. The very idea of issuing a subpoena to the president of the United States was "very improper."[6]

Cooper countered that government officials, up to and including the president, are first and foremost citizens. "It is the duty of every good citizen for the furtherance of justice, to give his testimony when duly called upon for that purpose," he said. Having carefully examined the Constitution for any wording that specifically exempted the president from testifying in court, Cooper had found no such exemptions, he argued. If the prosecutor or judge "will be kind enough to point out any such exemption, I shall most willingly retract my error," he added sanctimoniously. Otherwise, "it is not in the power of this court" to create exemptions out of whole cloth.

It's hard to imagine any judge, let alone Samuel Chase, taking kindly to such a lecture in his own courtroom. Chase warned Cooper that he was only tolerating such nonsense because Cooper was representing himself; no actual attorney would be permitted to advance such foolishness. Did Cooper seriously intend to ask a sitting president to take the witness stand and defend his presidential decisions? "Sir, this cannot be permitted," Chase said, "and if you had been a lawyer you would not have made the request."

And Chase was surely correct. How could a president be expected to endure courtroom cross-examination and justify his policies before every private citizen who happened to question his wisdom and motives? Yet Chase was, in effect, making Cooper's larger point, exposing the capricious and absurd quality of the Sedition Act itself. For if the president could not be compelled to appear in court, how could any defendant accused of criticizing the president hope for a fair trial, having thus been denied the opportunity to face his accuser? Federalists claimed that the defendants were on trial for subverting *the government* (and by implication the American people) rather than for criticizing specific officials. But under the veneer in each case there lurked thin-skinned politicians using the coercive power of government to punish their critics. Judge Richard Peters, hearing the case alongside Chase refused likewise to summon Pickering or the members of Congress. "If the gentlemen will voluntarily appear, it is well," he said; "if not, we cannot compel them."

Because the Sedition Act highlighted truth as a defense, Cooper had also requested from Pickering and the president copies of presidential speeches and other documents that he believed would help him "prove" Adams's bungling performance in office. When Pickering claimed that he had none of the documents and Adams did not reply, Cooper had written to William Shaw, the president's nephew and private secretary. Shaw, too, declined to help.

"Under the circumstances I have related, I do not think it possible for me safely to go on, while the person who may fairly be considered in some degree as my prosecutor, holds in his possession the legal evidence on which I must rest my defence," Cooper told the court. He asked to delay the trial until he could procure the necessary documents on his own.

"You are mistaken in supposing the prosecutor of this indictment is the President of the United States. It is no such thing," Chase replied. Cooper's prosecutor was the United States. Chase also refused his request for an extension. In denying Cooper's right to gather evidence from his accusers, Chase cited a remarkable legal requirement that he seems to have invented out of whole cloth. Anyone criticizing a government official, Chase said, should anticipate being prosecuted for sedition and prepare a defense, including all documentary proof, before setting pen to paper. Gathering supporting evidence prior to writing is a basic part of responsible journalism. But here was Chase essentially arguing that the defendant had a legal responsibility to anticipate every conceivable objection—and, once charged, had no right to demand further evidence from his accusers, nor help from the court.

In his opening statement, prosecutor William Rawle invoked the now-familiar position that an attack on individual politicians was an attack on those who elected them—and, in turn, on the United States itself. Cooper, Rawle said, must be made an example of, so that others with a "tolerable facility at writing" would think twice before using their skills to destroy public confidence in the men whom the citizenry had chosen to represent them. Such writing stood "in direct opposition to the duties of a good citizen."

Cooper denied that his writings were malicious or seditious. "Have we advanced so far on the road to despotism in this republican country," he asked, "that we dare not say our President may be mistaken?" He added, "I know that in England the king can do no wrong, but I did not know till now that the President of the United States had the same attribute."

Stripped of his witnesses and documentation, Cooper argued as well as he could for the "truth" of his writings. Regarding his assertions that Adams had sought to build a standing army and navy, he said, "Is it necessary that I should enter into a detail of authorities to prove that the sun shines at noon day?"

For all of its buildup, the trial lasted less than a day and featured a lone witness, called by the prosecution. A Northumberland resident testified that Cooper had showed him the pamphlet shortly after publication, establishing a point that Cooper already acknowledged—he, and not someone else, had written the pamphlet. In the end, that was all the prosecutor felt he needed for conviction, and his summation was perfunctory. With a forceful character such as Samuel Chase on hand, the jurors didn't need the superfluous words of William Rawle in order to know what was expected of them. During his final instructions, Chase essentially commanded them to return a verdict of guilty.[7]

In order to be acquitted, Chase said, Cooper had to prove "to the marrow" that every line in his pamphlet was true. If he failed in even a single point, and the jurors believed that Cooper had malice in his heart, they must convict. The obedient jury retired and reappeared twenty minutes later with the verdict Chase sought.[8]

To set an appropriate fine, Chase asked Cooper to disclose his personal finances. When Cooper declined, Chase suggested that unnamed members of "the party" (i.e., Republicans) might be footing the bill. If so, Chase assured Cooper, the court would impose the maximum fine. An indignant Cooper replied that he had never stooped to being a "party writer," answering instead to his own conscience.[9]

The next day, Chase sentenced Cooper to a $400 fine and six months in prison, with the further command, as an inducement to "good behavior" in jail, that he post a surety of $1,000 for himself, plus two $500 sureties from others.

Federalist editors applauded the justice system for its wisdom, and the fairness it had showed to this "imported incendiary," as one editor described Cooper. "Every one is happy that we have courts which do justice on such culprits—and everyone must be convinced of the mildness and impartiality of that justice."[10] In the *Columbian Minerva* of Dedham, Massachusetts, a correspondent identified only as "Reflector" praised Chase's handling of the proceedings. Had Cooper faced a judge under similar charges in "his own country, chains and confinement would have been his lot for years to come. Happy country, where culprits can escape so well."[11]

# CHAPTER TWENTY-FIVE

Samuel Chase had no time to waste gloating over Thomas Cooper's conviction and imprisonment. Only two weeks after the end of that trial Chase traveled to Virginia intent on eliminating one of the most nagging of all the Republican voices, that of Scottish-born journalist James T. Callender. Callender had been a thorn in the side of Federalists virtually from the moment he arrived from Scotland. From the relative safety of Republican Richmond since 1798 he had continued to hurl invectives their way as editor of the *Richmond Examiner*.

Earlier in the year, Callender had collected and amplified his anti-Adams screeds into a book called *The Prospect Before Us*. From the very first sentence of his preface, Callender made no effort to hide his intentions: "The design of this book is to exhibit the multiplied corruptions of the Federal Government, and more especially the misconduct of the President, Mr. Adams."[1] Though Callender, at his best, could be a dogged and incisive reporter, *The Prospect Before Us* contains one over-the-top statement after another. Secretly funded and egged on by Thomas Jefferson, Callender seems to have emptied his notebooks of every vile thing he could think of in relation to the president.

Toss a dart just about anywhere in Callender's dense, 184-page treatise and you will strike something that could be framed as actionable under the language of the Sedition Act. Here, he lambasts Adams's December 1798 speech to Congress as "distinguished by vague and virulent invective against the republic."[2] There, he accuses Adams of padding the personal coffers of his son John Quincy Adams by sending him on successive missions to Europe on the taxpayers' tab.[3] Among the more irresponsible and unfair charges was Callender's claim that Adams desired not just a war with France, but a civil war within the United States.[4] Such assertions understandably infuriated Adams and his supporters. But, once again, Federalist overreaction helped create a martyr.

Chase would do more than just preside over the trial of James T. Callender; he was one of its chief orchestrators. Preparing for his trip to Richmond, he boasted to an acquaintance that he would "teach the people to distinguish between the liberty and licentiousness of the press." With the proper jury "of good and respectable men," Chase vowed that the court "would certainly punish Callender."[5]

The prosecution hinged on quotes from Callender's book that, while inflammatory, were no more or less outrageous than the sum of the document itself. He had written, for example, "The reign of Mr. Adams has been one continued tempest of malignant passions. As President, he has never opened his lips, or lifted his pen without threatening and scolding; the grand object of his administration has been to exasperate the rage of contending parties, to calumniate and destroy every man who differs from his opinions."[6] Adams was, in Callender's judgment, "a professed aristocrat" who "had proved faithful and serviceable to the British interest."

Whatever one thinks of Callender as a journalist and a man, it's hard to argue with his characterization of the Adams presidency as a "tempest of malignant passions." In three short years, the national government had sunk to the depths of partisan bickering and rancor. And while conflicting relations with the English and French made things endlessly difficult, there was no getting around the depressing fact that the rancor involved Americans against Americans. Just a decade earlier, George Washington had inaugurated his presidency on a promise of unified purpose. Citizens would express their preferences when voting, and, once they had made their choices, leaders would govern in the interest of all the people. Three years into the Adams presidency that vision seemed like a distant and hazy memory. Generations of historians have pointed to Adams's personal shortcomings—his thin skin, his quick temper, his inability to form strong alliances within his own party, let alone with opponents—and a cold, distant persona that meant as one historian noted, "he was not the kind of politician admired by the masses."[7]

Yet it's hard to imagine things turning out differently under anyone else. By the end of Washington's presidency the idea of national unity (at least the way Washington had envisioned it) was already crumbling; Washington was frequently despondent over the rivalries and bad blood flowing not just among the citizenry and in the press but in his own cabinet. Even an Adams hater such as Callender believed that Adams "only completed the sense of ignominy which Mr. Washington began." Washington's presumption that free people charged with governing themselves would do anything but bicker and fight and jockey for position had proven to be hopelessly flawed. Any man consigned to the thankless role of second president was doomed to preside over the expulsion of 3 million Americans from Eden. The mistake that Adams and Federalists made was not in the rancor itself, but in their response to it—their intransigence in the face of dissent and criticism. As they saw the vision of national unity on important issues slipping away, they held ever more furiously to the ideal.

On the journey south to Richmond by stage, Chase discussed Callender with a fellow passenger, a Virginian. Chase remarked, "It is a pity you have not hanged the rascal."[8] But if Samuel Chase was going to operate yet another sham sedition trial, he would not have the luxury of doing so against another hapless defendant piecing together his own case. Not here in Republican Virginia. That message came from the very top. Vice President Jefferson wrote to Virginia's governor, James Monroe, advising, "I think it essentially

just and necessary that Callender should be substantially defended."
Jefferson raised the possibility of public demonstrations against the
trial, and of private contributions to Callender's defense. He urged
Monroe, who would go on to become the nation's fifth president, to
whip up support for the defendant among state legislators.[9]

Jefferson had more than a passing interest in Callender's case
and *The Prospect Before Us*. In September 1799, Jefferson had sent the
author fifty dollars to help him complete the book—an act that, by
itself, could have exposed the vice president to charges of sedition.
After all, the law had declared it illegal even to "willingly assist or
aid" in the creation of seditious materials. Jefferson asked Callender
to send him two or three copies when it appeared, and more upon
request.[10] Callender frequently mailed Jefferson advance pages from
the book, as they were written. In October, when Callender apparently requested some research information, Jefferson responded with
a long letter containing his personal recollections of negotiations
with France dating to 1786, and observations about the electoral
voting system in various states.[11]

Jefferson didn't sign the letter, and his explanation speaks volumes about the tense, if not paranoid, tenor of the times, and what
he saw as the sensitive nature of his communications with Callender:
"You will know from whom this comes without a signature: the omis-
sion of which has rendered almost habitual with me by the curiosity
of the post offices. Indeed a period is now approaching during which
I shall discontinue writing letters as much as possible, knowing that
every snare will be used to get hold of what may be perverted in the
eyes of the public."[12]

As a Republican, Jefferson was virtually alone in the Adams
administration. Framers of the Sedition Act had conspicuously isolated
the vice president by omitting him from the list of governmental leaders whom it was illegal to criticize. If he was concerned enough about
his security to believe postal officials were opening his mail, it's fair to
wonder if Jefferson now feared becoming a target of the Sedition Act.

Federalists had already shown themselves willing to try and imprison a sitting member of Congress. Why not the vice president?

Whether Jefferson entertained such fears, he was clearly eager to see that Callender receive a vigorous defense. Indeed, Callender went to trial with by far the strongest defense team of any Sedition Act defendant. Philip N. Nicholas was the state's attorney general. William Wirt was the clerk to the Virginia House of Delegates. George Hay, the third and final member of the defense, was the Petersburg attorney who, as "Hortensius," had a year earlier attracted the attention of Jefferson and many others with his impassioned *Essay on the Liberty of the Press.*

The three attorneys had to know, given the wording of the act, the judicial tactics of Samuel Chase, and the likelihood of a jury stacked with Federalists, that they had little if any chance of winning. But they also recognized the opportunity to make a larger case against the Federalists and the Sedition Act. In a sense, they saw Chase as riding into their trap.

During the trial, prosecutor Thomas Nelson questioned why people would ever want to say mean things about someone else. He asked, "Cannot a good thing be said of one individual, without saying black and damnable things of another?"[13] It was a weak and silly platitude on which to rest a federal prosecution; then again, Nelson was under no pressure to make a coherent case. Callender was clearly the author of the book in question. In the view of Justice Chase, the burden lay on the defense to prove Callender's innocence by establishing that the opinions advanced therein were factually correct.

For the defense, Hay focused on Callender's assertion that Adams had exhibited a "continued tempest of malignant passions." Had Callender accused Adams of stealing horses, such might be easily proved or disproved, Hay asserted. "About evidence in a question of this sort, all men of common understanding would form the same opinion." But how could one prove or disprove that the president's "passions" were "malignant"? "The circumstances to which the writer might allude, and which satisfied his mind that Mr. Adams was intemperate and passionate, would only prove to a man of different political complexion, that he was under the influence of a patriotic, honest and virtuous sensibility."[14]

Taking a page from Thomas Cooper's defense strategy, Philip Nicholas called witnesses from among the highest ranks of the government, including Timothy Pickering, who had recently left his position as secretary of state, and Congressman William B. Giles. These witnesses, Nicholas asserted, were essential to corroborate Callender's assertion that Adams was a closet aristocrat. According to Nicholas, Adams had once told Giles that he "wished that the executive had power to control the public will."[15] But Giles refused to appear in court, and Chase refused to subpoena him.

Even when witnesses agreed to testify, Chase stalled and blocked. For example, Nicholas called Colonel John Taylor, a prominent Republican politician from Virginia and a close friend and political ally of Thomas Jefferson. Chase demanded that Nicholas submit his questions for Taylor first to the court, in writing. Improper questions might sway the jury, the judge explained.[16]

When Nicholas submitted the questions, Chase decreed that Taylor would not be permitted to testify, since Taylor would only be asked to corroborate some of Callender's statements about Adams, rather than all of them. A partial endorsement "would, by misleading the jury under such illegal testimony, destroy public treaties and public faith; and nothing would be more uncertain than law, were such an illegal excuse admitted in courts of law."[17]

Next, Chase declared that the jury would not have the right to decide whether the law under which the defendant was charged was just or unjust. William Wirt rose and addressed the jury, complaining that the defendant had been rushed into trial without sufficient time to prepare a defense. When Chase admonished Wirt not to reflect on the conduct of the court, Wirt replied wryly that he did not mean to comment on the court, but only to apologize for the weak defense that circumstances had forced him into presenting. He then asked the jury to consider whether the Sedition Act was a just or an unjust law. Chase countered that the jury had no right or power to judge the constitutionality of a law, only to judge the facts. Did the offending act occur or not?

Wirt argued that a jury deciding a murder case must be empowered to decide not just the facts of the case, but whether those facts amounted to a murder. In other words, mustn't that jury do more than simply agree on facts? Mustn't it also mull and sift those facts in order to decide whether the defendant has committed a punishable crime? When Chase conceded the point, Wirt pounced: "Since, then, the jury have a right to consider the law, and since the constitution is law, the conclusion is certainly syllogistic, that the jury have a right to consider the Constitution."

Now it was Samuel Chase's turn to squirm. He still controlled the courtroom, but his iron-fisted control of the debate was beginning to slip. He responded weakly, "A *non sequitur*, sir."[18]

Nicholas built on Wirt's constitutionality argument, saying, "[A] law contrary to the Constitution is void." He added, "I do not deny the right of the court to determine the law, but I deny the right of the court to control the jury . . ."[19]

Chase fell back on his narrow interpretation of the jury's role and its responsibility to convict unless Callender could systematically prove the validity of twenty separate seditious items in his book. "I cannot possibly believe that Congress intended, by the statute, to grant a right to a petit jury to declare a statute void," he said. "The man who maintains this position must have a most contemptible opinion of the understanding of that body; but I believe the defect lies with himself."[20]

It hardly mattered in the end whether this particular jury had the authority to question the constitutionality of the law. After just two hours it returned a guilty verdict. The court sentenced Callender to nine months in prison and a fine of $200.[21]

Callender was hauled off to the Richmond jail, where he lived in deplorable conditions. From his dank cell, the prisoner buoyed himself by working on volume two of *The Prospect Before Us*, and pouring his heart into letters to Thomas Jefferson, one of the few political figures he unabashedly admired. The letters, jaunty and spirited at first, grew more strained and urgent as the weeks dragged on. "In one end of the lower Story, the blacks are singing psalms," Callender wrote. "In the other, a boy, who has gone crazed, is shrieking in lunacy. The sailors laughing. *Sic transit mundus!*"[22] Brave vows of vengeance against Federalist enemies were intermixed with naked despair, made more poignant by his handwriting—small words conserving precious paper, sentences snaking around tears and splotches.

Most frustrating for Callender was Jefferson's perplexing silence. "For some time past, I have regularly sent you, as far as they were printed, the Sheets of the 2d volume of *The Prospect*, because I flattered myself that, although neither the Stile nor matter could be exactly conformable to your ideas, or taste, yet that upon the whole, they would not be disagreeable," he wrote. "Whether I was right or wrong, or whether indeed You received my letters, I do not know."[23]

# Chapter Twenty-Six

As resistance to the Sedition Act mounted, one of the principal Federalist justifications for oppressing opposition Republicans—fear of a full-scale war with France—was beginning to fade. Armed with three new, powerful frigates—the *Constitution*, *Constellation*, and *United States*—and a host of smaller ships, Americans were at last finding some parity on the high seas. They chased French privateers away from U.S. coastal waters and provided greater protection for merchant ships bound for the West Indies. Insurance rates began to return to affordable levels. A string of naval battles that came to be known as the Quasi-War gave the country a bona fide naval hero in the person of Thomas Truxton, commander of the *Constellation*. In a dramatic standoff in early 1799, Truxton had chased and ultimately captured a larger French frigate, the *Insurgente*.[1]

As vital as such victories were to U.S. maritime interests and American morale, a quasi-war was still a quasi-war, fought sporadically and distant from the daily experience of most U.S. citizens. With each passing month it became clearer that the French had too many troubles of their own—from containing rebellion in Saint-Domingue to fighting on multiple fronts in Europe—to be planning any invasions of the U.S. mainland. It was, practically speaking, impossible to maintain a nation on indefinite alert in the absence of a full-blown war.

John Adams ultimately brokered peace with France. It was perhaps his finest act of statesmanship and his greatest display of political
courage. While being goaded toward war by Federalist hawks, and
berated daily as a warmonger (and monarchist and British toady) by
the Republican press, Adams had walked the finest of lines. In 1799
he opened a clear path to peace by nominating William Vans Murray, the U.S. minister to The Hague, as minister plenipotentiary to
France.[2] The move, greeted cordially by France, opened the door to
a gradual warming of relations between the two countries and eased
fears of an imminent war. Murray, with two other Adams representatives—Oliver Ellsworth and William R. Davie—reached a peace
agreement with France. The agreement, known as the Convention
of 1800, called for "firm, inviolable, and universal peace" between the
countries, and for the return of confiscated property.[3]

By bringing the French threat to a close, the president ironically undermined the strength of his own party even as it made
the country safer and more secure. Federalist hardliners who had
been so cheered by Adams's provocative opening speech to Congress
in the spring of 1797 were appalled, none more so than Secretary
of State Pickering. Adams's diplomacy only confirmed Pickering's
worst fears—that the president was weak and incapable of leading
the country through crisis.

Republicans by contrast were happily surprised by Adams's
efforts, but none of this did anything to improve the president's
flagging prospects come his reelection bid in the fall of 1800. Everywhere there were rising signs of Republican popularity. In 1799,
Republican Thomas McKean had defeated a Federalist hardliner to
become governor of Pennsylvania. In the spring of 1800 Republicans captured the state legislature of New York, practically assuring,
because of the electoral system, that Adams would lose New York in
the coming presidential election.[4]

Adams and Pickering had never really liked or trusted each other.
Pickering felt Adams too insular and reliant on his own judgment

rather than the opinions of experts such as himself. Pickering had undermined Adams when he resisted appointing Hamilton second-in-command of the army under George Washington, and had openly advocated for hostilities against France.[5,6]

The breaking point came when Pickering, doubting Adams's ability to be reelected, began scheming for an alternate candidate.[7] When Adams got wind of this, he wrote to Pickering on May 10, 1800, asking for his resignation.[8] Pickering responded two days later, informing Adams that because of "several matters of importance" requiring his "diligent attention" he had no intention of doing so. Considering that Adams was his direct supervisor and had specifically asked him to leave, the response was not just arrogant but a direct challenge to the president's authority. To this he added a further insult: "I had, indeed, contemplated a continuance in office until the fourth of March next, when, if Mr. Jefferson were elected President (an event which, in your conversation with me last week, you considered as certain), I expected to go out, of course."[9]

After receiving Pickering's notice, Adams had no choice but to fire him, which he did the next day. When R. G. van Polanen, the U.S. minister from the short-lived Batavian Republic (the Netherlands) wrote Pickering a letter of sympathy, Pickering sniffed that he was in no need of consolation. Pickering attributed his dismissal to his own excessive honesty and candor. "I confess that the manifestation of villainy, whether private or public, has ever been wont to excite my indignation; and I am not used to conceal what I feel."[10]

With the removal of Pickering, the Federalist anti-sedition machine lost its most enthusiastic enforcer. It was about that time that William Rawle, the Federalist U.S. district attorney who had so eagerly done Pickering's bidding, resigned. In New York, the Republican *American Citizen* headlined its article about these developments "The Hydra Dying."[11] The Pickering episode only put more distance between Adams and the hard-line Federalists. Federalist newspapers mourned the loss of a man "whose firmness has withstood the storm which threatened for the last few years, to lay waste the fair inheritance of his countrymen."[12]

Republicans rejoiced. The *Aurora* noted, "If ever a man went out of a public station loaded with the universal execrations of an injured country, it is Mr. Timothy Pickering. He is an uncommon instance of the mischief that may be done in a country, even by small and contemptible talents and a narrow mind, when set on fire by malignity."[13] To the *New York Daily Advertiser*, the *Aurora*'s brazenness was disheartening evidence that Federalists were losing their fighting spirit: "How can a government expect to be permanent that has not the power of protecting its worthiest citizens from such villainous abuse as this"?[14]

The next fissure was more serious still, for it involved a clash of titans: Adams and Hamilton. The relationship had at the best of times been strained, but by the summer of 1800 any pretense of cordiality was gone. The two plainly detested each other.

In September 1800 Hamilton wrote a fifty-four-page pamphlet, *Letter from Alexander Hamilton, Concerning the Public Conduct and Character of John Adams, Esq. President of the United States.* When he imprudently mailed the document to some two hundred prominent Federalists, the letter inevitably made its way into the Republican press, including the *Aurora* and other newspapers. The letter, which would ultimately help cripple Adams's reelection chances, aired all the dirty laundry between the two men, and then some. Much like Thomas Cooper, in his own pamphlet, Hamilton claimed to have been an admirer of the president at the outset of Adams's term. "My imagination had exalted him to a high eminence, as a man of patriotic, bold, profound, and comprehensive mind." But his vanity, anger, and lack of judgment (or so Hamilton believed) had helped convince Hamilton of Adams's "unfitness for the station" of president.[15]

Toward the end of his rambling letter, which described the president as vain and prone to ignoring the advice of those around him, Hamilton wrote, "Mr. Adams has committed some positive and serious errors of Administration." Adams was, Hamilton averred, a man prone to "ill humors and jealousies" that had divided and alienated his supporters and emboldened his enemies. Under such continuing maladministration, the entire government might "totter, if not fall."[16]

In tone, malice, and tendency to undermine the president and his ability to function in office, Hamilton's letter was at least as strident as the writings for which Sedition Act defendants were being hauled up on charges. And while Hamilton paid lip service to his intention to keep his letter out of the hands of Republicans who might use it to damage the president, the fact that he had the document printed and sent it to some two hundred Federalists virtually assured it would quickly reach a mass audience.

From the confines of his Philadelphia jail cell, Thomas Cooper recognized the publicity value to be had from this internal Federalist struggle. Cooper had continued to speak out from prison. His account of his trial, to this day the most complete record, appeared in mid-May. The sixty-four-page booklet, *An Account of the Trial of Thomas Cooper, of Northumberland*, was painstakingly re-created from shorthand notes taken by an unnamed recorder, with a preface, notes, and appendix provided by Cooper.[17] By May 15 the *Aurora* was advertising copies at twenty-five cents each, available at its Philadelphia offices.[18]

Some of Cooper's Northumberland neighbors, including Federalists, organized a petition for a pardon. In a letter to the *Aurora*, republished in other newspapers, Cooper responded that, as happy as he would be to leave his prison cell, he had no intention of accepting forgiveness for pretended crimes. "I am of the opinion with Mr. Adams that 'repentance should precede forgiveness,'" Cooper wrote in reference to Adams's earlier refusal to pardon an unrepentant Matthew Lyon. But Cooper believed that it was Adams who must apologize. "And until I receive myself, and hear that Dr. Priestley has received a satisfactory acknowledgment from Mr. Adams of the impropriety of his conduct to us, I may be turned out from hence, but I will not leave the place under the acceptance of a favor from President Adams."[19]

Although Adams had never and would never pardon a Sedition Act defendant, Republican editors preemptively ridiculed the very idea. "It is too late—it is forever too late," wrote one. "The whig [i.e., patriotic] spirit is roused to action, and when roused it never has, it never will fail to accomplish its object . . . We hope it will not be many months before Mr. Adams will retire."[20]

While Cooper put a brave face on his imprisonment, his inability to practice law or teach for six months put his wife and children in financial straits. In Richmond, Virginia, printer Meriwether Jones solicited donations for the Coopers. "The family of this gentleman relied upon his industry for their support; and at this fatal moment, while his children may be wounding the feelings of a distressed mother for their daily bread, his body is immured in the cell of some gloomy jail," Jones wrote in an article that was republished around the country. The printer promised to collect any contributions sent to Richmond, and forward them to Cooper and his family.[21]

Jones, as it turned out, was not overstating the difficulties the "distressed mother," Cooper's wife, faced with her husband in jail. Sometime not long before Cooper's release from prison on October 8, 1800, she died. History does not record the circumstances or cause, so it is impossible to know to what extent the stresses on holding her family together hastened her demise. Yet what is undeniable is that when she died, her husband of twenty-one years, for the crime of using his First Amendment right to criticize the president of the United States, was unable to be by her side.[22]

Cooper emerged from prison as belligerent and as convinced of the rightness of his positions as ever. His logician's mind enabled him to find and exploit inconsistencies in his enemies and to turn their own words against them. In the weeks after his release, infighting in the ranks of the Federalists gave him the perfect opportunity to drive a wedge within the party in power and demonstrate his conviction, in no uncertain terms, that the Sedition Act was at heart a political law rather than a necessary measure to protect the public. By the end of October, Cooper was on his way to New York City to drum up sedition charges against Alexander Hamilton. If Cooper could be found guilty of seditious written attacks on the president, why not Hamilton?[23]

Cooper personally visited Hamilton's home, intent on asking if he had, in fact, written the anti-Adams screed that bore his name. It was the same standard of guilt that Chase and other judges had applied to the Sedition Act defendants, which is to say: proof of authorship was proof of guilt. Discovering that Hamilton was in Albany at the time, Cooper sent him a letter the next day, by stage. Having suffered prison time and a fine for sedition, Cooper wrote, he was curious to find out whether the law applied equally to Federalists such as Hamilton, whose own writings about Adams were at least as disparaging about the president, and almost certainly more damaging. "I therefore have determined that in one way or other you shall be brought before the public on this account," Cooper wrote.[24]

Hamilton ignored Cooper's letter, and no prosecutor in the land was going to haul the chief architect of the Federalist party into court. The Federalist *New York Gazette* ridiculed the effort, saying Cooper "has an experimental knowledge of the nature of the sedition act, and would willingly see it put in force against one of the best friends of the government."[25] But Cooper had logic on his side if nothing else. During his visit to New York, Cooper was feted at a hotel dinner by a meeting of Republicans. They hailed him as "the conspicuous victim of the sedition law, the friend of science, and the able advocate of universal liberty."[26]

# Chapter Twenty-Seven

The presidential election of 1800 was the first that officially recognized party politics not as an aberration to be blotted out, but as a reality to be reckoned with and accommodated—a tacit admission that a free country is also by definition a fractious one. Republicans still believed Federalists were royalists trying to sell the country to the British; Federalists still believed Republicans were Jacobin traitors. But by now fewer people were suggesting that their political opponents could be legislated out of existence, or their critics thrown in jail.

The campaign lasted for months. Jefferson won the popular vote over Adams and Charles Pinckney by 61.3 percent to 38.7 percent.[1] Yet because of peculiarities of the electoral system, Jefferson and Aaron Burr wound up tied with 73 electoral votes apiece (Adams and Pinckney finished with 65 and 64, respectively, while John Jay garnered 1). The House of Representatives was charged with breaking the tie. Each of the sixteen states had a single vote, with nine needed to name the next president. The tension dragged on through thirty-five ballots as Federalists, determined to stall the Republican victory, insisted on supporting Burr over Jefferson.

Alexander Hamilton, who hated Jefferson but hated Aaron Burr even more, used his political capital to help sway the vote toward Jefferson.[2] Burr's fury at Hamilton's actions would help incite their fatal duel four years later. On February 17, 1801, on the thirty-sixth ballot, two states switched their votes. One was Vermont. Through the previous thirty-five ballots, the state had split its one vote, with Lyon supporting Jefferson, and Morris, the Federalist representative from the eastern side of the mountains, stubbornly pushing for Burr. On the thirty-sixth vote, Morris at last withdrew, and Lyon tipped Vermont (and thus the presidency) to Jefferson.[3]

In the same election season, Republicans swept to victory in the House and the Senate, capping a sweeping reversal in power from which the Federalist party would never recover.

The election left John Adams bitter at everybody. Federalists, Republicans, and the whole world had seemed to conspire against him. He was in no mood to forgive and forget his enemies, including those who were still behind bars under the Sedition Act. James T. Callender remained locked up in his cell in Richmond throughout the election season. So, too, did David Brown, the longest-serving prisoner of all, the forgotten and powerless wanderer who had offended the wrong Federalist in Dedham, Massachusetts.

Brown's sentence ran out in December 1800, but that didn't make him a free man. There was still the matter of his $480 fine, which he had no way to repay from his jail cell. He had applied to President Adams for a pardon in July 1800. Adams denied the request. Now, with his sentence expired, Brown continued to stew in jail for want of $480. In February 1801, he again applied to Adams. Counting the time he spent in jail before his trial, he had been incarcerated for a month shy of two years. He explained to Adams that since he had no way to pay off the fine in jail, he might never be released. Adams, with just a few weeks left as president, again refused.[4]

It was about that time, in early 1801, that Adams delivered a parting shot to President-elect Jefferson with a slew of last-minute appointments for government positions, including sixteen judges to federal courts. These "midnight judges" were Federalists and no friends of Jefferson. Historians debate whether Adams's appointments were the actions of an embittered man desperate to make life difficult for his foe, or natural and prudent steps by a principled man to fill important posts while he still had the chance. No doubt, there is an element of truth to both assessments, and some of Adams's choices, such as John Marshall as chief justice of the Supreme Court, were inspired.

But the moves, hastily approved by a lame-duck Federalist Senate, infuriated Republicans and Jefferson in particular. It was, he later told Abigail Adams, the one action in their long, complex relationship at which he took deep offense. "I did consider his last appointments to office as personally unkind," he wrote. "They were from among my most ardent political enemies, from whom no faithful co-operation could ever be expected . . ."[5]

Overshadowed by those famous judicial appointments was a series of last-minute military and political appointments. Adams used his final days to name a surgeon's mate for the First Regiment of Infantry, a collector of the port for Bristol, Rhode Island, and register of wills for Alexandria, Virginia. While patronage appointments certainly didn't begin or end with John Adams, one of these in particular raised a fury, as smelling of direct quid pro quo for one of the more contemptible characters of the Sedition Act.

On January 14, 1801, Adams sent the following letter to the senate:

> *Gentleman of the Senate:*
>
> I nominate Lucius Horatio Stockton, Esq. of New Jersey, to be Secretary of War, in the place of the Hon. Samuel Dexter, promoted to be Secretary of the Treasury.[6]

In a little more than two years as U.S. attorney for New Jersey, Stockton, still in his midthirties, had hardly distinguished himself as a major figure on the American stage, or one for whom the next logical step was high national office. But in one way that seems to have mattered to John Adams, he had demonstrated his fealty to the president and to the Federalist party. It was Stockton who had pursued the case against Luther Baldwin for his drunken joke about ceremonial cannon fire.

The image that Adams himself would carefully promote, of the reluctant onlooker to Sedition Act prosecutions, is belied by a maneuver so brazen that even the lame-duck Federalist Senate questioned it, despite having dutifully rushed through so many of Adams's other last-minute appointments. Senator Gouverneur Morris, a New York Federalist who had signed the Articles of Confederation in 1778, served in the Continental Congress, and helped frame the Constitution, reportedly exclaimed in dismay, "O Lord! O! Lord! O Lord!," when he learned of Stockton's nomination.[7]

Republican editors ridiculed the nomination, predicting that Stockton, if confirmed, would soon be fired by incoming President Jefferson.[8] But it never came to that. Within two days the Senate moved to indefinitely postpone any consideration of Stockton's nomination.[9] Shortly thereafter, Stockton asked Adams to withdraw his name.[10]

The Republican press would hound Stockton for years with the charge that he was little more than a Sedition Act hatchet man for Adams. By 1802, the *American Citizen* of New York had forgotten the office Stockton was nominated for, but not the reason. "Luther Baldwin was found guilty of the singular but dreadful charge; fined and imprisoned. And Lucius Horatio Stockton, for the zeal with which he managed the prosecution, was afterwards nominated by John Adams for the office of Secretary of State! . . . How shocking to humanity!!"[11] Two years later, the still-irate editors called the Stockton nomination "so outrageous an insult on all decency, that even Gouverneur Morris exclaimed against it."[12]

After the Stockton nomination collapsed, Adams followed on January 29 by placing in nomination a name even more odious to Republican ears: that of Roger Griswold, the Connecticut congressman who in 1797 had fought Matthew Lyon on the floor of Congress.[13] Though Griswold, like Stockton, requested that his name be withdrawn, Adams had made his point. It's hard to see the Griswold nomination as anything but a middle finger delivered to the outgoing president's bitterest foes, in particular, his most vocal congressional critic, Matthew Lyon. But Lyon, as it happens, was already planning an elaborate gesture of his own, one designed to ensure that he, rather than Adams, would have the last word.

On March 3, 1801, the Sedition Act quietly expired after two years, seven months, and seventeen days. The expiration had been written into the law when it was passed, to coincide with the last day of Adams's term in office, and the last day of sessions for the Sixth Congress. Incoming Republicans were content simply to let the measure die.

On the final day of the Federalist majority in Congress, Speaker Theodore Sedgwick led the House of Representatives through a flurry of bureaucratic resolutions involving stipends for the House clerk, the doorkeeper, and the sergeant at arms, and higher salaries for district judges. Members broke for dinner, then returned at 6 P.M. and worked into the night in an atmosphere of strained civility.

Not once did the momentous subject of the end of the Sedition Act arise.

But tensions simmered just below the surface, and could not in the end be contained. As the evening drew to a close, Federalists used their final majority vote in a resolution to thank Speaker Sedgwick for his services. Sedgwick, a hard-line Federalist from Massachusetts, had taken over as Speaker in 1799. A former senator, he had been among the eighteen who voted for the Sedition Act on July 4, 1798. Gabriel Christie, a Republican from Maryland, rose and announced that he would "not point out the improprieties in the conduct of the Speaker while in the Chair," except to vote against the thanks. The House erupted in angry voices until Sedgwick cried, "Order! Order!" In a narrow, partisan vote, the House approved the thanks. The House sent his final message to President Adams, a notice that they intended to adjourn. From the presidential residence, Adams sent his "wishes for the health and happiness of the members, and a pleasant journey on their return to their homes and families."[14]

The practical thing for Matthew Lyon to do at this point in his career was to luxuriate in victory. He had come through jail and not only been reelected, but cast the symbolic deciding vote in Congress that assured Thomas Jefferson's election as president. After half a century on earth, he could have eased into his role as elder statesman of Vermont and a powerful force in national government. He had transformed from a reviled outsider, suspect even in his own party, to a fixture, a symbol of strength and resilience. He had become an inevitable presence, even to his enemies. Matthew Lyon had won.

But something in him remained the rebellious pioneer. The western side of the Vermont mountains was becoming civilized, in spite of itself. New settlers brought churches, schools, and order. It was all becoming safe and pleasant and, perhaps, too much like the eastern side of the mountains. As he had as a young man in Connecticut, Lyon began looking for a new frontier.

While campaigning for Jefferson in the presidential election, Lyon had visited Andrew Jackson in Tennessee and marveled at the benevolent climate and wild spaces with nary a fence to be seen. "Your country is far superior to any I have ever seen and it has never been long out of my thought since I saw it," Lyon wrote to Jackson. "To enjoy the blessings of such a country, such a soil, and such a climate in a good neighborhood is what is most wished for by your Devoted friend."[15]

Lyon began wrapping up his business affairs in Vermont and selling his remaining mills in Fair Haven. He purchased nearly six thousand acres in Kentucky and mobilized family, friends, and workers for a massive trek southwest. He would, however, remain in office long enough to attend, in person, the Jefferson inauguration. Perhaps politics had lost its essential edge for him now that his enemies were in the minority.

In parting, Lyon could not resist sending a letter to his old foe, John Adams, conspicuously postmarked "City of Washington, 59 minutes before one, a.m. March 4, 1801." The timing was to pointedly note that, as of precisely one minute earlier, both he and the president had become mere citizens.

"Fellow Citizen," the letter began, "Four years ago this day, you became President of the United States, and I a Representative of the people in Congress . . ."

He bid the president "a hearty farewell," noting deliberately that while they both were retiring, Lyon was doing so "of my own accord." He was heading, he announced, "to the extreme western parts of the United States, where I had fixed myself an asylum from the persecutions of a party, the most base, cruel, assuming and faithless, that ever disgraced the councils of any nation. That party are now happily humbled in 'dust and ashes, before the indignant frowns of an injured country,' but their deeds never can be forgotten."[16]

Lyon savaged President Adams over taxes, the naval buildup, corrupt judges, and the supposed proliferation of "useless and expensive embassies." Yet he was only warming up to his inevitable discussion of the Sedition Act: "Perhaps in no one instance has our Constitution, our sacred bill of rights, been more shamefully, more barefacedly trampled on, than in the case of the passage of the bill called the Sedition Law," which Lyon described as Adams's "darling hobby horse." "By this law you expected to have all your follies, your absurdities, and your atrocities buried in oblivion. You thought by its terrors to shut the mouths of all but sycophants and flatterers, and to secure yourself in the Presidency at least; but how happily have you been disappointed,—the truth has issued from many a patriot pen and press,—and you have fallen, never, never to rise again."

# PART III

# THE FEVER BREAKS

# CHAPTER TWENTY-EIGHT

On March 4, 1801, Thomas Jefferson entered the expansive new Senate chamber in Washington, D.C., to take the oath of office. He was the first president to be inaugurated in the new capitol, located a little over a hundred miles from his Virginia hilltop home, Monticello. Chief Justice John Marshall, a Federalist and fellow Virginian, administered the oath. John Adams chose not to attend. With the oath complete, Jefferson turned to the audience of about one thousand, including members of Congress and guests. He began tenuously, with a perfunctory declamation of his small abilities, his unworthiness in the face of the momentous task ahead, and the help he would need from those in the audience in order to have any hope of success.[1] Jefferson did not enjoy public speaking and was by all accounts not very good at it. His voice was thin and wavering. Many of the guests struggled to make out his exact words.[2]

And yet the rest of his speech was a wonder. Two hundred and ten years later the words remain vibrant, optimistic, and young. For years, Federalists and Republicans alike had felt the republic to be on the verge of breaking apart. The rancor had been so strong, so angry, and so constant that many people doubted that the form of government laid out so recently in the Constitution could survive. It was not the Federalists' fault, per se. In a sense, they simply had the misfortune to be the first party in power. And, as such, they responded to criticism and opposition the way the powerful had throughout history—by vilifying it and doing everything in their power to stamp it out.

"We are all Republicans, we are all Federalists," Jefferson famously declared. But he was not, in the brittle Federalist fashion, calling for national unity around shared political views. In a more mature conception America was to be a nation unified by its disunity, a country that had been through fire and been tempered and proven strong enough to accommodate the seeming danger and disorder of clashing ideas. The speech contained no declarations of Republican victory or plan, nor any suggestion that, with the Federalists vanquished, the country could finally move forward in the correct, Republican way.

Just four years had passed between Washington's farewell address in 1797 and Jefferson's inaugural. But the leap forward spanned light-years. Washington's address, the heartfelt reflections of a man who had shepherded the infant country into and through its earliest days of independence, had warned against the overriding dangers of faction and argued for a country governed by wise leaders unified in their purpose, unified in their philosophy of government, disagreeing only on particularities of implementation. His farewell address resembled nothing so much as a world-weary lecture to wayward sons, from a loving father who had done everything he could but was losing hope that they would ever get along.[3]

Jefferson's speech, by contrast, implicitly recognized that the ideological struggles would continue as long as the nation continued, and that this was a good thing rather than bad. At the heart of this was the principle that free speech meant, perhaps most important, freedom for the other guy to speak. Jefferson even left room under that broad umbrella for true radicals. "If there be any among us who would wish to dissolve this Union or to change its republican form, let them stand undisturbed as monuments of the safety with which error of opinion may be tolerated where reason is left free to combat it," he said. Where others saw fractious, chaotic voices as cause for alarm, Jefferson found reassurance. "I believe this, on the contrary, the strongest Government on earth."

With subtle confidence he diminished Hamiltonian pessimism about the competency of average men. "Sometimes it is said that man cannot be trusted with the government of himself. Can he, then, be trusted with the government of others? Or have we found angels in the forms of kings to govern him? Let history answer this question."[4]

The election of 1800 is widely cited as one of the most crucial elections in American, if not world, history. That's true not so much because of the specific personalities involved but because it represented, for the first time, the peaceful, orderly transition of power from one political faction to another. After twelve years of Federalist authority, bitter rivals would occupy not just the presidential mansion but the majority of seats in the Senate and the House, without so much as a mob action or the firing of a musket. The people had spoken. Nobody was hanged, guillotined, or locked up in the dungeon. John Adams handed over the keys to the executive branch and rode off in "peace and retirement"—as the Dedham liberty pole had wished for—to his beloved farm in Massachusetts.

By the time the Sedition Act expired, the total number of men tried and convicted for speaking their minds amounted to fewer than a dozen. It's impossible to be precise, because court records and newspaper accounts are spotty and incomplete, and because there was disagreement even at the time whether certain defendants (such as Luther Baldwin) had been prosecuted under the Sedition Act or common law. In some ways, the greatest victims of the Sedition Act were the Federalists who had passed the law. Tossed from power in no small part because of mounting disgust over the law, they would never again hold a majority in any branch of the federal government. Within a few short years, the Federalist party would cease to exist.

As for the defendants themselves, it's true that their numbers were small and their punishments, in an age that gave the world the guillotine, were comparatively mild. But their sufferings had been real. Beyond the fines and prison sentences, they had suffered a fundamental violation of rights they had been told were unalienable. And through their sufferings they had helped the country find sure footing on the path to freedom.

David Brown, the man responsible for that liberty pole, was at last to become free. As one of his first acts as president, Jefferson issued a general pardon for any person who had been convicted under the Sedition Act. The pardon automatically freed the two prisoners who remained in jail: James T. Callender and David Brown.

Brown seems to have slipped back into an existence as unremarkable as his everyman name, uncelebrated, unheralded, unrecognized. It's unclear what he did after his jail term, how he lived, or where and when and how he died. We don't know whether he continued to agitate against Federalists, or turned his attention to the now-powerful Jefferson administration. Or perhaps he had tilted at enough windmills.

Brown's erstwhile tormenter, Fisher Ames, spent the remainder of his life convinced that the American experiment had failed and that the nation was doomed. Always a priggish moralist, he grew if anything more brittle over time, more unwaveringly certain that he and a shrinking handful of pious Federalists were all that stood between the republic and eternal damnation. Over the next several years, as his health steadily deteriorated, Ames continued to write regularly, primarily for the Boston newspapers. In 1805, the Corporation of Harvard College offered Ames the presidency of the college. Though still in his forties, he was forced to refuse because of declining health.[5]

Nathaniel Ames was elated by the rise of Jefferson and the triumph of the Republicans. But his elation was tempered and even. He remained a crotchety country doctor, faithfully recounting in his diary the endless change of seasons, gathering apples and winter pears in October, sleighing in January.[6] He praised Jefferson and wondered at the lingering resentments toward him and the Republicans in the remaining Federalist strongholds. Nathaniel recorded in minute detail medical conditions of countless patients, among them his brother, Fisher Ames. Throughout their bitter political and even personal differences, the bonds of brotherhood were never entirely broken. They seem to have maintained a sort of love or affection at some level. They were remarkably circumspect when it came to criticizing each other in public. And as Fisher's condition inevitably worsened, it was Nathaniel he turned to. As would Thomas Jefferson and John Adams eighteen years later, Fisher Ames left the world on the symbolic day of July 4, in 1808. Fisher died at 5 A.M. Even through Nathaniel's typically unsentimental writing it's impossible not to note a touch of emotion in his record for the day: "Fisher Ames my only Brother died this morn. at 5. Atrophy."[7]

The next day, when Fisher's Federalist colleagues convinced his wife to allow the body to be taken to Boston for a proper Federalist service, Nathaniel was incensed: "My Brother's body snatch'd by the Junto deluding the Widow to order the funeral at Boston!"[8]

A few days later, an article appeared in Boston's *Independent Chronicle*, assailing the move by the Federalists. Though the article contained no byline, historians have suggested the author was Nathaniel Ames. "Pageantry may answer the purposes of party; but when it is displayed to the outrage of every domestic sensibility, we pity those who sincerely mourn the loss of friends that they are made subservient to such cruel exhibitions."[9]

Nathaniel would continue his diary for another fourteen years. On July 21, 1822, he died of pneumonia at the age of eighty-two. The death warranted a rare obituary in the local newspaper, which usually noted deaths with a single line, but "Dr. Ames was not an ordinary man," the article acknowledged. In the end, the piece noted, Nathaniel Ames was driven by one overriding passion: "He always showed a strong predilection for that government which allows the greatest degree of popular freedom, and any unnecessary restraint and attack upon that, met in him a high spirited opposer."[10]

*    *    *

Luther Baldwin, the Sedition Act's unlikeliest hero, remained to Republicans a powerful rallying cry, a symbol of the dark days the nation had endured. Federalists, in full flight from responsibility for a law that had helped dismantle their party, insisted that Baldwin had been charged under common law rather than the Sedition Act. Alexander Hamilton's *Evening Post* noted with exasperation: "Luther Baldwin.—Once more, and for the last time, Luther Baldwin was not prosecuted under the Sedition Act."[11]

The after-the-fact claim was dubious. Stockton, the prosecutor, was a U.S. attorney, after all, and Baldwin's arrest and indictment had taken place during the heat of the Sedition Act. As one Republican editor noted, "It is immaterial to the victim, in what shape the *federalists* sent their destroying angel, whether as a wolf or a tiger . . . It is enough for us to state, that Luther Baldwin fell prey to federal wrath."[12]

It's too bad for Baldwin that he didn't experience his accidental celebrity a couple of centuries later. One can imagine him capitalizing in the twenty-first century with talk show appearances, his own reality show, and a line of bass fishing boats with logos featuring his name and a smoke-puffing cannon. But in the early eighteenth century, there was little to do when his case ended except return to what he knew best, the precarious rhythms of life and commerce on the water. In 1801 he narrowly escaped death when his sloop flipped over on a voyage between Governors Island and Staten Island in the chilly November waters of New York Harbor. Baldwin and his passengers clambered into the sloop's spare boat and made their way safely to shore.[13]

In the spring of 1804, he sailed his boat about 150 miles up the Hudson River to Albany on a lumber-buying expedition. He was fifty-two—an old man by the standards of the day. By the time his sloop docked in Albany he was feeling unwell. A few days into his trip, Baldwin was inspecting some timber stored on a boat. Walking the deck, he reached down to lift a low-hanging cable out of his way. As he lifted the cable over his head he felt something snap inside of him, according to a friend who was with him in Albany. Soon after he developed a bloody cough.

The friend summoned a physician, but Baldwin's condition deteriorated. A few days later he was taken from his boat to a nearby house. "I sat up with him," his friend said. "He got out of bed himself and got in again; and in half an hour after, was a corpse."[14] The cause of death, according to newspaper reports, was a burst blood vessel.

In its obituary, the *Aurora* could not resist one more dig at Adams, now more than three years into his post-presidency and retired to his farm in Quincy, Massachusetts. "This was the man," the *Aurora* noted of Baldwin, "whom Lucius Horatio Stockton of Jersey indicted for *wishing the wadding* of a gun had struck a little great man's posteriors."[15]

# Chapter Twenty-Nine

This is a story of freedom, not of heroes. Or, rather, the hero of this story is freedom. The supporting characters were a mixed lot. Raised to the level of martyrdom if not sainthood during their trials, they returned when the excitement was over to lives that were all too human. Some came to contradict the values for which they had suffered.

Of all the Sedition Act defendants, Thomas Cooper, with the possible exception of Matthew Lyon, went on to achieve the greatest renown and success. Somehow, the British intellectual, who had failed at business in his home country, failed as a newspaper editor in the United States, and seemed by his actions and demeanor bent on alienating as many of his adopted countrymen as possible, always managed to fail upward.

With the Republicans in power, Cooper rose to a level of high esteem in the now-dominant party, and in the country as a whole. He became an intimate of President Jefferson's. He served briefly as a judge in his adopted hometown of Northumberland, Pennsylvania, and then embarked on a university career that would enable him to combine his skills in science and politics. He served successively at Dickinson College in Pennsylvania (where he founded the chemistry department), the University of Pennsylvania, and the University of Virginia (where founder Thomas Jefferson secured him a position).

His final academic post would be South Carolina College (now the University of South Carolina).

Although he continued to beat the drums for free speech and religious expression, he became an ever deeper adherent of states' rights as reigning supreme over federal authority—a position that turned ugly on the issue of slavery. Cooper's concept of states' rights would lead him to adopt the doctrine of nullification, a form of passive resistance that became the lynchpin of the South's fight against the abolition of slavery.[1] Nullification held that states could simply ignore federal laws they deemed unconstitutional and in violation of their own rights—a point Jefferson had made, albeit in a different context, with his Kentucky Resolutions.

Cooper, who had criticized American slavery as a young man in England, and avoided slave states as possible homes when he first immigrated,[2] now became enamored of nineteenth-century Southern life and customs, and came to adopt a deep resentment of Northerners whom he saw as bent on destroying a precious way of life. In his zeal to protect states and the agrarian South, he ultimately came to see slavery not as a necessary evil, a regrettable institution without which the economy would collapse, but as a force for good. And he insisted that slaves were better treated in the United States than in most other countries, including those of Africa.[3]

His newfound views on race and slavery were more than just personally hypocritical; they were deeply damaging, because from his perch at the university, and because of his celebrated background, his outspoken views gave Southern slaveholders intellectual cover. His ideas, published in historical and political journals and republished in daily newspapers, were influential among Southern thinkers and gentry, who welcomed the opportunity to attach their own thinking to his. Cooper even bought slaves of his own, forever tarnishing that shining moment when he, as a victim of the Sedition Act, understood the essence of individual rights and fought to maintain them.[4]

When James Callender emerged from the Richmond jail in 1801, he must have imagined that he was at last embarking on a bright new phase of life. He expected to be greeted as a returning hero, one of a handful of brave souls who, in his own words, had "promoted the restoration of American liberty."[5] At the very least he expected a patronage job from a grateful President Jefferson, for all he had written and suffered to promote the Jeffersonian cause. The position as postmaster of Richmond carried with it a $1,500 stipend that would have relieved him for the first time in his life of the grinding poverty of journalism. And the position had a satisfying symbolic meaning, since Federalist postmasters had often used their positions to disrupt the spread of Republican newspapers distributed by mail.

Jefferson had been only too happy to have Callender's poison-tipped pen on his side when he was the challenger, the outsider to Adams's Federalist administration. But he was the president now, a man who in his inaugural address had declared, "We are all Republicans, we are all Federalists." For Jefferson, there was no advantage in appointing a ragged, unhinged alcoholic with a history of combativeness to a position requiring management skills and at least a modicum of diplomacy. Jefferson unceremoniously cut Callender, his half-mad Falstaff, loose.


When Callender's entreaties to Jefferson went unanswered, he traveled the hundred miles north of Richmond to press his case in Washington. Unable to arrange a face-to-face meeting, Callender did manage to call on Jefferson's secretary of state and close friend, James Madison. Madison let Callender down as gently as he could, but there were only so many ways to say nicely that Callender would get no appointment, as postmaster of Richmond or anything else. Madison noted in a letter to James Monroe after the meeting that Callender seemed "implacable" on the subject.[6] Jefferson later recalled, "I knew him to be totally unfit for it . . ." In a gesture that could only have deepened Callender's bitterness, Jefferson arranged to give Callender fifty dollars—the same amount he had once paid to keep the journalist writing his anti-Adams screeds.[7]

Callender stewed and boiled on the long ride back to Richmond. Though his disappointment was real, it's hard to imagine things turning out any other way for him. It was not in his makeup to become a loyal foot soldier of the party in power. He chafed at power, fought it, and was suspicious of those who had it. Jefferson's snub confirmed his suspicions, simmering since his days as a lowly clerk in Edinburgh, of the corrupting influence of power.

Primed for another righteous fight, Callender broke from his old newspaper, the *Richmond Examiner*, which had published so many of his attacks on Adams and defended him through his trial. He joined a moribund newspaper called the *Richmond Recorder*, and in no time he converted it into a fire-breathing anti-Republican sheet. Here in Jefferson's home state, Callender and the *Recorder* became one of the president's fiercest critics. Callender accused Jefferson of ingratitude to the souls who had suffered under the Sedition Act and helped secure for Jefferson the presidency and its "twenty-five thousand dollars *per annum*, for four years, to a person who was not, beforehand, overburdened with riches."[8]

In response to Callender's venom, Jefferson began to revise their mutual history, claiming he had supported Callender only as a charity case, in the same way that he supported many besieged Republican writers against Federalist tyranny. Furthermore, he declared Callender's writings about American politics useless and unenlightening. This directly contradicted Jefferson's earlier words of praise. "Such papers cannot fail to produce the best effect," Jefferson had written of Callender's *The Prospect Before Us*. "They inform the thinking part of the nation . . ."[9]

One by one, Callender's erstwhile Republican friends deserted him. The *Aurora*, once his champion, accused him of betraying the cause of liberty. Closer to home, Callender traded daily insults with the publishers of the *Examiner*, Meriwether and Skelton Jones, who until recently had hailed Callender as a martyr and a hero. Now, column after column was filled with vicious invective, much to the delight of the Richmond readership. To the Jones brothers, Callender's newspaper was "*The Recorder* of lies."[10]

But it was Callender's report in the *Recorder* on September 2, 1802, that would make Jefferson truly sorry he had ever known the man, generating a scandal that continues to make headlines today. The item, tucked discreetly on an inside page, began, "It is well known that the man, whom it delighteth the people to honor, keeps, and for many years has kept, as his concubine, one of his own slaves. Her name is Sally. The name of her eldest son is Tom. His features are said to bear a striking resemblance to those of the president himself."[11] With that, James Callender became the first journalist to accuse Jefferson directly of having carried on a sexual relationship with one of his slaves, Sally Hemings.

"By this wench Sally, our president has had several children. There is not an individual in the neighborhood of Charlottesville who does not believe this story, and not a few who know it," Callender wrote. He poked fun at Jefferson, whose *Notes on the State of Virginia* had described in great (and, to modern eyes, excruciating) detail what he saw as the inherent inferiority of slaves. "'Tis supposed that, at the time when Mr. Jefferson wrote so smartly concerning negroes, when he endeavoured so much to *belittle* the African race, he had no expectation that the chief magistrate of the United States was to be the ringleader in shewing that his opinion was erroneous; or that he should chuse an African flock whereupon he was to engraft his own descendants."

The story had previously been hinted at (though never explicitly) in Federalist newspapers. As a good Republican and a believer in Jefferson, Callender claimed, he had initially discounted such rumors. But mounting evidence had changed his mind. "The African Venus is said to officiate, as housekeeper at Monticello," Callender wrote. He added, "When Mr. Jefferson has read this article, he will find leisure to estimate how much has been lost or gained by so many unprovoked attacks upon J.T. Callender."

Jefferson never responded publicly to Callender's charges, but he was deeply stung. In a letter to Robert R. Livingston a month after the article appeared, he called Callender "a lying renegado from republicanism." The president noted with bitter satisfaction that Federalists had committed political suicide through "their own foolish acts, sedition laws, alien laws, taxes, extravagance & heresies . . . Callender, their new recruit, will do the same. Every decent man among them revolts at his filth . . ."[12]

With Jefferson facing reelection the following year, Callender predicted that the revelations would so shock political leaders and the voting public that the president would be tossed out of office. Indeed, subscriptions to the *Recorder* soared in the wake of such reports.[13] But so did the intensity of animosity against its editor. About three months after his Sally Hemings revelations, Callender was in a local store when he was struck from behind with a cane, opening a gash on his forehead. With blood streaming down his face, Callender managed to make out his attacker. It was George Hay, one of the three attorneys who had defended him in his Sedition Act trial. Hay, a friend and admirer of Jefferson's, had been incensed by Callender's attacks on the president. But there was a personal element as well: Callender had sharply criticized Hay in print.[14]

With his violent attack, Hay assaulted not just James Callender but his own principles. Recall that, in addition to defending Callender at trial, Hay had written eloquently about free speech in his *Essay on the Liberty of the Press*—especially on the need to protect the rights of those voicing noxious opinions. With Hay, as with so many others, the noble ideal of liberty had run headlong into the messiness of liberty played out in real life. Following the attack, Hay compounded his hypocrisy by suing in a Virginia court to have Callender restrained from printing any further critical comments about him. William

Duane of the *Aurora*, despite having lost all affection for Callender, warned that Hay's shortsightedness would only keep Callender in the public eye and endanger free speech. Hay's legal efforts fizzled.[15]

But Callender's internal battles in the end proved more formidable than any he waged against journalists or politicians. The part of him that was the soaring rhetorician, dogged reporter, and fearless defender of a free press could never overcome the darker, more self-destructive Callender, the one who poisoned every friendship and opportunity and seemed bent on proving to the world that he was, in John Fenno's unkind words, nothing more than "a dirty little toper." In the wee hours of July 17, 1803, Callender was spotted drunk and wandering the streets of Richmond near the James River. Later, local residents spotted the body of a man floating in three feet of water. They hauled him to shore and attempted to revive him, but they were too late. The coroner determined Callender had died of accidental drowning while drunk.[16]

# CHAPTER THIRTY

Considering the impact James Callender had in local and national politics, his obituaries in the Virginia press were subdued and understated. In the *Virginia Argus*, his death occasioned only a small notice at the bottom of page three, conspicuously below that for a local house painter named Simon Schultz. The Callender item noted: "Drowned, in James river, opposite this city, on Sunday last, where he went, it is supposed, for the purpose of bathing, JAMES THOMSON CALLENDER, for four or five years past an inhabitant of this city."[1] Another account said: "His remains were decently interred on the same evening, and on the day following the funeral rites were performed by the Rev. Mr. Blair."[2]

Owing to his many enemies and the lack of eyewitnesses, an air of mystery has always surrounded Callender's death. While it's not beyond imagination that one of his many enemies did him in, no evidence emerged to support the idea. At the *Richmond Examiner*, his friends turned mortal enemies Meriwether and Skelton Jones could not help suggesting, with barely concealed satisfaction, that the long list of those unable to abide James T. Callender had at last come to include Callender himself: "Our own opinion is, that Callender's drowning was not 'accidental' but *voluntary*."[3]

Callender was carried from the Richmond riverfront up a steep hill to a church cemetery resting at one of the highest points of the town. He was buried July 18, 1803, the day after his drowning.[4]

There was a nice symmetry to the burial place. Twenty-eight years earlier, in the church adjacent to the cemetery, Patrick Henry had famously stirred his fellow Virginians with the words, "I know not what course others may take; but as for me, give me liberty or give me death!" In death, Callender was free at last from the great torments that defined his life. His reporting was destined to live again, in what may go down as the political scandal with the longest gestation period in American history.

Although Federalist papers around the country reprinted Callender's accusations about Jefferson and Hemings, the nation responded with a collective shrug. Contrary to Callender's predictions, Jefferson not only won reelection in 1804 over Federalist challenger Charles Cotesworth Pinckney, but he did so by an electoral landslide of 162-14. Jefferson even captured such Federalist strongholds as New Hampshire, Massachusetts, and Rhode Island. Only Delaware and Connecticut held out for the Federalist ticket.[5]

For nearly two hundred years, Jefferson biographers and historians wrote off the Hemings story as the ramblings of a lying, bitter hack. When first making the allegations, Callender himself had accurately predicted the line that Jefferson's defenders would take: "Depend upon it, sir, the whole must be a lie. It cannot possibly be true. A thing so brutal, so disgraceful! A thing so foreign to Mr. Jefferson's character! The scoundrel [i.e., Callender] has been disappointed and affronted, you know, and this way, he seeks revenge."[6]

Among African Americans, stories of offspring from the Hemings-Jefferson relationship have had much stronger credibility. In 1873, James Madison Hemings, one of Sally's children, published an as-told-to memoir in a newspaper in Ohio, where he had settled as a carpenter and farmer after being freed by decree of Jefferson's will in 1826. In a long, dispassionate, and detailed account, Hemings described his mother's long-standing relationship, which started a few years after the death of Jefferson's wife, when Jefferson was serving in Paris as minister to France. (Sally Hemings was just sixteen years old; Jefferson forty-three). "During that time my mother became Mr. Jefferson's concubine . . . ," Hemings recalled. He later added, "Of my father, Thomas Jefferson, I knew more of his domestic than his public life during his life time."[7]

Through much of the twentieth century, Jefferson historians dismissed such claims as a bid by African Americans to bask in the reflected light of an iconic figure. "Passed down through generations the tale has acquired the garnishings of tongue and time," wrote historian Charles A. Jellison in 1959, "until today it boasts a gospel-like authority among Negro families who proudly claim the blood of the great Virginian in their veins."[8]

Then, in 1998, researchers used the emerging technology of DNA analysis to establish a firm Y chromosome link between the Jefferson and Hemings clans. Originally published in the journal *Nature*, the findings, using genetic material from descendants of Jefferson's uncle and of Hemings's son Eston, established with near certainty that some member of the Jefferson family had fathered Eston Hemings.[9]

The evidence doesn't prove conclusively that the third president was *the* Jefferson (dissenters point out the many possibilities for other males of the line to have connected with Sally Hemings). But the DNA, combined with the preponderance of other oral and documentary evidence going back to James T. Callender, was enough to convince the Thomas Jefferson Foundation at Monticello, Jefferson's Virginia estate. "TJF and most historians believe that, years after his wife's death, Thomas Jefferson was the father of the six children of Sally Hemings mentioned in Jefferson's records," the organization concluded.[10]

New books such as Jon Meacham's admiring biography *Thomas Jefferson: The Art of Power*, Henry Wiencek's critical *Master of the Mountain*, and Annette Gordon-Reed's *The Hemingses of Monticello*, attain a richer complexity and meaning by embracing the Hemings story and dealing openly with its implications, while still presenting

Jefferson as a figure worthy of our enduring fascination and respect. Callender has had no such luck.

In a book-length dissent from the presumption of a sexual relationship between Jefferson and Hemings, a group of Jefferson historians called the Scholars Commission in 2011 devoted an entire chapter to trashing Callender. It quoted several of his more prominent detractors and added its own colorful epithets: "self-confessed liar" and "an unprincipled drunkard and a vile racist."[11] What's truly remarkable about the chapter is its visceral anger, reading as though written to rebut a report delivered yesterday to millions on cable television rather than 210-plus years ago in a small-town newspaper. One imagines James Callender enjoying the knowledge that he can still arouse such fresh passions, and regretting only that he can't leap back into the fray.

There was another posthumous development in which Callender played a key role. On February 4, 1805, Supreme Court justice Samuel Chase, the Sedition Act's most notorious judge, sat down for another trial, this one his own. After debating through late November and early December, the Republican-led House of Representatives on December 4, 1804, approved eight articles of impeachment against Chase, five of them pertaining directly to Chase's behavior during Callender's sedition trial in Richmond.[12]

It's fair to ask why Republicans who had so come to loathe Callender during his life would go out of their way to avenge his honor in death. The answer lies not in latent regard for the journalist, but in the expert defense that his three high-powered attorneys had laid down in the trial four years earlier. The impeachment articles communicated little real concern for injustice done to the defendant. As always, it seemed, Callender was useful when he was useful and despised when he was not.

The Chase impeachment was more about the Republicans pressing for political advantage than concern over righting Sedition Act wrongs. The motivation can be found tucked away in the eighth and final article of impeachment, citing an "intemperate and inflammatory political harangue" that Chase had delivered in 1803 before a Baltimore grand jury.[13]

Republicans, including Jefferson, were still smoldering over Adams's "midnight judge" appointments, and the corresponding Judiciary Act, which had created a layer of Federalist judges across the states. Eager to best the one remaining branch of government still dominated by Federalists, the Republicans decided to go after the loudest and most brazen Federalist they could find. Chase's 1803 charge to the grand jury had held the stubborn Federalist line that the people were largely unfit to govern themselves, "for the bulk of mankind are governed by their passions and not by reason."[14]

With this and other politically charged observations, Chase "then and there, under pretence of exercising his judicial right to address the said Grand Jury . . . did, in a manner highly unwarrantable, endeavor to excite the odium of the said Grand Jury, and of the good people of Maryland, against the Government of the United States," the impeachment stated. For a Republican Congress that had stood enraptured while Thomas Jefferson declared, "We are all Republicans, we are all Federalists," the wording of the eighth article of impeachment, with its admonishments against exciting the people against their government, sounded ominously like the Federalists' Sedition Act. This wasn't a free speech case, precisely: the Republicans were challenging that Chase had stepped over the line of his authority in a speech delivered to a grand jury, thus abusing his power. Still, the article lent an undeniable political nature to the proceedings.

For precisely that reason, the ensuing trial never rose to become a debate of conscience, the sort of moral retrospective on free speech that the Sedition Act defendants deserved. The Chase trial evolved instead into another important lesson for the new country about the separation of powers. As a political case of two Republican branches of government (legislative and executive) going after a third (judicial), the case raised alarms about the ongoing stability of government. Chase would be acquitted, and that was a good thing, wrote Supreme Court chief justice William H. Rehnquist. "First, it assured the independence of federal judges from congressional oversight of the decisions they made in the cases that came before them. Second, by assuring that impeachment would not be used in the future as a method to remove members of the Supreme Court for their judicial opinions, it helped to safeguard the independence of that body."[15]

Still, there's irony in the fact that an important check on government power had to be established through the acquittal of a man such as Samuel Chase. One can't help but feel that Chase was impeached for the wrong reason. Nowhere in the two large volumes recounting the impeachment proceedings will one find the name of the most grievously wronged Sedition Act defendant of them all, David Brown,[16] the drifter guilty only of having strong opinions about his leaders, and for having the temerity to express them openly and persuade others to his way of thinking. Brown stood naked and defenseless before Chase's court in Massachusetts, pleaded guilty and threw himself upon the mercy of the court, only to endure the mockery of a phony trial. There's no escaping the image of a stern-faced Justice Chase bullying the defenseless defendant. For his conduct in that case, if for nothing else, Samuel Chase stands forever guilty of abusing his powers and corrupting justice.

Matthew Lyon pushed on westward, settling with his train of followers in an area of Kentucky along the Cumberland River, where he founded the town of Eddyville. Lyon's party included about seventy relatives and workers, including his wife, grown children, and skilled artisans. The party moved by covered wagon as far as Pittsburgh, and then by flatboats from the Ohio River to the Cumberland. Lyon had brought along his printing press and equipment from Fair Haven and, as he had in that town, quickly began making use of the natural resources that were abundant in the Kentucky wilderness. He built kilns, sawmills, limestone quarries, ironworks, and a tannery and leather works. He couldn't stay long out of politics, either. Within a year of his arrival, Lyon had been elected to the Kentucky legislature. In 1802 he was elected to the U.S. Congress once again.

Lyon would serve three terms, solidly representing his adopted state before retiring from politics for good in 1811. He would never create the sort of fireworks that he had as a young representative from Vermont. He remained an ally of President Jefferson. But what brought his Kentucky political career to an end was his staunch opposition to the War of 1812. However combative in his personal life, Lyon remained opposed throughout his life to wars and to the use of military power. His objection to the looming war put him into the camp of the Federalists with whom he had shared such an ongoing hatred for so many years. And it brought him to a breaking point with Jefferson and Madison; to Lyon, the Republican party had abandoned its ideals and become what it had once fought against.[17]

His Kentucky neighbors refused to reelect him to office in 1812. But that was just as well, for already Lyon was restlessly looking for new adventures. Perhaps even Kentucky was beginning to feel too contained. In 1820, President James Monroe appointed Lyon as U.S. factor to the Cherokee Indians, a position that entailed serving as the official trade liaison between the tribe and the government.[18] It was a position that Lyon might have administered from his home in Kentucky, which certainly would have made sense for a man now in his seventies. But Lyon had not yet lost his taste for adventure.

He made his way southwest to the Arkansas Territory. Lyon had once told President Madison that Indians had no more right to claim ownership of American land than did "the Bears and the Wolves"—an irony apparently missed by the man who had been called the wild Lyon of Vermont.[19] Yet when he actually met and began working with Cherokees, his mind changed. His biographer writes of Lyon attending a Cherokee dance and being moved by the common bonds between the cultures.

He was, appropriately, out in the wild when he died in 1822.

Lyon's son, Chittenden Lyon, named in honor of the former governor of Vermont, went on to be a fixture in Kentucky politics. A longtime member of the U.S. Congress, Chittenden Lyon would have the honor of having the Kentucky county where his father landed named Lyon County. Grandson Hylan B. Lyon would go on to become a general in the U.S. Army and a hero of the Civil War. Thus Matthew Lyon, in his own right and through family legacy, became a full force and product of the American dream. But nothing he or his descendants ever did could match the contribution he made by standing up to power and getting himself arrested and then reelected to Congress from jail, and helping to turn the tide away from the Sedition Act and toward freedom of speech.

In 1834, following a petition by Lyon's surviving children, the Twenty-third Congress passed a resolution fully exonerating its former member. "The committee are of the opinion, that the law above recited, was unconstitutional, null, and void, passed under a mistaken exercise of undelegated power," it stated. Returning the fines was a way for legislators "to place beyond question, doubt, or cavil, that mandate of the Constitution, prohibiting Congress from abridging the liberty of the press . . ."[20]

It was a lovely idea, that by the advanced year of 1834 lawmakers recognized "beyond question, doubt, or cavil" that freedom of the press was not to be abridged. Yet the human desire to shut other people up, and the conviction that opposing opinions are dangerous to society, would prove to be just as enduring. This had been the first great battle, but it would not be the last.

# PART IV

# THE PARCHMENT BARRIER

# CHAPTER THIRTY-ONE

Sedition laws are alive and well in the twenty-first century, though not in the United States. The Singapore Sedition Act outlaws "any act, speech, words, [and] publication" that may "excite disaffection against the Government" along with expressions promoting "feelings of ill-will and hostility between different races or classes."[1] A court in Thailand sentenced a Thai-born American to two and a half years in prison in 2011 for translating and publishing excerpts of a biography suggesting that King Bhumibol Adulyadej was a barrier to democracy. Even clicking "share" or "like" on an online item disrespectful to the Thai royal family may land a subject in jail.[2]

In Zimbabwe, a member of the Movement for Democratic Change nodded at a portrait of President Robert Mugabe in a court building and asked, a bit too jauntily, "How are you, Father? How is your health?" He was charged with insulting the president, carrying a maximum sentence of a year in jail.[3] A Moroccan court sentenced a twenty-four-year-old student to three years in prison for "violating the sacred values" of the kingdom after a video captured him insulting the king.[4] In 2012, three Vietnamese bloggers were charged with antigovernment propaganda for writings that, according to a state-run Vietnamese newspaper, "distorted and opposed the State."[5] And in China, citizens enjoying extraordinary new economic freedom have quickly learned those liberties do not extend to questioning government policies. One dissident was sentenced to ten years in prison in 2011 for "inciting subversion" through online essays. A year later, the government began requiring Internet users to register by name, and in 2013 a prominent Chinese American investor who had dared to speak out appeared in handcuffs on state-run television where he meekly confessed to having "contributed to an 'illegal and immoral' atmosphere on the Chinese internet," according to the *Financial Times*. Chinese authorities explained, "Acts of jeering and stirring up trouble easily lead to mass incidents and create grave upsets of public order."[6]

Elsewhere, rulers hand out harsh penalties to those who question state-approved religious orthodoxies. In 2012, an Iranian rapper based in Germany faced a potentially deadly fatwa under sharia law, issued by Iranian clerics for the crime of "blasphemous music."[7] A Saudi Arabian social media editor faced seven years in jail and six hundred lashes for "founding an Internet forum that violates Islamic values and propagates liberal thought."[8] In Turkey, often hailed by the West for its secular modernism, internationally celebrated pianist and composer Fazil Say committed the crime of criticizing the Islamic faith in a series of Twitter posts. A court sentenced him to ten months in prison.[9]

Few Western nations punish speech critical of politicians. But many have identified a new form of de facto sedition—speech that violates government-imposed standards of niceness and harmony. The European Union's Charter of Fundamental Rights proclaims, "Everyone has the right to freedom of expression."[10] Yet one European nation after another, whether EU member or not, has declared that official tolerance of speech takes a backseat to tolerance defined as the right of listeners and readers not to be offended. Denmark, for example, mandates up to two years in prison for public statements in which "a group of people are threatened, insulted or degraded on account of their race, color, national or ethnic origin, religion or sexual inclination."[11] In Finland, website operators may be committing a crime if they don't take down racist content posted on their sites.[12] Anyone who would make fun of a person for being blind is a boor, but is he also a criminal? Yes, say the Dutch, who include "physical, visual, or mental handicap" in the list of groups whom one may be fined or imprisoned for insulting.[13] And Iceland classifies a racist or homophobic insult or ridiculing remark as an "assault" punishable by up to two years in prison.[14]

"I love Hitler," a celebrated fashion designer announced in a bizarre, anti-Semitic rant in a Paris bar in 2011. He cruelly insinuated that the Nazis had gassed one patron's parents.[15] When an online video of the incident went viral, the designer's shocked employers quickly fired him. The man lost his private fashion label and the respect of his industry—and, one hastens to add, rightly so.[16] But making racist comments is also a crime in France. The man was tried and convicted of making "public insults based on origin, religious affiliation, race or ethnicity," which carries a maximum penalty of six months in prison and fines of up to 22,500 euros (the sentence was suspended).[17]

Even countries that Americans might assume to be close cousins on matters of individual rights have outlawed offending people's group identities. After a Canadian standup comic berated an audience member with crude remarks about her sexual orientation, the British Columbia Human Rights Tribunal conducted two years of hearings before slapping the comedian and the club owner with a total of $22,500 in fines for injuring the woman's "dignity, feelings and self-respect."[18] In Australia, a federal court ordered the *Herald Sun* newspaper to print apologies next to the work of a columnist who had mocked light-skinned "political Aborigines" as emphasizing Aboriginal ties because it seemed fashionable or for personal gain. When the case ended, a victorious plaintiff proclaimed to reporters that discussions of racial identity are permissible in Australia as long as they are "based on truth and fact" rather than malice.[19, 20] Which raises the very question that so vexed American Sedition Act defendants back in 1798: How do you prove the "truth and fact" of your opinions?

\*    \*    \*

None of these cases would have gotten far in the United States, where "We can denounce our rulers, and each other, with little fear of the consequences," wrote journalist and free speech champion Anthony Lewis.[21] The Canadian comic's insensitive treatment of an audience member has a well-known U.S. equivalent—*Seinfeld* veteran Michael Richards's tirade against an African American audience member in West Hollywood in 2006.[22] Public reaction to the admired comedian's racially charged outburst ranged from shock to sadness to outrage, and it did lasting damage to his career and public image—but nobody hauled him before a "human rights tribunal." The reason, of course, is that Americans are protected by the Bill of Rights. In the United States, as Lewis noted, "Hateful and shocking expression, political or artistic, is almost all free to enter the marketplace of ideas."[23]

More than 220 years after its adoption, the First Amendment continues to protect American rights with a strength, tenacity, and resilience that would have gratified and surprised its principal author. Though James Madison believed protecting free speech and other "rights of Conscience" to be the most vital function of government, he wondered in his gloomier moments whether a bill of rights set down on paper could long withstand the real-world desire of those in power to shut people up. Reflecting on bills of rights passed in Virginia and elsewhere, Madison wrote to Thomas Jefferson in 1788, "Repeated violations of these parchment barriers have been committed by overbearing majorities in every State."[24]

Yet this parchment barrier remains our indispensable tool for understanding our basic rights and for settling disputes in ways that preserve rather than destroy them. Though the Bill of Rights is sometimes characterized as being the source of our rights, Madison would have been the first to say that our rights don't come from that document, or from the minds of the Founders or any men. Central to the very idea of rights is that they are unalienable, an inherent part of being human. The best that a government created by people can do is to respect and defend those rights.

The Bill of Rights' first great accomplishment was to formally declare rights off-limits to government meddling. The second was to provide us, in a few simple words, with the means to determine when we've gone astray. Ernest Hemingway colorfully observed that any good writer needs a "built-in, shockproof, shit detector."[25] A nation needs the same thing—at least, a nation bold enough to dedicate itself to an ideal such as liberty. The Declaration of Independence is often described as our national mission statement, and the Constitution as our owner's manual. The Bill of Rights, then, is our "built-in, shockproof, shit detector," enabling us (compelling us) to identify and eliminate contradictions when some ambitious new law, however "well-meaning," seeks to advance this or that agenda at the expense of our liberties.

The detection process is not perfect, and correction can be agonizingly slow to materialize. At every phase of our history, some Americans have had their liberties violated in spite of the Bill of Rights. Even excluding the most obvious and shameful example of slavery, which denied a large segment of Americans of every conceivable right, the United States has failed specifically on the subject of free speech many times throughout its history.

Often, these failures have come during times of war, when the nation's survival seemed to be imperiled. The Civil War, World War I, and World War II each saw curtailments that strike us now as obviously wrong. An extreme example came in 1918, when a nation terrified of its foreign enemies and unmindful of its own history passed a new Sedition Act.

The Sedition Act of 1918 made it illegal to "willfully utter, print, write, or publish any disloyal, profane, scurrilous, or abusive language about the form of government of the United States."[26] This act and its forerunner, the Espionage Act of 1917, unleashed inquisitions reminiscent of 1798 and resulted in hundreds of arrests of citizens who dared to question U.S. foreign policy or even to criticize the government's handling of the war.

U.S. attorney general Thomas W. Gregory channeled the worst elements of John Adams's secretary of state, Timothy Pickering. Like Pickering, Gregory maintained a network of citizen informers around the country responsible for "keeping an eye on disloyal individuals and making reports of disloyal utterances."[27] U.S. postmaster general Albert Sidney Burleson suppressed suspect publications by refusing to mail them and by forcing foreign-language newspapers to submit English translations to authorities for prior review.[28] At the peak of hysteria, Socialist Party leader Eugene Debs was sentenced to ten years in prison under the Espionage Act merely for voicing his opinion in a speech that three fellow Socialists, themselves languishing in jail for assailing the draft, had been given a raw deal.[29]

Later, of course, fear of the Soviet Union and the spread of communism led to the abuses of the McCarthy era and the House Un-American Activities Committee. Thanks to the Bill of Rights, free speech has survived these and untold other efforts by political leaders bent on making the country better by silencing people whose opinions they don't like. The Sedition Act of 1798 may have been the first great test of whether the nation intended to live up to its ideal of liberty, but Americans continue to fight these battles every day.

For more than a decade, the country has been consumed with a fear that is to us today every bit as real and urgent as the fears of France and England that consumed Federalists and Republicans back in 1798. In the years since the September 11, 2001, terrorist attacks, with the looming threat of further attacks seemingly everywhere, we've been forced to live along that tense, uncertain border between protecting the immediate safety of our country and preserving the principles that make us who we are.

In April 2012, a twenty-nine-year-old American of Middle Eastern descent was sentenced to more than seventeen years in prison after being found guilty on several counts of supporting terrorists.[30] The defendant was not accused of actually participating in or funding actions against the United States, and had spoken out against attacks on civilians. Still, his statements in online chats, in speeches, and elsewhere were often deeply offensive (dead American troops in Iraq were "Texas BBQ"). Central to the prosecution's case was the defendant's translation of a text, written by a Saudi religious scholar, called "39 Ways to Serve and Participate in Jihad." "The act of translating this text is far from incitement to violent action," wrote Andrew March, an associate professor of political science at Yale, who testified on the defendant's behalf at his trial. He continued: "We have the resources to prevent acts of violence without threatening the First Amendment."[31] Nevertheless, a federal appeals court in late 2013 upheld the conviction.[32]

At the other end of the political spectrum, extremist voices spout venom aimed at Muslims. Consider the 2012 Koran burning by Florida pastor Terry Jones. Jones's hateful stunt offended any person of Islamic faith, and complicated the already hazardous and arduous jobs of American personnel serving in Afghanistan or Iraq. Prior to the burning, an exasperated Republican senator, Lindsey Graham, said, "I wish we could find a way to hold people accountable. Free speech is a great idea, but we're in a war."[33]

Graham is hardly alone. Across the spectrum of politics, society, and culture, there's no shortage of people who believe we'd be better off if we could only eliminate this or that dangerous, repellent voice; who believe, in other words, that free speech is a great idea—but.

To millions of Americans, the death of Osama bin Laden in 2011 at the hands of U.S. forces represented an appropriate end for an incalculably evil man. But to Noam Chomsky, the MIT linguist and prominent left-wing political activist, the killing represented an unjustified "assassination" of an "unarmed victim" who may have been innocent of the 9/11 atrocities, even though bin Laden himself claimed credit for them.[34] Whatever Chomsky hoped to accomplish, many believed the professor succeeded only in making himself look, as one article put it, "stupid and ignorant."[35] But does that mean Chomsky should be banned from teaching? A columnist in the *Wall Street Journal*, a paper that is usually a reliable defender of First Amendment rights, suggested as much by comparing Chomsky with German philosopher Martin Heidegger. Heidegger's Nazi sympathies prompted French occupation forces in postwar Germany to ban him from teaching for five years. With Chomsky in mind, the *Wall Street Journal* column pined for the days when "a self-confident West had no trouble demanding that Heidegger be banned."[36]

Conservative radio host Rush Limbaugh regularly infuriates as many if not more Americans on the Left than Noam Chomsky does those on the Right. His use of "slut" and "prostitute" to describe a young woman demanding that contraceptives be included in health care plans cost Limbaugh several high-profile sponsors and prompted a rare on-air apology. Not enough, said feminists Jane Fonda, Robin Morgan, and Gloria Steinem in an article the three cowrote. They demanded formal action from the Federal Communications Commission.[37] Limbaugh has "hidden behind the First Amendment" for too long, the authors wrote. Warning that "what's at stake is the fallout of a society tolerating toxic, hate-inciting speech," they claimed that free speech does not give Limbaugh a right to "the people's airways." The most notable aspect of the authors' demand that Limbaugh be silenced was the unacknowledged truth that all three had, in a different context and era, stood proudly upon their own First Amendment rights to express themselves in ways guaranteed to shock, outrage, and offend millions of Americans.

Meanwhile, in 2010 a Republican state senator in Michigan found his fifteen minutes of fame by proposing to register journalists through a new bureaucracy, the Board of Michigan Registered Reporters, asking journalists to provide evidence of good moral character, knowledge of industry ethics, and writing samples. "Legitimate media sources are critically important to our government," the politician explained.[38]

Thankfully, the parchment barrier has proved strong enough to withstand most such efforts. They collapse under the weight of those forceful words in the Bill of Rights that distinguish the United States from the rest of the world. Exceptionalism on individual rights has been a source of pride to generations of Americans, and a drawing card for millions of freedom-seeking immigrants. It's a quality that has made the United States proudly unique among nations, lending richness and resonance to phrases such as "land of liberty" and "let freedom ring."

But are these values, and America's uniqueness, still to be treasured? Over the past two decades, a chorus of voices has suggested it's past time for the United States to drop its stubborn insistence on the supremacy of free speech and join the greater community of nations. In this view, American exceptionalism isn't a source of pride; rather, "it's troubling," the founder of the Yale Initiative for the Interdisciplinary Study of Anti-Semitism told National Public Radio in 2011. Citing Europe and Canada as models, he said, "There is a need to curtail some forms of speech and it's just, how do we make the balance?"[39]

A Dartmouth philosophy professor in 2012 delivered an address in Hanover, New Hampshire, calling American free speech exceptionalism "disconcerting rather than cause for celebration." She explained, "Free speech is not a special right. There is no sound philosophical basis for giving such a right a priority when it comes in conflict with other values, such as the right to equality." One might have expected these remarks, delivered at a leading liberal arts university in a state bearing the motto "Live Free or Die," to elicit at least a few forceful rejoinders from the audience on behalf of free speech. If so, such was not recorded in a lengthy account of the event in the school newspaper. One student was quoted as saying that the speech "raised some really interesting ideas," while another wanted a better idea of what changing the First Amendment "would tangibly mean." A colleague from the philosophy department, meanwhile, praised the professor's "criticism of absolutism."[40]

"Absolutism" is a favored term among those proposing new limits on the First Amendment. By marginalizing free speech advocates as fringe fundamentalists lacking any sense of proportion, reformers claim the warm middle as moderates who merely wish to "balance" free speech against "other values." Yet it is the reformers whose limitations on speech, if enacted, would radically alter not just American discourse, but the underlying compacts that define so much of American life—from our relationships with one another to the relationship between the individual citizen and his or her government. Before we follow reformers down the path to becoming nicer, more civil, more European, Canadian, and Australian, it's important to consider what they are proposing, and what we stand to lose.

Jeremy Waldron, a New Zealand–born, British-educated law professor at New York University who has spent much of his career in America, is one of many scholars urging the United States to consider outlawing hate speech in the interest of protecting "vulnerable groups."[41] *The Harm in Hate Speech*, his 2012 book, argues that people have an inherent right to dignity, defined as freedom from being exposed to degrading comments about their group identity. The government, he suggests, should curtail such comments.

One need not strain for connections between Waldron's hate speech proposal and the Sedition Act of 1798—Waldron draws them himself. While noting its potential for abuse, he writes that the Sedition Act seemed necessary at a time when the republic was so fragile that survival was an open question, a time when "federal authority . . . was at the mercy of public opinion, and public opinion was looking well-nigh ungovernable."[42] Only when the government grew stronger and more self-confident could it withstand harsh and divisive voices. As Waldron sees it, minority groups in twenty-first-century America are as vulnerable today as the federal government was in 1798. Acceptance of minorities as equal members of society is "a recent and fragile achievement in the United States," Waldron posits—so fragile, in fact, that such groups may require sedition-style laws to protect them from being "denounced or bestialized" by voices of intolerance.[43]

Waldron is correct that the U.S. government was in deep crisis in 1798. Federalists and Republicans alike had good reason to fear for the future of their country. But he discounts the salient lesson that those early Americans learned at hard cost and bestowed as a gift to every subsequent generation: the way out of peril was through more freedom, not less. Irish immigrant Matthew Lyon, the Sedition Act's first victim, was routinely denounced and bestialized for much of his career. He found his place in America not by seeking to limit the constitutional rights of his critics but by claiming those rights as his own. Americans have never been a fragile people, and immigrants and minorities have consistently proven themselves to be the least fragile among us. Like Lyon, wave after wave has responded to scorn and verbal abuse from ignorant corners of the republic by planting both feet in the soil and reminding a sometimes forgetful nation that rights belong to everybody.

Though the desire to coerce others into silence is associated with no particular party or ideology, over the past twenty years or so the call to rethink the place of free speech in American society has come in the form of an intellectual movement from the Left. That's disheartening because the Left lays claim to the term "liberal," which, if it means anything, means a dedication to liberty. Yet to this new way of thinking, classical liberalism and its embrace of individual rights are anachronistic if not hopelessly naive. Waldron, for one, dismisses traditional, old-guard liberals ("white liberals," he calls them) as people who advocate free speech by way of boasting of their open-mindedness—and who can afford to do so because they've never felt the sting of prejudice.[44]

Amid such thinking, one all the more cherishes such lions of traditional liberalism as Nat Hentoff, at this writing still going strong in his late eighties. And one mourns the passing of figures such as Anthony Lewis, who died in 2013, and Pete Seeger, who died in 2014. Seeger was no cocktail party lefty but a fighter who put his values and his personal freedom on the line again and again. Nor was he personally "tolerant" of ignorance. He was in his own way a militant whose banjo bore the defiant words "This machine surrounds hate and forces it to surrender."[45]

Hounded by the House Un-American Activities Committee in the 1950s and banned for a time from performing on network television, Seeger never tried to turn the tables to silence his foes. He banked on his ability to play louder and sing a better song. Even those repelled by Seeger's politics, especially his early fascination with communism, might find something deeply and sweetly patriotic in the way he spread his message. "Isn't that the wonderful thing about America? You got a right to be wrong," he told one audience. "Where else in the world can you do it like we can do it here?"[46] Asked by his son near the end of his life if he ever feared being imprisoned for his views, Seeger reflected, "I really believed, and I think I was right, that in the long run, this country doesn't go in for things like that."[47]

The call to regulate speech usually comes paired with the proposition that today's challenges are so extreme and unprecedented as to require special action. Citing "astonishing economic and technological changes," University of Chicago professor Cass Sunstein warned, "we must now doubt whether, as interpreted, the constitutional guarantee of free speech is adequately serving democratic goals." In a book called *Democracy and the Problem of Free Speech*, Sunstein proposed a "New Deal for speech," regulating major media companies to ensure a more wholesome, healthy, and democratic exchange of ideas. And just what were those technologically advanced communications goliaths that so worried Sunstein when he wrote his book in 1993? "Newspapers and broadcasting stations."[48]

You can't fault Sunstein, who went on to serve as President Barack Obama's chief regulatory officer and now teaches at Harvard, for not foreseeing the Internet's massive disruption of the communications industry. Few people did. Still, it must be noted that the media bogeymen whose terrible powers warranted, to his mind, radical rethinking of the First Amendment, have been brought down to size without intervention by government regulators. On the contrary, it happened thanks to the very forces that worried Sunstein in the first place: astonishing economic and technological change and the vast, unrestrained marketplace of ideas. The Internet, like any technological advance, does present new issues and concerns over freedom. Yet as revelations about the National Security Agency's widespread surveillance of Americans' electronic communications attest, these concerns may be better focused on the government's use of technology to monitor citizens, and where we draw the line between national security and personal privacy.

Would-be reformers mistrust individual rights and dismiss the marketplace of ideas as a sort of sly excuse for the strong to consolidate power over the weak. Owen Fiss, a law professor at Yale University, has advanced a "democratic theory of speech" calling for an interpretation of the First Amendment that "emphasizes social, rather than individualistic, values." The "public freedom" Fiss advocates requires active government involvement to elevate some voices and shut others down. "Sometimes," he writes, "there is simply no other way."[49]

Stanley Fish, a law professor at Florida International University, argues a similar line, referring to himself as a First Amendment "consequentialist"—someone who believes that "you may have to regulate speech in order to preserve its First Amendment value."[50] According to Fish, consequentialists such as Supreme Court justice John Paul Stevens, now retired, view some speech as "noxious weeds" that must be eradicated "so that your garden can begin to grow again."[51] In 1787, Federalist John Jay used a similar speech-as-weeds analogy to help lay the intellectual foundation for the Sedition Act, suggesting that "a good Government is as necessary to subdue the one, as an attentive gardener or husbandman is to destroy the other."[52]

Such proclamations leave hanging the vital question of who gets to be the gardener. When it comes to ideas, one man's weeds are another's dandelion wine. Who determines when a particular voice has reached its permissible volume level and must be turned down or silenced? Phrases such as "First Amendment value" and "public freedom" promote the idea that speech rights exist primarily to advance collective purposes, such as a better, more participatory government.[53] Yet while open, healthy political debate is certainly a benefit of free speech, the suggestion that individual rights exist in order to protect the political system would seem to get it backward. Essential to the idea of free speech, as expressed so cogently in the First Amendment, is that the government exists to protect the rights of each individual—whether or not others, including those in government, find what an individual says to be edifying or useful.

It is up to each person to decide, singly or in voluntary association with others, what the "purpose" of free speech is, what the First Amendment is "for." One woman uses her speech rights to advance a political agenda, another writes haikus; one man angrily blogs that George W. Bush is a fascist or Barack Obama a communist, another writes cookbooks. One yearns to leave a mark on the world and will keep shouting until someone listens, another is content to live in solitude and not be heard at all. The purposes of freedom are as multitudinous as the imaginations of more than 300 million Americans. Yet as far as government is concerned, there can be only one. The purpose of freedom is freedom.

People who wish to remain free for long must acknowledge that no right, including speech, is absolute. If the government had no authority to punish speech, someone could directly instruct an angry mob to destroy your home and later claim that all he did was talk. Or, to cite the ubiquitous example, you could falsely shout "Fire!" in a crowded theater without fear of prosecution, even if the resulting stampede caused injury or death. Yet in reality, anyone charged with either offense would be tried and, if convicted, sent to jail. Far from conflicting with freedom, the principle that you can't use your own rights to destroy someone else's is essential to maintaining freedom. It applies not just to speech but to any other right. A reasonable person may cherish her right to move about as she pleases, while still understanding the need to arrest a burglar who abuses that right by entering someone's home and walking off with the jewelry.

We need a strong, vigorous government empowered to adjudicate, enforce, and punish in cases where rights clash. Over the years the Supreme Court has wrestled with the infinitely complex question of just where those boundaries lie, giving us terms such as "fighting words" and "clear and present danger" to determine when speech truly goes too far. But there is one thing that cannot coexist with freedom, and that is declaring that people have a right against being offended, even deeply offended, by someone else's words. Such a declaration automatically transfers the right of speech from the speaker to the listener, who now enjoys the power not just to say, "I don't like your opinion," but "I won't allow you to say that."

Compare the words of the First Amendment ("Congress shall make no law . . .") with those of the Australian Human Rights Commission in explaining that nation's Racial Discrimination Act (under which the *Herald Sun* newspaper was forced to print an apology for offending Aboriginal readers). In order to balance free speech against the right not to be offended, the act "outlines some things that are not against the law, provided they are 'done reasonably and in good faith.'"[54]

People who consult a government checklist to determine which speech is "not against the law" speak by permission rather than right. In Australia, France, Denmark, and Canada, permissions are wide and punishments for transgressions mild; in China, Saudi Arabia, and Iran, permissions are narrow and punishments are harsh. But permission is permission—alienable, impermanent, and, unlike rights, derived from other people.

Because everyone who voices a controversial opinion is bound to give offense to someone, speech granted by permission is essentially a political privilege. The trick isn't to avoid giving offense; rather, it is to avoid offending the wrong people. Modern Western governments may believe they have identified topics (race, gender, sexual orientation) so uniquely sensitive as to require special government restrictions. But keep in mind that the Federalists of 1798 believed just as strongly in the values they wanted to protect, and they were just as convinced that those values—and their way of life—were being directly imperiled by the toxic words of their Republican opponents. Both sides wrote and said outrageous things. Yet for the brief reign of the Sedition Act, Republicans went to jail and Federalists remained free—not because one side had a lock on wisdom, but because one side enjoyed political cover while the other did not.

Just about anybody can think of people he or she wishes would shut up and go away. Allowing offensive speech doesn't connote approval. Nor do we defend wrongheaded thinking under the bromide that everyone's opinions matter, or that the mere act of forming and expressing ideas entitles those ideas to respect. Ignorance and hatefulness can and should be confronted and shot down, but with reason and with better words. Rigorous confrontation of bad ideas is a process that author Jonathan Rauch calls "liberal science."

In his classic book, *Kindly Inquisitors*, Rauch, who is Jewish and gay, defended the rights of anti-Semites and homophobes to spout their hurtful nonsense. "The only way to kill a bad idea is by exposing it and supplanting it with better ones," Rauch wrote. Tolerance, he noted, is not a gift; it is an investment in one's own ongoing freedom of expression. "Today, true, the regulators may take gay people's side," he noted. "But the wheel will turn, and the majority will reassert itself, and, when the inquisitorial machinery is turned against them, homosexuals will rue the day they helped set it up."[55]

Each generation faces wars, recessions, and political, religious, or racial strife so seemingly perilous that even freedom-loving Americans may feel called upon to forcibly shut one another up. As Supreme Court justice Thurgood Marshall observed, "History teaches that grave threats to liberty often come in times of urgency, when constitutional rights seem too extravagant to endure."[56] It's human nature to believe ourselves ever to be standing on the precipice of disaster, holding tight to our values and our way of life. If previous generations seem by comparison to have lived in peace or harmony, that's only because their crises by now rest calmly in the history books, whereas our own seem so immediate and uncertain.

A passion for liberty and individual rights is not about hating the government, nor denying its essential place in our lives. On the contrary, it's about loving the government enough to protect it from ambitious souls who year after year migrate to the capital to run it for us, and who find in each new crisis a fresh opportunity to regulate and control. Most of the concerns that inflame us today will soon enough reside as historical footnotes alongside the XYZ Affair of 1798. What remains as the measure of a generation is not the policies it enacted to surmount temporary difficulties, nor the restrictions it imposed on its most repugnant voices. The true measure of greatness of any generation is the degree of wisdom it showed in looking beyond the moment and handing down liberty, intact and unfettered, to the next.

# SOURCES AND ACKNOWLEDGMENTS

My personal journey to the eighteenth century began by getting much better acquainted with the leading Founders than I had been before. We can't know these men personally, of course, but readers today can come close thanks to a stream of large, thorough, and highly readable modern biographies. Works by David McCullough (Adams), Ron Chernow (Hamilton and Washington), Walter Isaacson and Edmund S. Morgan (Franklin), Jon Meacham (Jefferson), and others have brought the principal Founders to vivid life for a new generation of readers. I'm indebted to all of them.

Two important books specifically on the Sedition Act, John C. Miller's *Crisis in Freedom* and James Morton Smith's *Freedom's Fetters*, appeared during the 1950s. While both are valuable, Smith's *Freedom's Fetters* stands out for its monumental primary research and was one of my constant companions during my research and writing. Another indispensable resource was historian Frank M. Anderson's slender but groundbreaking 1912 paper, "The Enforcement of the Alien and Sedition Laws," which I first learned of in *Freedom's Fetters*. Other extremely useful resources included works directly about individual Sedition Act defendants, especially *American Aurora* by Richard N. Rosenfeld, *"With the Hammer of Truth"* by Michael Durey, and *Matthew Lyon, "New Man" of the Democratic Revolution* by Aleine Austin.

The participants in the Sedition Act drama were fighting for their own lives rather than for ours, yet the writings they left behind in the form of newspaper articles, political speeches, personal correspondence, and essays provide an extraordinary window into a generation struggling to understand, in a practical sense, what it means to live in freedom. All Americans owe them a debt for enduring their struggles and emerging at the end affirming free speech and setting the country on a true course.

Thanks to the efforts of modern scholars at government agencies and private institutions, many of those writings are readily available online—from the Annals of Congress, to the papers of Jefferson, Adams, and other Founders, to complete issues of eighteenth-century newspapers. Any discussion of threats to freedom in America must start with an acknowledgment of our nation's extraordinary culture of openness.

Considering the plethora of online historical resources now available, what is notable is that libraries, historical societies, and flesh-and-blood experts are more important than ever.

In Philadelphia: Sue Habgood, a historian and professional tour guide, walked me around the older sections of her favorite city, suggested resources, introduced me to key experts, and helped bring Congress Hall, the offices of the *Aurora*, and the Philadelphia of Franklin, Bache, and Adams to life before my eyes. Thanks to the American Philosophical Society for access to the Benjamin Franklin Bache papers. Thanks to Karie Diethorn, Anna Toogood and Christian Higgins of the Independence National Historical Park Library in Philadelphia. Anna generously shared her personal files on period history, including essential diaries and letters from the yellow fever epidemic of 1798, and Benjamin Franklin Bache's home. In Northumberland, Pennsylvania, John L. Moore, Ron Blatchley, and Jo Ann Long, opened up the Joseph Priestley House, a hidden treasure in the landscape of American historical sites, for a special tour. John shared his own research into Thomas Cooper, while Ron shared his extensive knowledge of Joseph Priestley.

In Massachusetts, thanks to the Dedham Historical Society for sharing and copying many historical documents on the town and on Fisher and Nathaniel Ames. And special thanks to historian Robert Brand Hanson for generous conversations and for giving me a walking tour of Old Dedham. Hanson's two-volume *Diary of Dr. Nathaniel Ames of Dedham, Massachusetts, 1758–1822* is a work of remarkable scholarship, full of historical detail and invaluable context. It is also a delight to read and is deserving of a much wider audience. Thanks to the Massachusetts Historical Society for access to the papers of Timothy Pickering.

At the Vermont Historical Society in Barre, special thanks to Paul A. Carnahan and the helpful library staff for access to extensive material related to Matthew Lyon, Nathaniel Chipman, and their times. Also in Vermont, thanks to Carolyn L. Tallen of the Bixby Memorial Library in Vergennes; historian Tyler Resch at the Bennington Museum; Dani Laramie Roberts and Lorraine Brown of the Fair Haven Historical Society; and the University of Vermont's Bailey/Howe Library. And to Vincent Feeney, author of *Finnigans, Slaters, and Stonepeggers: A History of the Irish in Vermont*, and Robert D. Rachlin, a Burlington attorney and historian who has written about Matthew Lyon and the east-west political divide in early Vermont.

Years ago, as a newspaper reporter, I covered the Virginia Historical Society's full emergence, under Charles Bryan, as one of the nation's premier historical museums and research institutions. It was a personal thrill to return to Richmond on my own research project and dive into the society's extraordinary collections. Thanks also to the Virginia State Library, whose period newspapers helped me piece together James Callender's tortured final days, and to Harrison Crews, for scouting sources in advance of my visit.

Over the course of two summer vacations from college, my daughter Natalie Slack worked as my researcher. Using the wonderful online resource America's Historical Newspapers, Natalie uncovered treasures on each of the cases. Her research into Luther Baldwin and his prosecutor, Lucius Horatio Stockton, enabled me to offer a fuller portrait than perhaps ever before on this vital and too-often-dismissed episode of the Sedition Act drama. Additionally, Natalie tracked down graduate theses and other materials in far-flung libraries. Working with Natalie and sharing excitement over each new finding has been one of my greatest joys on this book, and in my career as a writer. My daughter Caroline lent music to my prose with her ever-present guitar and, aging perfectly into the role, will be on deck as my next researcher, if she'll agree to it.

Nelson D. Lankford, historian at the Virginia Historical Society and editor of the *Virginia Magazine of History and Biography*, graciously read my manuscript and offered valuable suggestions and corrections. Mary A. Vogler, a physician in the division of infectious diseases at Weill Cornell College of Medicine in New York, shared her own knowledge, sent me journal articles, and read my pages on yellow fever. Others who read portions of the manuscript include lawyer-friends Lamar Flatt and Walter Gans (on the common law), and friends Claudio Phillips and Ed Goldfinger. Professional fact-checker Charles Kotsonis reviewed Part IV of this book. His careful work saved me from some embarrassing errors and challenged several assumptions in ways that forced me to strengthen the manuscript. Dean King read parts of the manuscript and offered, as he has throughout my career, indispensable writer-to-writer encouragement, advice, and friendship. Any errors are mine.

My parents, Carolyn and Warner Slack, provided constant encouragement. My father, who through a life of courageous words and actions has upheld the highest ideals of classical liberalism, read and reread the manuscript. His ongoing enthusiasm always kept my spirits from flagging. Thanks to my agent of many years, Andrew Blauner, for getting and staying behind this project, and to Grove Atlantic for taking it on. To have landed with a legendary publisher such as Morgan Entrekin and a superb young editor such as Jamison Stoltz (ably assisted by Allison Malecha) was humbling. Jamison's challenging and incisive comments helped me greatly improve the manuscript. Thanks to Nancy Tan for an especially thorough and careful copyedit.

Most of all, thanks to my wife, Barbara, who read the manuscript, kept me going, shared all of my highs and endured the lows, and remains the love of my life.

# NOTES

## PART I: THE ROAD TO SEDITION
## CHAPTER ONE

1   Alexander Hamilton wrote Washington's Farewell Address. It was intended to be read rather than heard, appearing first in *Claypoole's American Daily Advertiser* on September 9, 1796. The copy from which this quote is taken is in Bloom, Sol, *The Story of the Constitution*, U.S. Constitution Sesquicentennial Commission, Washington, D.C., 1937, p. 140.

2   Schlesinger, Arthur M., et al., eds., *A History of American Life*, rev. and abr., Scribner, New York, 1996, p. 419.

3   7 Annals of Cong., 430 (1797).

4   McLaughlin, James Fairfax, *Matthew Lyon, the Hampden of Congress*, Wynkoop Hallenbeck Crawford Co., New York, 1900, pp. 7–8.

5   Austin, Aleine, *Matthew Lyon, "New Man" of the Democratic Revolution, 1749–1822*, Pennsylvania State University Press, University Park, 1981, pp. 8, 10.

6   Ibid., p. 13.

7   Randall, Willard Sterne, *Ethan Allen: His Life and Times*, W. W. Norton & Co., New York, 2011, pp. 288–289.

8   One of the best and most succinct analyses of the political differences imposed by the mountains may be found in Rachlin, Robert D., "The Sedition Act of 1798 and the East-West Political Divide in Vermont," *Vermont History* 78, no. 2 (Summer/Fall 2010): 123–150.

9   Sherman, Michael, Gene Sessions, and P. Jeffrey Potash, *Freedom and Unity: A History of Vermont*, Vermont Historical Society, Barre, 2004, p. 85.

10    Austin, *Matthew Lyon*, p. 13.

11    Austin, *Matthew Lyon*, pp. 15, 16.

12    Adams, Andrew N., *A History of the Town of Fair Haven, Vermont*, Leonard & Phelps, Fair Haven, VT, 1870, p. 417.

13    Austin, *Matthew Lyon*, p. 18; Ward, Christopher, *The War of the Revolution*, vol. 2, Macmillan, New York, 1952, p. 539.

14    Order of the Court of Confiscation, Apr. 30, 1778 (Vermont Historical Society).

15    Austin, *Matthew Lyon*, pp. 23-24.

16    Adams, *A History of the Town of Fair Haven, Vermont*, pp. 18, 35, 38.

17    Ibid., pp. 35, 416, 417. See also Allen, Richard Sanders, "Matthew Lyon, Soldier, Politician, Pioneer and Iron-Maker," unpublished account (Vermont Historical Society).

18    Smallwood, Frank, *Thomas Chittenden: Vermont's First Statesman*, New England Press, Shelburne, VT, 1997, pp. 26, 27.

19    Adams, *A History of the Town of Fair Haven, Vermont*, p. 419.

20    Ibid., pp. 103–104.

21    Austin, *Matthew Lyon*, p. 45.

22    Sherman, Sessions, and Potash, *Freedom and Unity*, p. 121.

23    Years later, when Chipman was a U.S. senator and Lyon a member of Congress, Chipman recounted the story in testimony to Congress, which was deliberating ejecting Lyon for misconduct, as described later in Part I. 7 Annals of Cong., 1000 (1798).

24    Sherman, Sessions, and Potash, *Freedom and Unity*, pp. 121–122.

25    James Madison to Thomas Jefferson, Oct. 17, 1788, reprinted in Madison, James, *Writings*, comp. Jack N. Rakove, Library of America, New York, 1999, p. 420.

26    Wood, Gordon S., *The Radicalism of the American Revolution*, Vintage Books, New York, 1991, p. 30.

27    See Gordon Wood's illuminating chapter "Equality" in *The Radicalism of the American Revolution*, pp. 229–243. On pp. 242–243 Wood discusses the relationship between Matthew Lyon and Nathaniel Chipman; see also Chipman, Daniel, *The Life of Hon. Nathaniel Chipman, LL.D.*, C. C. Little and J. Brown, Boston, 1846, pp. 5–7.

28   *Porcupine's Gazette*, June 6, 1797, quoted in Wharton, Francis, *State Trials of the United States During the Administrations of Washington and Adams*, Carey & Hart, Philadelphia, 1849, p. 338.

## CHAPTER TWO

1   Stewart, Donald H., *The Opposition Press of the Federalist Period*, SUNY Press, Albany, NY, 1969, p. 118.

2   Kelley, Joseph J., Jr., *Life and Times in Colonial Philadelphia*, Stackpole Books, Harrisburg, PA, 1973, p. 224.

3   Hébert, Catherine, "The French Element in Pennsylvania in the 1790s: The Francophone Immigrants' Impact," *Pennsylvania Magazine of History and Biography* 108, no. 4 (Oct. 1984): 451–469.

4   Hébert, Catherine, "French Publications in Philadelphia in the Age of the French Revolution: A Bibliographical Essay," *Pennsylvania History* 58, no. 1 (Jan. 1991): 37–61.

5   "John Jay's Treaty, 1794-95," U.S. Department of State, Office of the Historian. history.state.gov/milestones/1784-1800/jay-treaty (accessed June 1, 2014).

6   Elkins, Stanley, and Eric McKitrick, *The Age of Federalism: The Early American Republic, 1788–1800*, Oxford University Press, New York, 1993, p. 377.

7   Elkins and McKitrick, *The Age of Federalism*, p. 389; Currie, David P., *The Constitution in Congress: The Federalist Period, 1789–1801*, University of Chicago Press, Chicago, 1997, p. 209.

8   "John Jay's Treaty, 1794–95," U.S. Department of State, Office of the Historian, history.state.gov/milestones/1784-1800/jay-treaty (accessed May 20, 2014).

9   Rosenfeld, Richard N., *American Aurora: A Democratic-Republican Returns*, St. Martin's Press, New York, 1997, p. 30.

10   5 Annals of Cong., 1239 (1796).

11   Ibid., p. 1245.

12   Ibid., pp. 1250–1251.

13   Estes, Todd, "'The Most Bewitching Piece of Parliamentary Oratory': Fisher Ames' Jay Treaty Speech Reconsidered," *Historical Journal of Massachusetts* 28, no. 1 (Winter 2000): 1–22.

14   5 Annals of Cong., 1291 (1796). Also, "Primary Documents in American

History: Jay's Treaty," Library of Congress, www.loc.gov/rr/program/bib/ourdocs/jay.html (accessed May 20, 2014).

15   Elkins and McKitrick, *The Age of Federalism*, p. 415.

16   Schama, Simon, *Citizens: A Chronicle of the French Revolution*, Knopf, New York, 1989, p. 619.

17   Ibid., pp. 632–635.

18   Adams, John, *Revolutionary Writings 1775–1783*, ed. Gordon Wood, Library of America, New York, 2011, pp. 303, 305.

19   McCullough, David M., *John Adams*, Simon & Schuster, New York, 2001, p. 443.

20   Schama, *Citizens*, p. 870.

21   McCullough, *John Adams*, pp. 443–444.

22   Chernow, Ron, "Citizen Genet," in *Washington: A Life*, Penguin Books, New York, 2010, 692.

23   Ibid. p. 692.

24   Ibid, p. 697.

25   The French Jacobins were named for a Parisian club known for radical politics; the Sans Culottes were French laborers, so named because they wore long workingman's trousers, in contrast to the knee-length silk culottes worn by the aristocracy.

26   Elkins and McKitrick, *The Age of Federalism*, p. 316.

27   Kelley, *Life and Times in Colonial Philadelphia*, p. 223.

28   "Historical Election Results: Electoral College Box Scores 1789–1996," U.S. Electoral College, www.archives.gov/federal-register/electoral-college/scores.html#1796 (accessed May 20, 2014).

## CHAPTER THREE

1   Quoted in DeConde, Alexander, *The Quasi-War: The Politics and Diplomacy of the Undeclared War with France, 1797–1801*, Scribner, New York, 1966, p. 10.

2   Ibid., p. 124.

3   Ibid., p. 16.

4   7 Annals of Cong., 54 (1797).

5  Ibid., p. 56.

6  Ibid., p. 57.

7  Ibid., p. 68.

8  "Gallatin, Albert (1761–1849)," Biographical Directory of the U.S. Congress, bioguide.congress.gov/scripts/biodisplay.pl?index=G000020 (accessed May 20, 2014).

9  7 Annals of Cong., 232 (1797).

10  House Journal, 5th Cong., 1st Sess. 21 (1797).

11  Ibid., p. 22.

12  7 Annals of Cong., 234–235 (1797).

13  Ibid., p. 235.

14  Ibid.

15  Nathaniel Chipman to Cephas Smith Jr., Nov. 24, 1797 (Vermont Historical Society).

16  7 Annals of Cong., 422 (1797).

17  Ibid., pp. 424–425.

18  Ibid., pp. 425–426.

19  Ibid., p. 430.

20  Austin, *Matthew Lyon*, pp. 93, 95.

21  7 Annals of Cong., 961–962 (1798).

## CHAPTER FOUR

1  7 Annals of Cong., 955–956 (1798).

2  Ibid., p. 967.

3  Lewis R. Morris to unidentified Vermont resident, Feb. 22, 1798 (Vermont Historical Society).

4  7 Annals of Cong., 997–998 (1798).

5  Ibid., p. 980.

6  Ibid., pp. 987–988.

7  Ibid., p. 974. The word "arse" was decorously omitted from the Annals.

8  Ibid., p. 1008.

9  Ibid., p. 1034.

10    Ibid., pp. 1034, 1049.

11    Ibid., p. 1036.

12    Ibid., p. 1066.

13    Ibid., p. 1067.

14    Ritchie, Donald A., *Press Gallery: Congress and the Washington Corre-spondents*, Harvard University Press, Cambridge, MA, 1991, p. 7; 1 Annals of Cong., 952 (1789); Dearmont, Nelson S., "Secrecy in Government: The Public Debate in Congress During the Formative Years of the American Republic," PhD diss., City University of New York, 1975, pp. 44–46.

15    Ritchie, *Press Gallery*, p. 7; 1 Annals of Cong., 948 (1789). In Burke's defense, his resolution did not propose punishing reporters or banishing them from the House chamber altogether. His point was that allowing them access to the floor of the House, rather than the public gallery, amounted to giving sanction to their erroneous reporting. Still, the episode offered a telling preview of the contentious relationship between politicians and reporters in the United States on into our own time: the difference between supporting a concept of free speech versus supporting free speech used against oneself.

16    Ritchie, *Press Gallery*, p. 7; 1 Annals of Cong., 955 (1789).

17    Dearmont, "Secrecy in Government," p. 51.

18    Brown, Walt, *John Adams and the American Press: Politics and Journalism at the Birth of the Republic*, McFarland & Co., Jefferson, NC, 1995, p. 43.

19    Ibid.

20    Miller, John C., *Crisis in Freedom: The Alien and Sedition Acts*, Little, Brown, Boston, 1951, p. 104.

21    *Connecticut Gazette*, Mar. 7, 1798. (Most newspapers cited can be found via America's Historical Newspapers.)

22    *Philadelphia Aurora*, Feb. 8, 1798. This newspaper underwent numerous name changes during its years of publication. For clarity, it is referred to in these pages simply as the *Philadelphia Aurora*, or *Aurora* . . .

23    7 Annals of Cong., 968 (1798).


CHAPTER FIVE

1    Tagg, James, *Benjamin Franklin Bache and the* Philadelphia Aurora, University of Pennsylvania Press, Philadelphia, 1991, pp. 4–5.

2   Schiff, Stacy, *A Great Improvisation: Franklin, France, and the Birth of America*, Henry Holt, New York, 2005, p. 3.

3   From Faÿ, Bernard, *The Two Franklins: Fathers of American Democracy*, quoted in Platt, John D. R., *The Home and Office of Benjamin Franklin Bache (America's First Modern Newsman)*, Office of History and Historic Architecture, Eastern Service Center, Washington, D.C., 1970.

4   Tagg, *Benjamin Franklin Bache and the* Philadelphia Aurora, p. 23.

5   Schiff, *A Great Improvisation*, pp. 13–14.

6   Ibid., p. 14.

7   Isaacson, Walter, *Benjamin Franklin: An American Life*, Simon & Schuster, New York, 2003, p. 327.

8   Schiff, *A Great Improvisation*, p. 14.

9   Isaacson, *Benjamin Franklin: An American Life*, p. 326.

10   Tagg, *Benjamin Franklin Bache and the* Philadelphia Aurora, p. 28.

11   Ibid.

12   Isaacson, *Benjamin Franklin: An American Life*, pp. 326, 334–342.

13   Tagg, *Benjamin Franklin Bache and the* Philadelphia Aurora, pp. 30-31.

14   Benjamin Franklin Bache to Benjamin Franklin, Oct. 25, 1799 (American Philosophical Society).

15   Benjamin Franklin Bache to Sarah Franklin Bache, Sept. 15, 1782 (American Philosophical Society).

16   Benjamin Franklin Bache to Sarah Franklin Bache, Feb. 9, 1785 (American Philosophical Society).

17   *The New Annual Register, or General Repository of History, Politics, and Literature for the Year 1782*, G. Robinson, Pater-noster-Row, London, 1797, p. 63.

18   Diary of Benjamin Franklin Bache, Oct. 9, 1782 (American Philosophical Society).

19   Ibid., Feb. 19, 1783.

20   Morgan, Edmund S., *Benjamin Franklin*, Yale University Press, New Haven, CT, 2002, p. 297.

21   Among the guests was a certain "Mr. Delon, who professes the power of animal magnetism," Bache wrote in May 1784. "The Academy has nominated several persons of consequence, among them my grandfather, at whose house the commissioners assembled to day. Mr. Delon, who after

magnetizing several sick persons, went out into the garden to magnetize the trees." Diary of Benjamin Franklin Bache, May 22, 1784 (American Philosophical Society).

22    Ibid., April 5, 1785.

23    Ibid., August 23 and 24, 1785.

24    Tagg, *Benjamin Franklin Bache and the* Philadelphia Aurora, p. 60.

25    Isaacson, *Benjamin Franklin: An American Life*, p. 457.

26    Benjamin Franklin Bache to Margaret H. Markoe, May 2, 1790 (American Philosophical Society).

27    Isaacson, *Benjamin Franklin: An American Life*, p. 473.

28    Tagg, *Benjamin Franklin Bache and the* Philadelphia Aurora, pp. 64–66.

## CHAPTER SIX

1    Brigham, Clarence S., *History and Bibliography of American Newspapers, 1690–1820*, vol. 2, American Antiquarian Society, Worcester, MA, 1947, p. 916.

2    Rosenfeld, *American Aurora*, p. 507.

3    *Historic Structures Report, Part I, on the Benjamin Franklin Tenant House, 322 Market Street*, prepared by Penelope Hartshorne, Helmuth Reich, and Robert Harris, U.S. Department of the Interior, National Park Service Eastern Office, Design and Construction, March 1963.

4    Tagg, *Benjamin Franklin Bache and the* Philadelphia Aurora, pp. 72–73.

5    Ibid., pp. 75-76.

6    Platt, *The Home and Office of Benjamin Franklin Bache*, p. 73.

7    Benjamin Franklin Bache to Le Veillard, Apr. 6, 1792, quoted in ibid., pp. 72–73.

8    Platt, *The Home and Office of Benjamin Franklin Bache*, pp. 73–74.

9    Tagg, *Benjamin Franklin Bache and the* Philadelphia Aurora, p. 40.

10    William Vans Murray to John Quincy Adams, Nov. 27, 1798, Annual Report of the American Historical Association for the Year 1912, Washington, 1914, pp. 489-490. E-book.

11    Quoted in Chernow, *Washington: A Life*, p. 562.

12    Van Doren, Carl, *The Great Rehearsal: The Story of the Making and Ratifying of the Constitution of the United States*, Viking Press, New York, 1948, pp. 1, 2.

13    Quoted in Tagg, *Benjamin Franklin Bache and the* Philadelphia Aurora, p. 158.

14    Miller, *Crisis in Freedom*, pp. 27–28.

15    Rosenfeld, *American Aurora*, p. 30; Chernow, *Washington: A Life.*

16    Chernow, *Washington: A Life.*

17    Rosenfeld, *American Aurora*, page 31.

18    Tagg, *Benjamin Franklin Bache and the* Philadelphia Aurora, pp. 296–297.

19    Described in a letter by Abigail Adams, quoted in Smith, James Morton, *Freedom's Fetters: The Alien and Sedition Laws and American Civil Liberties*, Cornell University Press, Ithaca, NY, 1966 [1956], p. 9.

20    Quoted in ibid.; Abigail Adams to Mary Cranch, Apr. 28, 1798, in Mitchell, Stewart, ed., *New Letters of Abigail Adams, 1788–1801*, Houghton Mifflin Co., Boston, 1947, p. 167.

21    Rosenfeld, *American Aurora*, p. 82.

22    Elkins and McKitrick, *The Age of Federalism*, p. 552.

23    Ibid., pp. 571–574.

24    DeConde, *The Quasi-War*, p. 93.

25    Miller, *Crisis in Freedom*, p. 63.

26    Ibid., pp. 61, 63.

27    8 Annals of Cong., 1972 (1798).

28    Bache, Benjamin Franklin, *Truth Will Out! The Foul Charges of the Tories against the Editor of the* Aurora *Repelled by Positive Proof and Plain Truth, and His Base Calumniators Put to Shame*, Nabu Press, Charleston, SC, 2010 [s.p., Philadelphia, 1798].

29    Ibid., pp. 1–2.

30    *Rutland Herald*, July 16, 1798.

31    McCullough, *John Adams*, p. 501.

32    Reprinted in the *Vermont Gazette*, Bennington, May 26, 1798.

## CHAPTER SEVEN

1    Durey, Michael, *"With the Hammer of Truth": James Thomson Callender and America's Early National Heroes*, University Press of Virginia, Charlottesville, 1990, p. 103.

2    Philip Schuyler to Alexander Hamilton, Aug. 19, 1802, from *The Papers of Alexander Hamilton: Volume XXVI, May 1, 1802–October 23, 1804*, ed. Harold C. Syrett, Columbia University Press, New York, 1979, p. 36.

3    *Gazette of the United States*, Aug. 9, 1798.

4    McCullough, *John Adams*, p. 583.

5    James T. Callender to Thomas Jefferson, Jan. 5, 180[1] (Thomas Jefferson Papers, Library of Congress).

6    McCullough, *John Adams*, p. 536.

7    Miller, *Crisis in Freedom*, p. 211.

8    Chernow, Ron, *Alexander Hamilton*, Penguin Press, New York, 2004, pp. 509, 529.

9    Quoted in Durey, *"With the Hammer of Truth,"* p. 127.

10    Ford, Worthington Chauncey, "Thomas Jefferson and James Thomson Callender," in *New-England Historical and Genealogical Register*, vol. 50, Boston, 1896, p. 321.

11    Dabney, Virginius, *Richmond: The Story of a City*, rev. ed., University Press of Virginia, Charlottesville, 1990, p. 64.

12    Durey, *"With the Hammer of Truth,"* p. 48.

13    Ibid., p. 103.

14    Cobbett, William, *Porcupine's Works*, vol. 5, Cobbett and Morgan, London, 1801, p. 204.

15    Wharton, *State Trials*, pp. 322, 326–327; Callender, James T., *Sedgwick & Co., or A Key to the Six Per Cent Cabinet*, printed for the author, Philadelphia, 1798, p. 18. Not surprisingly, Callender's principled defense of Cobbett did the unfortunate Callender no good. It angered his fellow Republicans, while Cobbett continued his attacks on Callender. Michael Durey's biography *"With the Hammer of Truth"* describes the episode in detail on pp. 108–110.

16    Callender, James T., *The History of the United States for 1796*, Snowden & M'Corkle, Philadelphia, 1797, p. 39.

17    Durey, *"With the Hammer of Truth,"* pp. 14–16.

18    Callender, James T., *Deformities of Dr. Samuel Johnson Selected from His Works*, printed for the author, Edinburgh, 1782. *Deformities* makes for fascinating reading. The inconsistencies Callender uncovers in no way detract from Johnson's monumental achievement. Indeed, it is Johnson's wry, often crotchety observations on life, rather than absolute lexicographic precision,

that give Johnson's *Dictionary* its stamp of genius and its enduring literary value. Still, *Deformities* sheds light on Callender's obsessive personality, his terrific attention to detail, and his inherent combativeness, all of which he would bring to bear with terrifying results for his celebrated American enemies.

19   Callender, James, *The Political Progress of Great Britain, or An Impartial Account of the Principal Abuses in the Government of This Country, from the Revolution in 1688*, Robertson & Berry, Edinburgh, 1792, p. 63.

20   Durey, *"With the Hammer of Truth,"* p. 53.

21   Chernow, *Alexander Hamilton*, p. 232.

22   James T. Callender to Thomas Jefferson, Sept. 22, 1798 (Thomas Jefferson Papers, Library of Congress).

23   Durey, *"With the Hammer of Truth,"* p. 8.

24   For a detailed analysis of this episode in Hamilton's life, see Chernow, *Alexander Hamilton*, esp. pp. 364–370.

25   Callender, *The History of the United States for 1796*, p. 204.

26   Quoted in Durey, *"With the Hammer of Truth,"* p. 102.

27   Full title: *Observations on Certain Documents Contained in No. V & VI of "The History of the United States for the Year 1796," in Which the Charge of Speculation against Alexander Hamilton, Late Secretary of the Treasury, Is Fully Refuted. Written by Himself.* Hamilton, Alexander, *Writings*, comp. Joanne B. Freeman, Library of America, New York, 2001, pp. 883–910.

28   Durey, *"With the Hammer of Truth,"* p. 103.

29   Thomas Jefferson to James Madison, May 3, 1798 (Thomas Jefferson Papers, Library of Congress).

30   Rosenfeld, *American Aurora*, p. 148.

31   Smith, *Freedom's Fetters*, pp. 200, 202.

32   Full texts of the three Alien Acts may be found online at the Library of Congress.

## CHAPTER EIGHT

1   Senate Journal, 5th Cong., 2d Sess. 518 (1798).

2   Ibid., pp. 527, 528.

3   Ibid., p. 527.

4   "Speech in the Constitutional Convention on a Plan of Government" (recorded by James Madison), from Hamilton, *Writings*, pp. 156–157.

5   Dearmont, "Secrecy in Government," p. 44.

6   Ibid., p. 70.

7   Ritchie, *Press Gallery*, p. 9-10.

8   Ibid., p. 10; ; "December 9, 1795, The Senate Opens Its Doors," www.senate.gov/artandhistory/history/minute/The_Senate_Opens_Its_Doors.htm (accessed May 31, 2014).

9   Senate Journal, 5th Cong., 2d Sess. 518 (1798).

10   *Newark (NJ) Centinel of Freedom*, July 17, 1798.

11   Quincy, Josiah, *An Oration, Pronounced July 4, 1798, at the Request of the Inhabitants of the Town of Boston, in Commemoration of the Anniversary of American Independence*, John Russell, Boston, 1798, pp. 8, 9.

12   Ibid., pp. 23–24.

13   Ibid., p. 18.

14   Bernhard, Winfred E. A., *Fisher Ames: Federalist and Statesman, 1758–1808*, University of North Carolina Press, Chapel Hill, 1965, p. 298.

15   The full text of the letter to John Adams may be found in a footnote in Ames, Nathaniel, *The Diary of Dr. Nathaniel Ames of Dedham, Massachusetts, 1758–1822*, vol. 2, ed. Robert Brand Hanson, Picton Press, Rockport, ME, 1998, p. 649.

16   Ames, *The Diary of Dr. Nathaniel Ames of Dedham, Massachusetts*, p. 650.

17   Ibid., pp. 649-650.

18   *Newark (NJ) Centinel of Freedom*, July 17, 1798.

19   Yeas and nays are recorded by last name in the Senate Journal for July 4, 1798. Names and party affiliations were checked against the Biographical Directory of the U.S. Congress, 1774–Present, at bioguide.congress.gov.

## CHAPTER NINE

1   8 Annals of Cong., 2094 (1798).

2   Ibid., p. 2098.

3   Ibid., p. 2100.

4   Ibid., p. 2103.

5  Tagg, *Benjamin Franklin Bache and the* Philadelphia Aurora, pp. 101, 291–292.

6  *Report of the Postmaster-General of the United States*, Government Printing Office, Washington, D.C., 1888, pp. 733, 734.

7  Miller, *Crisis in Freedom*, pp. 30–31.

8  8 Annals of Cong., 2104 (1798).

9  Ibid., p. 2105.

10  Ibid., p. 2106.

11  Ibid., p. 2107.

12  Ibid., p. 2108.

13  Ibid., p. 2109.

14  Ibid., p. 2111.

15  Ibid., p. 2112.

16  Ibid.

17  Ibid., p. 2133.

18  Ibid., p. 2134.

19  Ibid., p. 2137.

20  Ibid.

## CHAPTER TEN

1  Clarfield, Gerard H., *Timothy Pickering and the American Republic*, University of Pittsburgh Press, Pittsburgh, PA, 1980, p. vii.

2  Ibid., p. 163; Elkins and McKitrick, *The Age of Federalism*, p. 625.

3  Quoted in Chernow, *Washington: A Life*, p. 735.

4  Clarfield, *Timothy Pickering and the American Republic*, pp. 158–162; McCullough, *John Adams*, p. 472; Rosenfeld, *American Aurora*, p. 483.

5  Timothy Pickering to Richard Harison, June 28, 1798 (Pickering Papers, reel 8, Massachusetts Historical Society).

6  Copies of original documents including the arrest warrant and indictment may be found at "*United States v. William Durrell*: Violating the Alien and Sedition Acts," National Archives, available at www.archives.gov/education/lessons/sedition.html (accessed May 21, 2014).

7    Brigham, *History and Bibliography of American Newspapers*, vol. 1, pp. 605, 606.

8    "*United States v. William Durrell*," National Archives.

9    *New York Weekly Museum*, marriage notice, May 26, 1798.

10    Smith, *Freedom's Fetters*, p. 386.

11    Wilson, David A., *United Irishmen, United States: Immigrant Radicals in the Early Republic*, Cornell University Press, Ithaca, NY, 1998, pp. 22–24.

12    Wilson's *United Irishmen, United States* offers a nuanced, balanced analysis of the United Irishmen, their formative influence on American life and politics in the late eighteenth and early nineteenth centuries, and, particularly, the mutual misunderstandings that colored relations between the Irishmen and the Federalists.

13    Wilson, *United Irishmen, United States*, p. 49.

14    *New York Time-Piece*, July 2, 1798.

15    Timothy Pickering to William Cobbett, Feb. 3, 1798 (Pickering Papers, reel 8, Massachusetts Historical Society).

16    Timothy Pickering to Richard Harison, July 7, 1798 (Pickering Papers, reel 37, Massachusetts Historical Society).

17    Miller, *Crisis in Freedom*, pp. 101-102.

18    8 Annals of Cong., 2139, 2140 (1798).

19    Ibid., p. 2113.

20    Ibid., p. 2171.

21    1 Statutes at Large, 5th Cong., 2d Sess. 596–597 (1789–1799).

22    Ibid.

23    Miller, *Crisis in Freedom*, p. 93.

24    *New Hampshire Gazette*, Aug. 7, 1798.

## CHAPTER ELEVEN

1    Adams, Charles Francis, ed., *The Works of John Adams, Second President of the United States*, vol. 9, Little, Brown, Boston, 1856, p. 289. (Available online through the Online Library of Liberty.)

2    Ibid., p. 291.

3   Ibid., p. 14n2.

4   David McCullough's masterful 2001 biography, *John Adams*, refers to Adams's signing of the Alien and Sedition Acts as "the most reprehensible acts of his presidency" (p. 504). Yet they earn mention on just a dozen of the biography's 651 pages. Page Smith's enormous, two-volume 1962 biography, *John Adams*, refers to the Sedition Act on just 6 of 1,138 pages.

5   "Adams National Historical Park, Massachusetts: John Adams," National Park Service, www.nps.gov/adam/historyculture/john-adams.htm (accessed May 21, 2014).

6   McCullough, *John Adams*, pp. 65–68.

7   Adams, *Revolutionary Writings 1755–1775*, p. 123.

8   Ibid.

9   From Adams's private journal, under "notes for an oration at Braintree," quoted by McCullough, *John Adams*, p. 70.

10   Gelles, Edith B., *Abigail & John: Portrait of a Marriage*, Harper Perennial, New York, 2010, p. 247.

11   Ibid., p. 248.

12   Howell, T. B., comp., *A Complete Collection of State Trials and Proceedings for High Treason and Other Crimes and Misdemeanors, from the Earliest Period to the Year 1783*, vol. 9, Longman, Hurst, Rees, Orme & Brown et al., London, 1816, p. 667.

13   Descriptions of Algernon Sidney's arrest, trial, and execution are drawn from the transcript available in ibid., pp. 818–950.

14   Thomas Jefferson to Mason L. Weems, Dec. 13, 1789 (Papers of Thomas Jefferson, Library of Congress). Also see Gowdy, J. David, *Jefferson & James Madison's Guide to Understanding and Teaching the Constitution*, 2nd rev. ed., Washington, Jefferson & Madison Institute, 2011, e-book, which offers an excellent analysis of Sidney's influence on the Founders.

## CHAPTER TWELVE

1   Levy, Leonard W., *Legacy of Suppression: Freedom of Speech and Press in Early American History*, Harper & Row, New York, 1963, p. 18.

2   Ibid.

3   Ibid., p. ix.

4   Blackstone, William, *Blackstone's Commentaries*, abr. 9th ed., Callaghan and Company, Chicago, 1915, p. 463.

5   Ibid.

6   Ibid, pp. 461–462.

7   Hamilton, Alexander, "Concerning the Dangers from War between the States," Federalist Paper no. 6, Nov. 14, 1787, from *The Essential Federalist and Anti-Federalist Papers*, Classic Books America, New York, 2009, p. 29.

8   Hamilton, Alexander, "Certain General and Miscellaneous Objections to the Constitution Considered and Answered," Federalist Paper no. 84, July 16, 26, and Aug. 9, 1788, from ibid., pp. 380–381.

9   Chernow, *Alexander Hamilton*, p. 259.

10   *Philadelphia Independent Gazetteer*, Nov. 10, 1787, reprinted as "Rebuttal to 'An Officer of the Late Continental Army': 'Plain Truth,'" in *The Debate on the Constitution*, vol. 1, comp. Bernard Bailyn, Library of America, New York, 1993, p. 107.

11   *Virginia Independent Chronicle*, Richmond, Jan. 30, 1788, reprinted as "Reply to Mason's 'Objections': 'Civis Rusticus,'" in ibid., p. 357.

12   *Norfolk and Portsmouth (VA) Journal*, Feb. 20–Mar. 19, 1788, reprinted as "Answers to Mason's 'Objections': 'Marcus' [James Iredell] I–V," in ibid., p. 364.

13   *Massachusetts Gazette*, Boston, Jan. 8, 1788, reprinted as "Resolutions of the Tradesmen of the Town of Boston," in ibid., p. 718.

14   *American Magazine*, Dec. 1787, reprinted as "On the Absurdity of a Bill of Rights: 'Giles Hickory' [Noah Webster] I," in ibid., pp. 670–671.

15   *Philadelphia Independent Gazetteer*, Jan. 2, 1788, reprinted as "'Centinel' [Samuel Bryan] VIII," in ibid., p. 687.

16   Thomas Jefferson to James Madison, Dec. 20, 1787, reprinted in Jefferson, Thomas, *Writings*, comp. Merrill D. Peterson, Library of America, New York, 1984, p. 916.

17   Thomas Jefferson to Alexander Donald, Feb. 7, 1788, reprinted in ibid.

18   Levy, Leonard W., *Emergence of a Free Press*, Ivan R. Dee, Chicago, 2004 [1985].

19   Sunstein, Cass R., *Democracy and the Problem of Free Speech*, Free Press, New York, 1993, p. xiv.

20   Dershowitz, Alan M., "Speaking Freely: Thomas Healy's 'Great Dissent,'" *New York Times Book Review*, Aug. 22, 2013.

21   Armstrong, John, "To the Senate and Representatives of the United States, in Congress Assembled." The full text of Armstrong's essay, in its original format, may be found at "An American Time Capsule: Three Centuries of Broadsides and Other Printed Ephemera," Library of Congress, memory.loc.gov/ammem/rbpehtml/ (accessed May 21, 2014).

## CHAPTER THIRTEEN

1   Rosenfeld, *American Aurora*, pp. 198–199.

2   DeConde, *The Quasi-War*, pp. 104–105.

3   Ibid., p. 102.

4   Chernow, *Alexander Hamilton*, pp. 555–559; McCullough, *John Adams*, p. 511.

5   Ursula Baier, historian at the Skyline Farm Carriage Museum in North Yarmouth, Maine, estimates that carriages plying the East Coast in the late eighteenth century averaged at best twenty-five miles per day. In a phone conversation, she kindly provided many of the descriptive details used in this paragraph.

6   Chernow, *Washington: A Life*, p. 453.

7   Smith, Page, *John Adams*, vol. 2, Doubleday, Garden City, NY, 1962, p. 980.

8   *New York Daily Advertiser*, July 12, 1798.

9   Thomas Jefferson to James Madison, May 3, 1798 (Thomas Jefferson Papers, Library of Congress).

10   *Greenleaf's New York Journal*, July 14, 1798.

11   *Newark (NJ) Centinel of Freedom*, Oct. 8, 1799.

12   *Thomas's Massachusetts Spy*, Worcester, Aug. 8, 1798; Smith, *Freedom's Fetters*, p. 270.

13   *Newark (NJ) Centinel of Freedom*, Oct. 8, 1799. This scene is based on the *Centinel*'s account, with minor changes for clarity. The article tactfully presents the president's hindquarters as his "a—." The word is restored here as "arse" since that's the term used in Baldwin's indictment.

14   Rosenfeld, *American Aurora*, p. 198.

15   Austin, *Matthew Lyon*, p. 107.

16   Rosenfeld, *American Aurora*, pp. 203–204.

17   Wharton, *State Trials*, p. 333.

18    *Scourge of Aristocracy, and Repository of Important Political Truths*, Oct. 15, 1798.

19    A native of Redding, Connecticut (the local high school bears his name), Joel Barlow was also a Revolutionary War veteran and diplomat who had fallen out of favor with Federalists over his support of the French Revolution.

20    Austin, *Matthew Lyon*, pp. 109–110.

21    James T. Callender to Thomas Jefferson, Sept. 22, 1798 (Thomas Jefferson Papers, Library of Congress).

22    Durey, *"With the Hammer of Truth,"* p. 111.

23    *Gazette of the United States*, Aug. 9, 1798.

## Chapter Fourteen

1    "Letterbook of David Montagu Erskine, 1798–1799," Jan. 1, 1799 (Independence National Historical Park Library, Philadelphia; original at University of Virginia).

2    "Buildings of the Department of State: State House, Trenton," U.S. Department of State, Office of the Historian, history.state.gov/department history/buildings/section18 (accessed May 22, 2014).

3    Griffitts, Samuel Powel, "Diary of the Epidemic of Yellow Fever in 1798" (Independence National Historical Park Library, Philadelphia).

4    McCullough, *John Adams*, p. 510.

5    Dr. Benjamin Rush to William Marshall, Sept. 15, 1798 (Independence National Historical Park Service Library, Philadelphia).

6    *Philadelphia Aurora*, Aug. 11, 1798.

7    Griffitts, "Diary of the Epidemic of Yellow Fever in 1798."

8    Staples, J. Erin, and Thomas P. Monath, "Yellow Fever: 100 Years of Discovery," *Journal of the American Medical Association* 300, no. 8 (2008): 960–962.

9    Monath, Thomas P., "Yellow Fever," UpToDate, www.uptodate.com/contents/yellow-fever (accessed May 21, 2014).

10    "Yellow Fever: Clinical and Laboratory Evaluation," Centers for Disease Control and Prevention, www.cdc.gov/yellowfever/healthCareProviders/healthCareProviders-ClinLabEval.html (accessed May 22, 2014); "Yellow Fever: Frequently Asked Questions," Centers for Disease Control and Prevention, www.cdc.gov/yellowfever/qa/index.html (accessed May 22, 2014).

11   Today, the disease has been generally eradicated from North America and much of the world through vaccines and control of mosquito populations, but outbreaks remain a persistent threat. And while modern medicines may make a patient more comfortable, victims unfortunate enough to contract the most serious form of the disease still die up to half the time.

12   Griffitts, "Diary of the Epidemic of Yellow Fever in 1798."

13   Ibid.

14   Ibid.

15   *Philadelphia Aurora*, Aug. 11, 1798.

16   Benjamin Franklin Bache to Richard Bache, Sept. 2–3, 1798, reprinted in Smith, Jeffery A., *Franklin and Bache: Envisioning the Enlightened Republic*, Oxford University Press, New York, 1990, p. 163.

17   Rosenfeld, *American Aurora*, p. 204.

18   Ibid., p. 217.

19   Ibid., p. 208.

20   Ibid., p. 209.

21   Ibid., p. 213.

22   Platt, *The Home and Office of Benjamin Franklin Bache*, p. 74.

23   Smith, *Franklin and Bache: Envisioning the Enlightened Republic*, p. 163.

24   Quoted in Miller, *Crisis in Freedom*, p. 96.

25   Timothy Pickering to Timothy Williams, Sept. 13, 1798 (Timothy Pickering Papers, reel 4, Massachusetts Historical Society).

26   John Adams to Benjamin Rush, June 23, 1807, quoted in Rosenfeld, *American Aurora*, p. 235.

27   Hoadly, Charles J., comp., *The Public Records of the State of Connecticut*, vol. 9, Press of the Case, Lockwood & Brainard Co., Hartford, CT, 1895, pp. 316–317.

28   Reprinted in the *Farmers' Register*, Chambersburg, PA, Sept. 19, 1798.

## Chapter Fifteen

1   "General Election Results—U.S. Representatives, 1791–1800 (Two Districts)" (Vermont Office of the Secretary of State, Vermont State Archives and Records Administration).

2   Ibid.

3   *Scourge of Aristocracy*, Oct. 1, 1798.

4   Ibid.

5   Ibid.

6   Ibid.

7   Wharton, *State Trials*, p. 333.

8   Haw, James, et al., *Stormy Patriot: The Life of Samuel Chase*, Maryland Historical Society, Baltimore, 1980, p. 178.

9   Ibid., p. 196.

10   "The Supreme Court of the United States—History," U.S. Senate Committee on the Judiciary, www.judiciary.senate.gov/nominations/supreme-court/history/ (accessed May 23, 2014); "History of the Federal Judiciary: The Supreme Court of the United States and the Federal Judiciary," Federal Judicial Center, www.fjc.gov/history/home.nsf/page/courts_supreme.html (accessed May 23, 2014).

11   Haw et al., *Stormy Patriot*, p. 177.

12   Wharton, *State Trials*, pp. 335–336. Smith-Lyon election history: "General Election Results—U.S. Representatives, 1791–1800 (Two Districts)" (Vermont Office of the Secretary of State, Vermont State Archives and Records Administration).

13   *Wharton, State Trials*, p. 339.

14   Ibid., p. 336.

15   Ibid., p. 335.

16   *Scourge of Aristocracy*, Oct. 15, 1798.

17   Wharton, *State Trials*, p. 335.

18   Ibid., p. 336.

19   Ibid.

20   Dispatch from the *Vergennes (VT) Gazette*, reprinted in the *Boston Columbian Centinel*, Nov. 3, 1798.

21   Wharton, *State Trials*, pp. 336–337.

22   Soltow, Lee, *Distribution of Wealth and Income in the United States in 1798*, University of Pittsburgh Press, Pittsburgh, PA, 1989, p. 53, table 10.

23   A 1793 study of selected Massachusetts towns' estimated life expectancy at 36.5 years, with no breakdown by gender. Hacker, J. David, "Decennial

Life Tables for the White Population of the United States, 1790–1900," *Historical Methods* 43, no. 2 (Apr. 2010): table 1.

24   *Scourge of Aristocracy*, Oct. 15, 1798 . . .

25   There were at least two men named Jabez Fitch living in Vermont at the time of Matthew Lyon's imprisonment. One was a *Mayflower* descendant and Revolutionary War veteran renowned for his diary of days aboard a British prison ship during the war. George Gadbois, a *Mayflower* descendant who had been transcribing Fitch's diary, very generously leaped ahead in his project and transcribed entries from 1798 to help me determine if the Fitches were one and the same. Alas, while the veteran Fitch did comment briefly upon the Lyon case, this was not Jabez Fitch the jailer.

26   Wharton, *State Trials*, p. 341.

27   Dispatch from the *Vergennes (VT) Gazette*, reprinted in the *Boston Columbian Centinel*, Nov. 3, 1798.

28   Wharton, *State Trials*, p. 341.

29   Smith, *Freedom's Fetters*, p. 239.

30   Ibid.

31   "Mason, Stevens Thomson (1760–1803)," Biographical Directory of the U.S. Congress, bioguide.congress.gov/scripts/biodisplay.pl?index=M000226 (accessed May 23, 2014).

32   *Scourge of Aristocracy*, Oct. 15, 1798.

33   Ibid.

## CHAPTER SIXTEEN

1   *Claypoole's American Daily Advertiser*, Philadelphia, June 22, 1799. This wording is taken from the Sedition Act indictment and a report titled *Circuit Court* that was widely reprinted. Other accounts included slight punctuation and wording changes; some included the words "Liberty, Equality" at the outset, and the concluding line, "may moral virtue be the basis of Civil Government."

2   "The Origins of Liberty Poles in New York," Liberty Pole, thelibertypole.org/liberty_poles/liberty_poles.htm (accessed May 23, 2014).

3   Hamilton, *Writings*, p. 87.

4   *Columbian Centinel*, Boston, Aug. 19, 1798, quoted in Smith, James

Morton, "The Federalist 'Saints' versus 'The Devil of Sedition': The Liberty Pole Cases of Dedham, Massachusetts, 1798–1799," *New England Quarterly* 28, no. 2 (June 1955): 198–215.

5    *Massachusetts Mercury*, Boston, Nov. 9, 1798.

6    *Massachusetts Mercury*, Boston, Nov. 9, 1798.

7    Hanson, Robert Brand, *Dedham, Massachusetts, 1635–1890*, Dedham Historical Society, Dedham, MA, 1976, p. 175.

8    *New London (CT) Bee*, Nov. 21, 1798.

9    *Russell's Gazette*, Boston, Nov. 11, 1798.

10   *Claypoole's American Daily Advertiser*, Philadelphia, June 22, 1799.

11   *Eastern Herald and Gazette of Maine*, Portland, June 24, 1799.

12   *Claypoole's American Daily Advertiser*, Philadelphia, June 22, 1799.

13   Ibid.

14   Ibid.

15   Fisher Ames to Christopher Gore, Dec. 18, 1798, and Fisher Ames to Jeremiah Smith, Nov. 22, 1798, reprinted in Ames, Seth, ed., *Works of Fisher Ames, with a Selection from His Speeches and Correspondence*, vol. 1, Little, Brown, Boston, 1854, pp. 240–241, 247.

16   Ames, *The Diary of Dr. Nathaniel Ames of Dedham, Massachusetts*, p. 656.

17   Hanson, *Dedham, Massachusetts, 1635-1890*, p. 167.

18   Ames, *The Diary of Dr. Nathaniel Ames of Dedham, Massachusetts*, pp. 443–446.

19   Ibid., pp. 438–439.

20   From an article by Fisher Ames in the *Independent Chronicle*, Boston, Oct. 12, 1787, quoted in Bernhard, *Fisher Ames: Federalist and Statesman*, p. 48.

21   Ames, *The Diary of Dr. Nathaniel Ames of Dedham, Massachusetts*, p. 589.

22   Hanson, *Dedham, Massachusetts, 1635–1890*, p. 170.

23   Ibid., p. 171.

24   Ames, *The Diary of Dr. Nathaniel Ames of Dedham, Massachusetts*, p. 283.

25   Ibid., pp. 527, 528.

26   Ames, Fisher, *Works of Fisher Ames, Compiled by a Number of His Friends*, T. B. Wait, Boston, 1809.

27   Ames, *The Diary of Dr. Nathaniel Ames of Dedham, Massachusetts*, p. v.

28    *The Dedham Historical Register*, vol. 5, Dedham Historical Society, Dedham, MA, 1894, p. 149.

29    Ames, *The Diary of Dr. Nathaniel Ames of Dedham, Massachusetts*, pp. 610, 639.

30    Ames, ed., *Works of Fisher Ames*, p. 247.


## CHAPTER SEVENTEEN

1    *Philadelphia Aurora*, Nov. 22, 1798.

2    Rosenfeld, *American Aurora*, p. 525.

3    *Farmers' Register*, Chambersburg, PA, Nov. 7, 1798.

4    *New-York Gazette and General Advertiser*, Nov. 22, 1798.

5    Reprinted in the *New-Hampshire Gazette*, Portsmouth, Nov. 21, 1798.

6    *Columbian Herald*, Charleston, SC, Oct. 18, 1787.

7    Stockton was married in April 1798 (*Gazette of the United States*, Philadelphia, Apr. 18, 1797). In early 1798 he was appointed by Adams as U.S. Attorney for New Jersey (*Gazette of the United States*, Feb. 14, 1798).

8    Pasler, Rudolph J., and Margaret C. Pasler, *The New Jersey Federalists*, Associated University Presses, London; Fairleigh Dickinson University Press, Rutherford, NJ, 1975, p. 83.

9    *Newark (NJ) Centinel of Freedom*, Nov. 6, 1798. Also, *Herald of Liberty*, Washington, PA, Nov. 3, 1800.

10    *Herald of Liberty*, Washington, PA, Nov. 3, 1800.

11    Stone, Geoffrey R., *Perilous Times: Free Speech in Wartime from the Sedition Act of 1798 to the War on Terrorism*, W. W. Norton & Co., New York, 2004, p. 66.

12    Smith, *Freedom's Fetters*, p. 274.

13    Rose, P. K., "The Founding Fathers of American Intelligence," CIA Center for the Study of Intelligence Library, www.cia.gov/library/center-for-the-study-of-intelligence/csi-publications/books-and-monographs/the-founding-fathers-of-american-intelligence/art-1.html (accessed May 23, 2014).

14    Drake, J. Madison, *Historical Sketches of the Revolutionary and Civil Wars*, Webster Press, New York, 1908, p. 110.

15    *Pennsylvania Evening Post*, Philadelphia, Mar. 25, 1782.

16  *New-Jersey Gazette*, Burlington, May 17, 1784.

17  *New York Evening Post*, June 4, 1803, and July 30, 1803; *Newark (NJ) Centinel of Freedom*, Aug. 9, 1803.

18  *Newark (NJ) Centinel of Freedom*, July 31, 1798.

19  Ibid., Aug. 16, 1803.

20  Ibid., Jan. 8, 1799.

21  *Newark (NJ) Centinel of Freedom*, Nov. 6, 1798.

22  *Albany (NY) Centinel*, Nov. 16, 1798; *Suffield (CT) Impartial Herald*, Nov. 20, 1798; *Georgetown (SC) Gazette*, Nov. 27, 1798.

23  *Salem (NY) Northern Centinel*, Nov. 27, 1798.

24  *Newark (NJ) Centinel of Freedom*, Dec. 18, 1798.

25  Ibid., Jan. 8, 1799.

## CHAPTER EIGHTEEN

1  *Scourge of Aristocracy*, Dec. 15, 1798.

2  Quoted in Wharton, *State Trials*, p. 342.

3  *Scourge of Aristocracy*, Dec. 15, 1798.

4  Ibid.

5  From an unidentified newspaper clipping, quoted in Austin, *Matthew Lyon*, p. 123.

6  Wharton, *State Trials*, p. 343; Lyon biographer Aleine Austin offers the same victory margin in her book *Matthew Lyon* (p. 124), citing a *Rutland Herald* newspaper article, as does James Fairfax McLaughlin's biography *Matthew Lyon, the Hampden of Congress*. The Office of the Vermont Secretary of State's historical elections database says the exact figures for that election can't be found, but that Lyon won by "a large majority."; "General Election Results—U.S. Representatives, 1791–1800 (Two Districts)" (Vermont Office of the Secretary of State, Vermont State Archives and Records Administration).

7  *Vermont Gazette*, Bennington, Jan. 31, 1799.

8  Austin, *Matthew Lyon*, p. 125. See also Thomas Jefferson to James Madison, Jan. 3, 1799, in Jefferson, Thomas, *The Works of Thomas Jefferson*, vol. 9, ed. Paul Leicester Ford, G. P. Putnam's Sons, New York and London, 1905, p. 4.

9  Randall, *Ethan Allen: His Life and Times*, pp. 498–504.

10   Wharton, *State Trials*, p. 684.

11   Smith, *Freedom's Fetters*, p. 243; McLaughlin, *Matthew Lyon, The Hampden of Congress*, page 376.

12   Unpublished history by J. D. Smith, grandson of Lyon's Vermont neighbors (Bixby Memorial Library, Vergennes, VT).

13   White, Pliny H., "Life and Services of Matthew Lyon," quoted in McLaughlin, *Matthew Lyon, the Hampden of Congress*, p. 378.

14   Daniel Church to Major Stephen Greenleaf, Mar. 4, 1799 (Vermont Historical Society).

15   9 Annals of Cong., 2884-2885; 2906–2907 (1799).

16   Ibid., p. 2934.

17   From *Porcupine's Gazette*, quoted in Wharton, *State Trials*, p. 343.

18   9 Annals of Cong., 2954 (1799).

19   Ibid., p. 2961.

20   Ibid., p. 2964.

21   Ibid., p. 2965.

22   Ibid., p. 2973.

## CHAPTER NINETEEN

1   Thomas Jefferson to James Monroe, Jan. 3, 1799, from Jefferson, *The Works of Thomas Jefferson*, p. 6.

2   Thomas Jefferson to James Monroe, July 17, 1802 (Thomas Jefferson Papers, Library of Congress).

3   Thomas Jefferson to John Taylor, Nov. 26, 1798 (Thomas Jefferson Papers, Library of Congress).

4   Madison, *Writings*, p. 902.

5   Jefferson, *Writings*, p. 1525.

6   Ibid., p. 451.

7   Ibid., p. 454.

8   Ibid., p. 453.

9   James Madison to Thomas Jefferson, Dec. 29, 1798, reprinted in Madison, *Writings*, p. 592.

10   "Virginia Resolutions against the Alien and Sedition Acts," Dec. 21, 1798, reprinted in ibid., p. 589.

11   James Madison to Nicholas P. Trist, Dec. 23, 1832, reprinted in ibid., p. 862.

12   *Albany (NY) Centinel*, Jan. 1, 1799.

13   *New York Daily Advertiser*, Jan. 7, 1799.

14   *Gazette of the United States*, reprinted in the *Courier of New Hampshire*, Concord, Jan. 12, 1799.

15   *Porcupine's Gazette*, Sept. 21, 1798, quoted in Stewart, *The Opposition Press of the Federalist Period*, p. 362.

16   *Oracle of Dauphin*, Harrisburg, PA, Jan. 2, 1799.

17   *Maryland Herald*, Jan. 31, 1799.

18   Hoadly, comp., *The Public Records of the State of Connecticut*, pp. 357–358.

19   "Political Reflections," *Philadelphia Aurora*, Feb. 23, 1799, reprinted in Madison, *Writings*, p. 600.

20   "Foreign Influence," *Philadelphia Aurora*, Jan, 23, 1799, reprinted in ibid., pp. 592–599.

21   "Political Reflections," *Philadelphia Aurora*, Feb. 23, 1799, reprinted in ibid., pp. 605, 606.

22   Hay, George, *An Essay on the Liberty of the Press*, rpt., Samuel Pleasants Jr., Richmond, VA, 1803 [s.p., Philadelphia, 1799], e-book.

23   Ibid.

24   Ibid.

25   Ibid.

## CHAPTER TWENTY

1   9 Annals of Cong., 2955, 2985 (1799). Calculations based on 69,887 voters in the November 1799 Pennsylvania gubernatorial race (www.ourcampaigns. com) and Pennsylvania population of 602,365 for 1800, and 12,702,379 for 2010 (www.npg.org/library/population-data/pennsylvania.html). See also en.wikipedia.org/wiki/Pennsylvania_gubernatorial_election,_1799.

2   Mark, Gregory A., "The Vestigial Constitution: The History and Significance of the Right to Petition," *Fordham Law Review* 66, no. 6 (1998): 2175–2177, 2200–2201.

3   Baker, Dillon, "The Massachusetts's Body of Liberties and the Spirit of the Puritans," *The University of Vermont History Review*, 2013-2014. A version of this paper, expanded post publication, deals specifically with the right to petition.

4   Mark, "The Vestigial Constitution: The History and Significance of the Right to Petition."

5   9 Annals of Cong., 2988 (1799).

6   Bloom, *The Story of the Constitution*, p. 140.

7   9 Annals of Cong., 2988–2989 (1799).

8   Ibid., p. 2990.

9   Ibid.

10   Ibid., pp. 2992, 3016.

## Chapter Twenty-One

1   Timothy Pickering to Robert Wharton, Apr. 26, 1799 (Pickering Papers, reel 37, Massachusetts Historical Society).

2   Timothy Pickering to William Rawle, July 5, 1799 (Pickering Papers, reel 11, Massachusetts Historical Society). Although his letter does not identify the German-language publication, Pickering was probably referring to *Der Unpartheyische Reading Adler*, established in Reading in 1796 by printers Jacob Schneider and Georg Gerrisch. Brigham, *History and Bibliography of American Newspapers*, vol. 2, p. 969.

3   *Porcupine's Gazette*, Philadelphia, June 21, 1799.

4   *A Plan of Dedham Village, Mass., 1636–1876*, Dedham Historical Society, Dedham, MA, 1883, p. 13.

5   For example, see MeasuringWorth at www.measuringworth.com/uscompare/.

6   *Massachusetts Mercury*, Boston, June 21, 1799.

7   Ibid., June 26, 1799.

8   Ibid.

9   *American Mercury*, Hartford, CT, June 27, 1799.

10   *Salem (MA) Gazette*, July 25, 1799.

11   Haw et al., *Stormy Patriot*, pp. 18, 58–64, 68.

12    Ibid., pp. 30, 144–156, 177.

13    Miller, *Crisis in Freedom*, pp. 86–87.

14    *Claypoole's American Daily Advertiser*, Philadelphia, June 22, 1799.

15    Ibid.

16    Chernow, *Washington: A Life*. p. 271.

17    Ames, *The Diary of Dr. Nathaniel Ames of Dedham, Massachusetts*, p. 684.

18    Warren, Charles, *Jacobin and Junto; or, Early American Politics as Viewed in the Diary of Nathaniel Ames, 1758–1822*, Harvard University Press, Cambridge, MA, 1931, p. 110.

19    Ames, *The Diary of Dr. Nathaniel Ames of Dedham, Massachusetts*, p. 778.

20    *Norwich (CT) Packet*, July 4, 1799.

21    Ibid.

## Chapter Twenty-Two

1    Based on memories of the Duc de La Rochefoucauld Liancourt, who visited the area in 1795, in Wood, T. Kenneth, "History in the Making of the West Branch—The Story of Samuel Wallis," *Proceedings of the Northumberland County Historical Society*, vol. 4, Northumberland County Historical Society, Sunbury, PA, 1932, pp. 62–63.

2    Kieft, Lester, *Joseph Priestley and the Priestley House*, booklet, Friends of the Joseph Priestley House, Northumberland, PA, 2006.

3    Johnson, Steven, *The Invention of Air: A Story of Science, Faith, Revolution, and the Birth of America*, Riverhead Books, New York, 2008, p. 100.

4    Slack, Charles, *Noble Obsession: Charles Goodyear, Thomas Hancock, and the Race to Unlock the Greatest Industrial Secret of the Nineteenth Century*, Hyperion, New York, 2002, p. 30.

5    Johnson, *The Invention of Air*, p. 54.

6    Ibid., p. 39.

7    Ibid., p. 178.

8    Ibid., p. 144.

9    Ibid., p. 187.

10    Malone, Dumas, *The Public Life of Thomas Cooper, 1783–1839*, University

of South Carolina Press, Columbia, 1961 [Yale University Press, New Haven, CT, 1926], p. 5.

11   Ibid., p. 17.

12   Cooper, Thomas, *Some Information Respecting America*, J. Johnson, London, 1794, p. iv. (Available online from Dickinson College Archives and Special Collections).

13   The house, owned by the state of Pennsylvania and operated and maintained by local volunteers in the small town of Northumberland, still stands. It's one of America's under-discovered historical treasures.

14   Malone, *The Public Life of Thomas Cooper*, p. 8.

15   *Sunbury and Northumberland Gazette*, Apr. 27, 1799, reprinted in *Philosophical Writings of Thomas Cooper*, vol. 2, ed. Udo Thiel, Thoemmes Press, Bristol, England; Sterling, VA, 2001, e-book.

16   "On the Sedition Bill" in ibid.

17   "Address to the Readers of the *Sunbury and Northumberland Gazette*, June 29, 1799," reprinted in ibid.

18   Smith, *Freedom's Fetters*, pp. 309–310.

19   Timothy Pickering to Charles Hall, Aug. 1, 1799 (Pickering Papers, reel 11, Massachusetts Historical Society).

## CHAPTER TWENTY-THREE

1   Timothy Pickering to John Adams, Aug. 1, 1799 (Pickering Papers, reel 11, Massachusetts Historical Society).

2   John Adams to Timothy Pickering, Aug. 13, 1799, Adams, *The Works of John Adams, Second President of the United States*, vol. 9, Little, Brown, Boston, 1854, p. 13.

3   Ibid., pp. 13-14.

4   Cooper, Thomas, *An Account of the Trial of Thomas Cooper, of Northumberland; on a Charge of Libel against the President of the United States*, J. Bioren, Philadelphia, 1800, p. 4. Cooper's own account, printed in April 1800, offers the best and most complete rendition of his Sedition Act trial.

5   Ibid., p. 7.

6   Indictment of Thomas Cooper printed in the *Philadelphia Gazette*, Apr. 21, 1800.

7    Cooper, *An Account of the Trial of Thomas Cooper*, p. 7.

8    *Philadelphia Gazette*, Apr. 26, 1800.

9    There's some discrepancy over the exact size of Baldwin's fines. While numerous newspaper accounts put the figure at $150 total, the *Centinel of Freedom* repeatedly put the amount at $400 ($250 for sedition; $150 in costs). It is also uncertain exactly how much time Baldwin spent in jail, combining both his initial arrest and punishment. The sentence mandated that the defendant remain in jail until his fine was paid.

10   *Philadelphia Independent Gazetteer*, Oct. 29, 1787, reprinted as "'To Lick the Feet of Our Well Born Masters': 'John Humble,'" in *The Debate on the Constitution*, p. 226.

11   *Greenleaf's New York Journal*, Oct. 19, 1799.

12   *New London (CT) Bee*, Oct. 16, 1799.

13   Reprinted in the *Constitutional Telegraph*, Boston, Oct. 26, 1799.

14   Ibid.

15   *Columbian Centinel*, Boston, Nov. 16, 1799.

16   *Constitutional Telegraph*, Boston, Oct. 26, 1799.

17   Smith, *Freedom's Fetters*, p. 406.

18   *Maryland Herald and Elizabeth-Town Advertiser*, Dec. 5, 1799.

19   *Dover (NH) Sun*, Dec. 18, 1799; Smith, *Freedom's Fetters*, p. 414.

20   Rosenfeld, *American Aurora*, p. 720.

21   Ibid., p. 820. Duane and Bache would remain married for thirty-five years. In keeping with the times, Duane assumed control over the editorial content of the paper, as Bache renewed her more traditional role of wife and mother. The two would have five children together (in addition to Margaret's four with her first husband). One of those children would take over the helm of the paper upon his father's retirement. Another son would go on to serve in the administration of President Andrew Jackson as secretary of the Treasury, the position first held (and given its definition) by the *Aurora*'s enemy, Alexander Hamilton.

## Chapter Twenty-Four

1    Wharton, *State Trials*, pp. 684-685.

2    Ibid., p. 687.

3   Resch, Tyler, "Anthony Haswell and Freedom of the Press." Transcript of speech by the librarian of the Bennington (VT) Museum, April 24, 2004.

4   Resch, "Anthony Haswell and Freedom of the Press."

5   *New York Republican Watch-Tower*, Apr. 23, 1800.

6   All following quotes from the trial in Cooper, *An Account of the Trial of Thomas Cooper*, pp. 9, 13–16, 20–21.

7   *United States v. Thomas Cooper*, 25 Fed. Cas. 631 (C.C.D.Pa. 1800), in *Law and Jurisprudence in American History, Cases and Materials*, 3rd ed., ed. Stephen B. Presser and Jamil S. Zainaldin, West Publishing Company, St. Paul, MN, 1995.

8   Cooper, *An Account of the Trial of Thomas Cooper*, p. 49.

9   Ibid., p. 51.

10   *Leominster (MA) Telescope*, May 15, 1800.

11   *Columbian Minerva*, Dedham, MA, May 8, 1800.

## CHAPTER TWENTY-FIVE

1   Callender, James Thomson, *The Prospect Before Us*, vol. 1, s.p., Richmond, VA, 1800, p. 3.

2   Ibid., p. 157.

3   Ibid., p. 53.

4   Ibid., p. 86.

5   *Trial of Samuel Chase: An Associate Justice of the Supreme Court of the United States*, vol. 1, printed for Samuel H. Smith, Washington, D.C., 1805, p. 193.

6   Wharton, *State Trials*, p. 688.

7   DeConde, *The Quasi-War*, p. 4.

8   *Trial of Samuel Chase*, p. 194.

9   Thomas Jefferson to James Monroe, May 26, 1800 (Thomas Jefferson Papers, Library of Congress).

10   Thomas Jefferson to James Callender, Sept. 6, 1799 (Thomas Jefferson Papers, Library of Congress).

11   Thomas Jefferson to James T. Callender, Oct. 6, 1799 (Thomas Jefferson Papers, Library of Congress).

12    Ibid.

13    Wharton, *State Trials*, pp. 705–706.

14    Ibid., p. 693.

15    Ibid., p. 694.

16    Ibid., p. 691.

17    Ibid., p. 707.

18    Ibid., p. 710.

19    Ibid., p. 711.

20    Ibid., p. 714.

21    Ibid., p. 718.

22    James T. Callender to Thomas Jefferson, Oct. 27, 1800 (Thomas Jefferson Papers, Library of Congress).

23    James T. Callender to Thomas Jefferson, Oct. 11, 1800 (Thomas Jefferson Papers, Library of Congress).

## CHAPTER TWENTY-SIX

1    DeConde, *The Quasi-War*, pp. 124–129.

2    McCullough, *John Adams*, p. 523.

3    Elkins and McKitrick, *The Age of Federalism*, p. 686.

4    Clarfield, *Timothy Pickering and the American Republic*, p. 212.

5    Ibid., pp. 182–183.

6    Timothy Pickering to George Washington, July 6, 1798. Timothy Pickering to George Washington, Sept. 1, 1798 (Pickering Papers, reel 9, Massachusetts Historical Society).

7    Clarfield, *Timothy Pickering and the American Republic*, p. 212.

8    John Adams to Timothy Pickering, May 10, 1800 (Pickering Papers, reel 13, Massachusetts Historical Society).

9    Timothy Pickering to John Adams, May 12, 1800 (Pickering Papers, reel 13, Massachusetts Historical Society).

10    Timothy Pickering to R. G. van Polanen, May 15, 1800 (Pickering Papers, reel 13, Massachusetts Historical Society).

11    *American Citizen*, New York, May 12, 1800.

12    *New York Gazette*, May 15, 1800.

13   *Aurora* article reprinted in *American Mercury*, Hartford, CT, May 15, 1800.

14   *New York Daily Advertiser*, May 12, 1800.

15   Hamilton, Alexander, *Letter from Alexander Hamilton, Concerning the Public Conduct and Character of John Adams, Esq. President of the United States*, John Lang, New York, 1800, p. 4.

16   Ibid., p. 50.

17   To the benefit of posterity, Cooper was sufficiently convinced of the righteousness of his cause to present the case in full, including the arguments of Justice Chase and prosecutor Rawles.

18   *Philadelphia Aurora General Advertiser*, May 15, 1800.

19   *J. Russell's Gazette*, Boston, May 26, 1800.

20   *Constitutional Telegraph*, Boston, May 31, 1800.

21   *Carolina Gazette*, Charleston, SC, May 5, 1800.

22   Malone, *The Public Life of Thomas Cooper*, pp. 136–137.

23   Ibid., pp. 140–142.

24   Ibid., pp. 141–142.

25   Quoted in ibid., p. 140.

26   Ibid.

## CHAPTER TWENTY-SEVEN

1   "7 Elections That Changed U.S. History: Election of 1800," Duke University Libraries, library.duke.edu/exhibits/sevenelections/elections/1800/winner.html (accessed May 24, 2014).

2   Currie, *The Constitution in Congress*, p. 293.

3   10 Annals of Cong., 1033 (1801). Also "7 Elections That Changed U.S. History: Election of 1800."

4   Anderson, Frank M., "The Enforcement of the Alien and Sedition Laws," *Annual Report of the American Historical Association for 1912*, American Historical Society, Washington, D.C., 1914, p. 125. Anderson's seminal paper was the first to reveal many of the Sedition Act cases, defendants, and punishments. In the case of David Brown, Anderson located Brown's pardon appeals and established that Adams read the July 1800 request at his farm in Quincy, before forwarding it to the State Department with no action.

5    Thomas Jefferson to Abigail Adams, June 13, 1804 (Thomas Jefferson Papers, Library of Congress).

6    Senate Executive Journal, 6th Cong., 2nd Sess. 368 (1801).

7    *Republican Watch-Tower*, New York, July 28, 1802.

8    *Guardian of Liberty*, Newport, RI, Jan. 31, 1801.

9    Senate Executive Journal, 6th Cong., 2nd Sess. 370 (1801). Also, *Philadelphia Gazette*, Jan. 22, 1801.

10    Senate Executive Journal, 6th Cong., 2nd Sess. 375 (1801).

11    *American Citizen*, New York, July 26, 1802.

12    *American Citizen*, New York, Jan. 1, 1804.

13    Senate Executive Journal, 6th Cong., 2nd Sess. 375 (1801).

14    10 Annals of Cong., 1079–1082 (1801).

15    Matthew Lyon to Andrew Jackson, Feb. 28, 1800, quoted in Austin, *Matthew Lyon*, p. 131.

16    The entire letter, from which this excerpt is quoted, appeared in the first full-length biography of Lyon: McLaughlin, *Matthew Lyon, the Hampden of Congress*, pp. 397–406.

## PART III: THE FEVER BREAKS
## CHAPTER TWENTY-EIGHT

1    Jefferson, *Writings*, pp. 492–496.

2    Meacham, Jon, *Thomas Jefferson: The Art of Power*, Random House, New York, 2012, p. 348.

3    "Washington's Farewell Address," reprinted in Bloom, *The Story of the Constitution*, p. 136.

4    Jefferson, *Writings*, pp. 492–496.

5    Bernhard, *Fisher Ames: Federalist and Statesman*, p. 342.

6    Ames, *The Diary of Dr. Nathaniel Ames of Dedham, Massachusetts*, p. 799.

7    Ibid., p. 889.

8    Ibid.

9    Ibid.

10   Ibid., p. 1184.

11   *New York Evening Post,* Jan. 1, 1804.

12   *Newark (NJ) Centinel of Freedom,* Aug. 17, 1802.

13   *Alexandria (VA) Advertiser and Commercial Intelligencer,* Nov. 9, 1801.

14   The letter, dated May 1, 1804, and attributed to "a gentleman in Albany," was subsequently published in the *Newark (NJ) Centinel of Freedom,* May 22, 1804. An editorial note explained that the letter was published "in order to correct reports, and for the satisfaction of his friends."

15   *Philadelphia Aurora,* May 12, 1804.

## CHAPTER TWENTY-NINE

1   Malone, *The Public Life of Thomas Cooper,* pp. 325–335.

2   Ibid., pp. 20–21, 76.

3   Ibid., pp. 288–289.

4   Ibid., pp. 284–285, 334, 377.

5   *Richmond (VA) Recorder,* Sept. 1, 1802.

6   Jellison, Charles A., "That Scoundrel Callender," *Virginia Magazine of History and Biography* 67, no. 3 (July 1959): 295–306.

7   Thomas Jefferson to James Monroe, July 15, 1802 (Thomas Jefferson Papers, Library of Congress).

8   *Richmond (VA) Recorder,* Sept. 1, 1802.

9   Thomas Jefferson to James T. Callender, Oct. 6, 1799 (Thomas Jefferson Papers, Library of Congress).

10   *Richmond (VA) Examiner,* June 2, 1802.

11   *Richmond (VA) Recorder,* Sept. 1, 1802.

12   Thomas Jefferson to Robert R. Livingston, Oct. 10, 1802 (Thomas Jefferson Papers, Library of Congress).

13   Durey, *"With the Hammer of Truth,"* p. 163.

14   Ibid., pp. 164–165.

15   Ibid., pp. 167–168.

16   Ibid., p. 171; *Richmond Examiner,* July 23, 1803.

CHAPTER THIRTY

1  *Virginia Argus*, July 20, 1803.

2  *Virginia Herald*, Fredericksburg, July 22, 1803.

3  *Richmond (VA) Examiner*, July 23, 1803.

4  The date of burial was confirmed via e-mail by Saint John's Church, Richmond, VA, the centerpiece of what is today Richmond's historic Church Hill neighborhood.

5  "Electoral College Box Scores 1789-1996," National Archives, www.archives.gov/federal-register/electoral-college/scores.html (accessed June 1, 2014).

6  *Richmond (VA) Recorder*, Sept. 22, 1802.

7  A copy of the article can be found at "The Memoirs of Madison Hemings, 1873," Frontline, www.pbs.org/wgbh/pages/frontline/shows/jefferson/cron/1873march.html (accessed May 24, 2014).

8  Jellison, "That Scoundrel Callender," p. 305.

9  "Assessment of DNA Study," *Report of the Research Committee of Thomas Jefferson and Sally Hemings*, Thomas Jefferson Foundation, Charlottesville, VA, January 2000.

10  "Thomas Jefferson and Sally Hemings: A Brief Account," Thomas Jefferson Foundation, www.monticello.org/site/plantation-and-slavery/thomas-jefferson-and-sally-hemings-brief-account (accessed May 24, 2014).

11  Turner, Robert F., ed., *The Jefferson-Hemings Controversy: Report of the Scholars Commission*, Carolina Academic Press, Durham, NC, 2011, pp. 95–103.

12  House Journal, 8th Cong., 2nd Sess. 31–33 (1804).

13  Ibid.

14  Presser and Zainaldin, eds., *Law and Jurisprudence in American History*, pp. 224, 225.

15  Rehnquist, William H., *Grand Inquests: The Historic Impeachments of Justice Samuel Chase and President Andrew Johnson*, Morrow, New York, 1992, p. 114.

16  *Trial of Samuel Chase*, p. 1805.

17  Austin, *Matthew Lyon*, p. 147.

18  Ibid., p. 149.

19   Ibid., pp. 149–150.

20   "Matthew Lyon—Heirs Of," rep. no. 218, 23rd Cong., 1st Sess. (1834).


PART IV: THE PARCHMENT BARRIER
CHAPTER THIRTY-ONE

1   "Sedition Act (Chapter 290)," Attorney-General's Chambers, Singapore, statutes.agc.gov.sg/aol/search/display/view.w3p;page=0;query=DocId%3A%221f6d9e4b-1cf1-4575-9480-da4bdeff9ef4%22%20Status%3Apublished%20Depth%3A0;rec=0 (accessed May 25, 2014).

2   Intarakratug, Vee, and Alisa Tang, "American Sentenced to Prison for Thai Royal Insult," Associated Press, Dec. 8, 2011.

3   Smith, David, "In Jail: Zimbabwe Police Sergeant Who Dared to Use Robert Mugabe's Loo," *Guardian*, May 27, 2011.

4   Schemm, Paul, "Moroccan Student Sentenced to 3 Years in Prison for Insulting King in Online Video," Associated Press, Feb. 14, 2012.

5   Quoted in "3 Vietnamese Bloggers Charged over Their Writing" Associated Press, Apr. 16, 2012.

6   Hennock, Mary, "China Jails Dissident Chen Xi for 10 Years," *Guardian*, Dec. 26, 2011; "China Requires Internet Users to Register Names," Associated Press, Dec. 28, 2012; Anderlini, Jamil, "China Intensifies Internet Crackdown," *Financial Times*, Sept. 16, 2013.

7   Dehghan, Saeed Kamali, "Iranian Rapper Faces Death Threats and Fatwa for 'Blasphemous' Song," *Guardian*, May 14, 2012.

8   "Editor Jailed for Seven Years and Sentenced to 600 Lashes after Starting 'Free Saudi Liberals' Website," *Daily Mail*, July 30, 2013.

9   Dombey, Daniel, "Turkish Musician Accused of Islam Insults," *Financial Times*, Oct. 18, 2012.

10   "Art 11. Freedom of Expression and Information," EU Charter of Fundamental Rights, www.eucharter.org/home.php?page_id=18 (accessed May 25, 2014).

11   Greene, Marilyn, ed., *It's a Crime: How Insult Laws Stifle Press Freedom*, World Press Freedom Committee, 2006, p. 24.

12   *ECRI Report on Finland (Fourth Monitoring Cycle)*, European Commission against Racism and Intolerance, Council of Europe, July 9, 2013.

13   *National Legal Measures to Combat Racism and Intolerance in the Member States of the Council of Europe*, European Commission against Racism and Intolerance, Council of Europe. See "The Netherlands," p. 7.

14   "General Penal Code of Iceland, No. 19, February 12, 1940," Legislation Online, Organization for Security and Co-operation in Europe, legislationline.org/documents/section/criminal-codes (accessed May 25, 2014).

15   Vinocur, Nick, "John Galliano to Attend Anti-Semitic Trial," Reuters, June 21, 2011.

16   "Lagerfeld 'Furious' over Galliano Outbursts," AFP, Mar. 3, 2011.

17   Barchfield, Jenny, "Court Convicts Galliano in Anti-Semitism Case," Associated Press, Sept. 8, 2011.

18   Crawford, Tiffany, and Andrea Woo, "Comedian Fined for Hurling Sexual Insults at Show," *Vancouver Sun*, Apr. 22, 2011.

19   Dunn, Mark, "Class Action against Columnist Andrew Bolt Succeeds in Federal Court," *Herald Sun*, Sept. 28, 2011.

20   "Andrew Bolt Penalty Handed Down," 3AW Radio, Oct. 19, 2011.

21   Lewis, Anthony, *Freedom for the Thought That We Hate: A Biography of the First Amendment*, Basic Books, New York, 2007, p. ix.

22   "'I'm Not a Racist,' Says Richards after Rant," *Chicago Tribune*, Nov. 21, 2006.

23   Lewis, *Freedom for the Thought That We Hate*, p. ix.

24   James Madison to Thomas Jefferson, Oct. 17, 1788, reprinted in Madison, *Writings*, p. 420.

25   Plimpton, George, ed., *Writers at Work: The* Paris Review *Interviews*, 2nd series, Penguin Books, New York, 1977 [1963], p. 239.

26   Stone, *Perilous Times*, p. 186. Stone's widely hailed book offers an indispensable look at efforts to suppress speech during times of conflict throughout the nation's history.

27   Kennedy, David M., *Over Here: The First World War and American Society*, Oxford University Press, Oxford and New York, 1980, p. 82.

28   Kennedy, *Over Here*, pp. 75-77.

29   Stone, *Perilous Times*, pp. 196–197.

30    March, Andrew F., "A Dangerous Mind?," *New York Times Sunday Review*, Apr. 21, 2012.

31    Ibid.

32    Andersen, Travis, "Federal Appeals Court Upholds Tarek Mehanna Terror Convictions," *Boston Globe*, Nov. 13, 2013.

33    "Graham: Explore Limits on Quran Burnings," *Politico*, Apr. 3, 2011.

34    Chomsky, Noam, "My Reaction to Osama bin Laden's Death," *Guernica*, May 6, 2011.

35    Hitchens, Christopher, "Chomsky's Follies," *Slate*, May 9, 2011.

36    Stephens, Bret, "From Chomsky to bin Laden," *Wall Street Journal*, May 10, 2011.

37    Fonda, Jane, Robin Morgan, and Gloria Steinem, "FCC Should Clear Limbaugh from Airwaves," CNN.com, Mar. 12, 2012.

38    Winter, Jana, "Michigan Considers Law to Register Journalists," FOXNews.com, May 28, 2010.

39    "Comparing Hate Speech Laws in the U.S. and Abroad," National Public Radio, Mar. 3, 2011. Later in 2011, Yale closed the Initiative for the Interdisciplinary Study of Anti-Semitism. Ironically, some critics of the decision suggested Yale had closed the program in part for too openly encouraging discussions on the sensitive subject of Muslims and anti-Semitism. In response to the criticism, a university official assured the student newspaper that "Yale is strongly committed to freedom of speech." See Burt, David, "Anti-Semitism Initiative to End," *Yale Daily News*, June 7, 2011. The university has since opened the Yale Program for the Study of Antisemitism (ypsa.yale.edu).

40    Dudding, Sasha, "Brison Discusses Free Speech Limits," *Dartmouth*, Jan. 17, 2012.

41    Hall, David, "Interview: Jeremy Waldron," *New Zealand Listener*, Feb. 18, 2012.

42    Waldron, Jeremy, *The Harm in Hate Speech*, Harvard University Press, Cambridge, MA, 2012, p. 25.

43    Ibid., pp. 31, 33.

44    Ibid., p. 33.

45    Rosen, Rebecca J., "'This Machine Surrounds Hate and Forces It to Surrender,'" *Atlantic*, Jan. 28, 2014.

46 *Music from* Pete Seeger, the Power of Song, CD (2-disc special ed.), Live Nation Worldwide, New York, 2007.

47 *Pete Seeger: The Power of Song*, American Masters, PBS, aired Jan. 30, 2014.

48 Sunstein, *Democracy and the Problem of Free Speech*, pp. xi, 16–17, 28.

49 Fiss, Owen M., *The Irony of Free Speech*, Harvard University Press, Cambridge, MA, 1996, pp. 2–4.

50 Fish, Stanley, "What Is the First Amendment For?," *New York Times*, Feb. 1, 2010.

51 Ibid.

52 Jay, John, "An Address to the People of the State of New-York," 1787, quoted in Miller, *Crisis in Freedom*, p. 16.

53 For example, Supreme Court justice Elena Kagan in 2011 declared "The First Amendment's core purpose is to foster a healthy, vibrant political system full of robust discussion and debate." From "*Arizona Free Enterprise Club's Freedom Club PAC et al. v. Bennett, Secretary of State of Arizona, et al.*," dissenting opinion by justice Kagan, joined by justices Ginsburg, Breyer, and Sotomayor, www.supremecourt.gov/opinions/10pdf/10-238.pdf (accessed August 9, 2014).

54 *Racial Discrimination: Know Your Rights*, Australian Human Rights Commission, Sydney, 2012, p. 8.

55 Rauch, Jonathan, *Kindly Inquisitors: The New Attacks on Free Thought*, University of Chicago Press, Chicago, 1993, pp. 160–162.

56 Marshall's quote (I read it first in Doris Kearns Goodwin's *Team of Rivals*) originated in a dissenting opinion to a 1988 drug case, *Skinner v. Railway Labor Executives' Association*. Particulars of the case and Marshall's opinion may be found at the Legal Information Institute, Cornell University Law School, www.law.cornell.edu/supremecourt/text/489/602 (accessed May 25, 2014).

# Selected Bibliography

## Primary Sources

Adams, John, *Revolutionary Writings 1775–1783*, ed. Gordon Wood, Library of America, New York, 2011.

Ames, Nathaniel, *The Diary of Dr. Nathaniel Ames of Dedham, Massachusetts, 1758–1822*, ed. Robert Brand Hanson, 2 vols., Picton Press, Rockport, ME, 1998.

Bache, Benjamin Franklin, *Truth Will Out! The Foul Charges of the Tories against the Editor of the* Aurora *Repelled by Positive Proof and Plain Truth, and His Base Calumniators Put to Shame*, Nabu Press, Charleston, SC, 2010 [s.p., Philadelphia, 1798].

Callender, James T., *The History of the United States for 1796*, Snowden & M'Corkle, Philadelphia, 1797.

———, *The Political Register, or, Proceedings in the Session of Congress Commencing November 3d, 1794, and Ending March 3d, 1795*, T. Dobson, Philadelphia, 1795.

———, *The Prospect Before Us, Volume 1*, s.p., Richmond, VA, 1800.

———, *Sedgwick & Co., or A Key to the Six Per Cent Cabinet*, printed for the author, Philadelphia, 1798.

Chipman, Daniel, *The Life of Hon. Nathaniel Chipman, LL.D.*, C. C. Little and J. Brown, Boston, 1846.

Cooper, Thomas, *An Account of the Trial of Thomas Cooper, of Northumberland; on a Charge of Libel against the President of the United States*, J. Bioren, Philadelphia, 1800.

———, *Some Information Respecting America*, J. Johnson, London, 1794.

*The Debate on the Constitution*, comp. Bernard Bailyn, 2 vols., Library of America, New York, 1993.

Franklin, Benjamin, *Writings*, comp. J. A. Leo Lemay, Library of America, New York, 1987.

Hamilton, Alexander, *Writings*, comp. Joanne B. Freeman, Library of America, New York, 2001.

Jefferson, Thomas, *Writings*, comp. Merrill D. Peterson, Library of America, New York, 1984.

Madison, James, *Writings*, comp. Jack N. Rakove, Library of America, New York, 1999.

Nelson, William, *An Enquiry whether the Act of Congress . . . Generally Called the Sedition Bill, Is Unconstitutional or Not*, S. Pleasants, Richmond, VA, 1798.

Wharton, Francis, *State Trials of the United States During the Administrations of Washington and Adams*, Carey & Hart, Philadelphia, 1849.

## SECONDARY SOURCES

Adams, Andrew N., *A History of the Town of Fair Haven, Vermont*, Leonard & Phelps, Fair Haven, VT, 1870.

Austin, Aleine, *Matthew Lyon, "New Man" of the Democratic Revolution, 1749–1822*, Pennsylvania State University Press, University Park, 1981.

Bernhard, Winfred E. A., *Fisher Ames: Federalist and Statesman, 1758–1808*, University of North Carolina Press, Chapel Hill, 1965.

Bowen, Catherine Drinker, *Miracle at Philadelphia: The Story of the Constitutional Convention, May to September 1787*, Little, Brown, Boston, 1966.

Brigham, Clarence S., *History and Bibliography of American Newspapers, 1690–1820*, 2 vols., American Antiquarian Society, Worcester, MA, 1947.

Brown, Stuart Gerry, *The First Republicans: Political Philosophy and Public Policy in the Party of Jefferson and Madison*, Syracuse University Press, Syracuse, NY, 1954.

Brown, Walt, *John Adams and the American Press: Politics and Journalism at the Birth of the Republic*, McFarland & Co., Jefferson, NC, 1995.

Chernow, Ron, *Alexander Hamilton*, Penguin Press, New York, 2004.

———, *Washington: A Life*, Penguin Press, New York, 2010.

Clarfield, Gerald H., *Timothy Pickering and the American Republic*, University of Pittsburgh Press, Pittsburgh, PA, 1980.

Currie, David P., *The Constitution in Congress: The Federalist Period, 1789–1801*, University of Chicago Press, Chicago, 1997.

DeConde, Alexander, *The Quasi-War: The Politics and Diplomacy of the Undeclared War with France, 1797–1801*, Scribner, New York, 1966.

Drake, J. Madison, *Historical Sketches of the Revolutionary and Civil Wars*, Webster Press, New York, 1908.

Durey, Michael, *"With the Hammer of Truth": James Thomson Callender and America's Early National Heroes*, University Press of Virginia, Charlottesville, 1990.

Elkins, Stanley, and Eric McKitrick, *The Age of Federalism: The Early American Republic, 1788–1800*, Oxford University Press, New York, 1993.

Ellis, Joseph J., *Founding Brothers: The Revolutionary Generation*, Vintage Books, New York, 2000.

Feeney, Vincent E., *Finnigans, Slaters, and Stonepeggers: A History of the Irish in Vermont*, Images from the Past, Bennington, VT, 2009.

Fiss, Owen M., *The Irony of Free Speech*, Harvard University Press, Cambridge, 1996.

Gelles, Edith B., *Abigail & John: Portrait of a Marriage*, Harper Perennial, New York, 2010.

Gordon-Reed, Annette, *The Hemingses of Monticello: An American Family*, W. W. Norton & Co., New York, 2008.

Haw, James, et al., *Stormy Patriot: The Life of Samuel Chase*, Maryland Historical Society, Baltimore, 1980.

Isaacson, Walter, *Benjamin Franklin: An American Life*, Simon & Schuster, New York, 2003.

Johnson, Steven, *The Invention of Air: A Story of Science, Faith, Revolution, and the Birth of America*, Riverhead Books, New York, 2008.

Kendall, Joshua C., *The Forgotten Founding Father: Noah Webster's Obsession and the Creation of an American Culture*, Berkley Pub Group, New York, 2012.

Kelley, Joseph J., Jr., *Life and Times in Colonial Philadelphia*, Stackpole Books, Harrisburg, PA, 1973.

Levy, Leonard W., *Legacy of Suppression: Freedom of Speech and Press in Early American History*, Harper & Row, New York, 1963.

———, *Origins of the Bill of Rights*, Yale University Press, New Haven, CT, 1999.

Malone, Dumas, *The Public Life of Thomas Cooper, 1783–1839*, University of South Carolina Press, Columbia, 1961 [Yale University Press, New Haven, CT, 1926].

McCullough, David, *John Adams*, Simon & Schuster, New York, 2001.

Meacham, Jon, *Thomas Jefferson: The Art of Power*, Random House, New York, 2012.

Miller, John C., *Crisis in Freedom: The Alien and Sedition Acts*, Little, Brown, Boston, 1951.

Morgan, Edmund S., *Benjamin Franklin*, Yale University Press, New Haven, CT, 2002.

Pasler, Rudolph J., and Margaret C. Pasler, The New Jersey Federalists, Associated University Presses, Cranbury, N.J., 1975.

Randall, Willard Sterne, *Ethan Allen: His Life and Times*, W.W. Norton & Co., New York, 2011.

Rauch, Jonathan, *Kindly Inquisitors: The New Attacks on Free Thought*, University of Chicago Press, Chicago, 1993.

Rehnquist, William H., *Grand Inquests: The Historic Impeachments of Justice Samuel Chase and President Andrew Johnson*, Morrow, New York, 1992.

Ritchie, Donald A., *Press Gallery: Congress and the Washington Correspondents*, Harvard University Press, Cambridge, MA, 1991.

Rosenfeld, Richard N., *American Aurora: A Democratic-Republican Returns*, St. Martin's Press, New York, 1997.

Schama, Simon, *Citizens: A Chronicle of the French Revolution*, Knopf, New York, 1989.

Schiff, Stacy, *A Great Improvisation: Franklin, France, and the Birth of America*, Henry Holt, New York, 2005.

Schlesinger, Arthur M., et al., eds., *A History of American Life*, rev. and abr., Scribner, New York, 1996.

Sherman, Michael, Gene Sessions, and P. Jeffrey Potash, *Freedom and Unity: A History of Vermont*, Vermont Historical Society, Barre, 2004.

Smallwood, Frank, *Thomas Chittenden: Vermont's First Statesman*, New England Press, Shelburne, VT, 1997.

Smith, James Morton, *Freedom's Fetters: The Alien and Sedition Laws and American Civil Liberties*, Cornell University Press, Ithaca, NY, 1966 [1956].

Smith, Jeffery A., *Franklin and Bache: Envisioning the Enlightened Republic*, Oxford University Press, New York, 1990.

Smith, Page, *John Adams*, 2 vols., Doubleday, Garden City, NY, 1962.

Stewart, Donald H., *The Opposition Press of the Federalist Period*, SUNY Press, Albany, NY, 1969.

Stone, Geoffrey R., *Perilous Times: Free Speech in Wartime, from the Sedition Act of 1798 to the War on Terrorism*, W. W. Norton & Co., New York, 2004.

Sunstein, Cass R., *Democracy and the Problem of Free Speech*, The Free Press, New York, 1993.

Tagg, James, *Benjamin Franklin Bache and the* Philadelphia Aurora, University of Pennsylvania Press, Philadelphia, 1991.

Turner, Robert F., ed., *The Jefferson-Hemings Controversy, Report of the Scholars Commission*, Carolina Academic Press, Durham, NC, 2011.

Van Doren, Carl, *The Great Rehearsal: The Story of the Making and Ratifying of the Constitution of the United States*, Viking Press, New York, 1948.

Waldron, Jeremy, *The Harm in Hate Speech*, Harvard University Press, Cambridge, 2012.

Ward, Christopher, *The War of the Revolution*, 2 vols., Macmillan, New York, 1952.

Warren, Charles, *Jacobin and Junto; or, Early American Politics as Viewed in the Diary of Nathaniel Ames, 1758–1822*, Harvard University Press, Cambridge, MA, 1931.

Wiencek, Henry, *Master of the Mountain: Thomas Jefferson and His Slaves*, Farrar, Straus and Giroux, New York, 2012.

Wills, Garry, *"Negro President": Jefferson and the Slave Power*, Houghton Mifflin, Boston, 2005.

Wilson, David A., *United Irishmen, United States: Immigrant Radicals in the Early Republic*, Cornell University Press, Ithaca, NY, 1998.

Wood, Gordon S., *The Radicalism of the American Revolution*, Vintage Books, New York, 1991.

———, *Revolutionary Characters: What Made the Founders Different*, Penguin Books, New York, 2006.

Young, Alfred F., Gary B. Nash, and Ray Raphael, eds., *Revolutionary Founders: Rebels, Radicals, and Reformers in the Making of the Nation*, Alfred A. Knopf, New York, 2011.

# INDEX